Love

in 90 Days

Love
in 90 Days

THE ESSENTIAL GUIDE TO FINDING
YOUR OWN TRUE LOVE

DIANA KIRSCHNER, PhD

REVISED EDITION

CENTER
STREET

New York   Nashville

Center Street
Hachette Book Group
1290 Avenue of the Americas, New York, NY 10104
centerstreet.com
twitter.com/centerstreet

Originally published in hardcover and ebook by Center Street in 2009
First revised edition: January 2019

Center Street is a division of Hachette Book Group, Inc. The Center Street name and logo are trademarks of Hachette Book Group, Inc.

The publisher is not responsible for websites (or their content) that are not owned by the publisher.

The Hachette Speakers Bureau provides a wide range of authors for speaking events. To find out more, go to www.HachetteSpeakersBureau.com or call (866) 376-6591.

"The Prayer for Beauty" from *Original Tribe Handbook of Angels* is reprinted by permission from JoAnne Karl, copyright © 1997 by JoAnne Karl. All rights reserved.

"Autobiography in Five Short Chapters" is reprinted by permission from *There's a Hole in My Sidewalk*, copyright © 1993 by Portia Nelson, Beyond Words Publishing, Hillsboro, Oregon. All rights reserved.

The Library of Congress has cataloged the hardcover edition as follows:
Kirschner, Diana Adile
Love in 90 days : the essential guide to finding your own true love / Diana Kirschner.—1st ed.
p. cm.
ISBN: 978-1-59995-122-5
1. Dating (Social customs). 2. Mate selection. 3. Love. 4. Single women—Psychology. 5. Women—Psychology. I. Title. II. Title: Love in ninety days.
HQ801.K565 2009
646.7'7—dc22

2008021916

ISBNs: 978-1-5460-8489-1 (revised edition, paperback), 978-1-5460-8491-4 (revised edition, ebook)

Printed in the United States of America

LSC-C

10 9 8 7 6 5 4 3 2 1

*To my husband and love partner, Sam, whose unseen hand lifts
and lights my soul and all that I do.*

*To my beloved mother, Concetta Adile, whose patient, undying
love surfaced through the dungeon gates of her childhood
and penetrated even the darkness of death.*

*To my beloved grandchildren, Siren Ortega,
Jacob Kirschner and Ethan Kirschner.*

CONTENTS

My Love in 90 Days Gratitude List   ix

Author's Note and Welcome to the Age of Abundant Love   xiii

Introduction   xvii

PART I

The First Month

1 Your Love in 90 Days Program   3

2 The Deadly Dating Patterns   22

3 Dating Games Men Play   44

4 Dating Three to Find the One   76

5 Secrets of Rapid Online and App Dating Success   98

Contents

PART II

The Second Month

6   Finding Love Mentors   131

7   Discovering and Using Your Diamond Self   152

8   One Simple Secret to Irresistible Self-Confidence and Getting the Love You Deserve   175

9   Field Report on DUDs and STUDs   193

10   Ditching Deadly Dating Patterns Forever   214

PART III

The Third Month

11   First Aid for Heartache   239

12   Beware of Frenemies   263

13   Love Secrets Just for You: African-Americans, Single Mothers, College-Educated or Successful Women, or Women Forty-Five and Over   282

14   How Happy Couples Work: The Eight Habits of Living Love   309

15   Launch to More Love   336

Appendix A: *Creating Your Own Team Love*   347

Appendix B: *Love in 90 Days: The Eight Steps*   351

Appendix C: *Love in 90 Days Online; Love in 90 Days Online University; Facebook*   352

Notes   355

Index   373

MY LOVE IN 90 DAYS
GRATITUDE LIST

———— ✧ ————

How blessed I have been to be able to create this work with channels of help coming through for me at every turn. It has changed me, honed me, made me more conscious, more observant, and more alive. Most of all the work has given me an enormous sense of opening in my heart, for which I am so very grateful. First I want to acknowledge all my clients and students, who were absolutely instrumental in helping refine the program.

I am very grateful to: my Beauty Mentors, hair artist extraordinaire Ruben Colon, and ultrastylist Edwin Pabon; Dave, my unbelievably great photographer at David Paul Photography; my writing teacher, Lew Hunter, and his fabulous wife, Pamela; my dear friend, mentor, and uber-supporter, Susan Batson; and acting coach, Jack Plotnick.

Very special thanks also to: Belle Grubert; Carol and Nolan Grubert; Beth Grubert; Betts and Eldon Mayer; Stan and Dr. Hildy Richelson; Jane Firth; Beth Coltoff Koren and Dr. Tedd Koren; Jo Singel; Andrea Andrews; Michele Ritterman, PhD; Susan Rosbrow-Reich, PhD; Susan Taylor; Susan

Shapiro; Melynda Fuller; Susan Unger; Helene Abrams; David Giller; Terry Barak; Bertha Hardt; Nancy Bird; Jane Brailove Rutkoff; Kim Parker; Adria Baratt; Joey Avniel; Mitchell Rigie; Ed Hale; Alicia Adema; Breck Baldwin; Peter Fogel; Melissa Horn; Lynya Floyd; Shauna Toh; Anastasia Furst; and Jill Dahne for many blessings, ideas, support, and belief in me and the project.

A big shout out to my brilliant, loving, and magically helpful friends: Lori Hammel, Sherri Tennant, Laura Marini, Cathy Kadets, Sandra Park, Nanci Deutsch, Deb Kalas, Linda Waters, Saidah Arrika Ekulona, Astrid Brouwer, Diane Kaldany, Marie Pastor, Marlene Landauer, and especially Susan Davies for her manuscript suggestions and Alexandra Desbrow, who contributed an exercise to the book.

Many thanks to my nourishing and uplifting spiritual commu-nity, especially Linda Vitta, Nanette Stavis, Zack Lewis, Suzy and Bill Schoonover, Carl Josel, Jacob Marcus, Chrystal Constant, Steve Hur-witz, Glenn V. Alper, and Harry S. Keats. My precious daughter, Con-cetta Kirschner, aka Princess Superstar, read parts of the manuscript and gave her invaluable input. My incredible son, Jason Kirschner, was terrifically encouraging, especially when he rescued me after multiple computer crashes!

Both of our children are now happily married and we have three grandchildren. A shout-out to my daughter-in-law, Rachel Kirschner, and my son-in-law, Miguel Ortega, for their support. I've dedicated this new edition to my grandkids, Siren, Jacob and Ethan, because, while everything will have changed when they start dating, the deep and time-less principles of finding and cultivating true love will be exactly the same!

My sweet soulmate friend, Sandra Robertson, patiently supported me all along the way, carried me through when I had doubts, and helped bring me back to my source mission.

Many thanks to Jacquie Jordan, my angel of television, who helped me develop and get on major shows to spread the word.

And to the incredible team at Center Street, whose mission married mine: Rolf Zettersten, Harry Helm, Gina Wynn, Jana Burson, Lori Quinn, Preston Cannon, Jody Waldrup, Karen Thompson, and the whole Hachette Book Group sales force. Heartfelt thanks for believing in me and doing such a fantastic job on the book and its promotion.

My original editor, Sarah Sper, is an angel with hawk-like vision! She went over every word of the manuscript and made it clearer, more user friendly, and just so much better. I was impressed by how much Sarah cared about you, the reader, and thought carefully about clearing your path to love.

My editor for this expanded version, Jaime Coyne, was infinitely helpful! She read over the original manuscript very carefully and suggested many updates that needed to be included to make this edition pop with the most current and most useful information out there.

What can I say about my agent, Wendy Sherman, the goddess charioteer who carried this work to you? She is the best in every way! Totally supportive, she gives me spot-on advice and holds an unwavering belief in me.

My beloved mentor, Dr. Arthur Stein, laid the foundation for this book long ago. He not only held the vision but also developed the basic strategies underlying the Love in 90 Days Program. I am also eternally grateful to the many other magnificent and truly inspiring mentors, teachers, and role models who generously gave of themselves, informing and enriching all that I may have to offer.

Many thanks to Emily Manning, who has been a brilliant social media and marketing strategist, as well as a prime mover and partner in the Love in 90 Days University. And great thanks to David Dachinger, the Prism of Absolute Light who wrote the music for the University.

My seriously brilliant, wise, loving and devoted team of Love Mentor® coaches have brought the magic of the Love in 90 Days approach to tens of thousands of women all around the world and they have refined and added to the approach over the past ten years. Immense gratitude to coaches Jim Delpino, Tamara Green, Judith Joshel, Joielle Shepherd, Ann Robbins, Betts Mayer, Susan Kalinowski, Judy Rappaport, Kate Forest,

Nicole and Gabriel Dicristofaro, Kim Quick, Betty Russell, Tinamarie
Bernard, Jenevieve Ybarra, Fernanda Beccaglia, Angelia Johnson, Kris-
ten Darcy, Pam Ross, Judy Gotlieb, Lindsey Halpern-Givens, Maya Diamond, Karen Holland, Lori Hammel, Alec Satin, Debbie Fumanti, and
Michelle Marchant Johnson.

Finally, I am most grateful to the two people who taught me the most
about love in action: Sam Kirschner, my dearest partner in sublime, and
my late mother, Concetta Adile, who at this moment is probably laughing, waving, and saying, "Luck, luck, luck, honey!"

AUTHOR'S NOTE AND WELCOME TO THE AGE OF ABUNDANT LOVE

The best love is the kind that awakens the soul and makes us reach for more, that plants a fire in our hearts and brings peace to our minds. That's what I hope to give you forever.
—*Nicholas Sparks*

Hi Love! I am so happy you picked up this book!!!! Because you now live in the Age of Abundant Love! Yes, the dating world has exploded in the past ten years since this book was published. Recent research has found that now one in three marriages in the U.S. begin online. Online relationships progress to marriage faster. And they are happier marriages! And they last longer! In America, divorce rates climbed until the birth of the internet and have actually fallen since.

Digital dating has changed the landscape of love.

An estimated 200 million singles globally now use digital dating services each month. Not only have dating websites grown exponentially but dating apps have brought thousands of single men right to the phone in the palm of your hand. Even Facebook is starting *Dating*, a new relationship-oriented matching feature within its app. Your dating choices are now almost unlimited.

Bottom line: Your chances of finding real soulmate love have never been better!

But, of course, there is a downside to all these "meet" markets. Ten percent of all new dating profiles do not belong to real people. Dating companies pad their numbers, especially in the startup phase, so that they can offer a better gender ratio or greater overall numbers. Spam and bot profiles are also common. And there are bots who are programmed to come across as real humans. Ghosting, where people abruptly disappear on you without warning and for no apparent reason, has become common. And there are cruel catfishers who misrepresent themselves just to play a game with another person's psyche. Last, but not least, we have seen the rise of romance scam con artists. In 2016, the FBI reported that singles (mostly women) lost more than $230 million through online dating scams. One woman lost over a million dollars, her whole retirement nest egg.

The rise of dating apps has created potential challenges for singles. These apps have launched a swiping culture, making an already difficult dating world even more confusing. They offer much less information on matches than dating sites. For example, Tinder only allows 500 characters in a profile. So it can be like decoding an encrypted secret message. Tinder, which started as a hookup app and then morphed into relationship matching, still attracts unsavory men who send unsolicited sexually explicit photos. Because digital dating is more impersonal, and users act in relative anonymity and isolation, there is more poor behavior without the social repercussions of dating "in real life."

There are other challenges with dating apps if you do not know how to use them. Users have become a more fickle crowd, as they face match after match to swipe on. Playing with an app can be like an addictive online game for guys, as they kill time or date shop just to see how many women like them. In addition, having more choices can be overloading to the brain, which is only wired to handle around 8 or 9 choices. It can be paralyzing to you and to the matches you are interested in. Texting is the new way of "meeting" a match and can go on endlessly without ever leading to an actual meeting. Some women report spending 10 to 14 hours on an app just to get one date. These problems have been dubbed *dating app burnout* or *battle fatigue* in numerous articles in the popular media.

But, the great news is that all these obstacles can be handled, so that you reap the benefits of dating in the Age of Abundant Love! And you will learn exactly how to do that in the updates that have been added to this expanded version of *Love in 90 Days*. I have also included a list of all the dating sites and apps that are most useful.

I've gathered so much knowledge about the dating scene in the last decade. In response to requests from all over the world, I assembled a team of professional Love Mentor® coaches who have used the Love in 90 Days Program with tens of thousands of women looking for soulmate love. This has allowed me to be up close and personal in terms of what is happening in the dating world and how to make it work out sublimely! I know how to avoid all the pitfalls that are now out there and how to maximize the opportunities to connect to marvelous guys from 21 to 71!

Another thing I have learned from the many women in our coaching program who have been wounded by abandonment, loneliness, and the heartbreak of betrayal, cheating, and other major disappointments is how important self-esteem, deservedness, and self-confidence are in terms of rising from the ashes of ruined love. And I am so excited to tell you that I have created a very powerful method that has helped women all around the world to bounce back from heartbreaking traumas and move into a whole new level of irresistible self-confidence and magnetic charisma. I cannot wait to share this secret with you in my new chapter, "One Simple Secret to Irresistible Self Confidence and Getting the Love You Deserve." I know you will find this tool extremely valuable. And not just in the love domain! I use it all the time, myself, in all areas of my life!

We have seen over and over how well the Love in 90 Days Program works! For instance, I had my own PBS Special, *Finding Your Own True Love*, where I presented just a few of the tips in this book. As a result, three single women in the studio audience alone were able to go ahead and get happily married. One of them, Midge Woolsey, documented her amazing love journey in an article in the *New York Times*. She was the PBS host who was asking for pledges during my program. A never-married fifty-something, she asked to try the program before she offered my DVD on air. Within sixty days she met the great love of her life, her dearest soulmate. I got to attend their glorious wedding celebration and it was filled with music, singing, and so much love!

Over the past ten years my Love in 90 Days coaching team has worked with many thousands of women of all ages around the world and we have found that the principles and techniques described in this book are truly life-transforming. The vast majority of our Love Mentor® coaching clients experience greater self-love and deservedness, as well as tremendous breakthroughs in self-confidence and dating know-how. They date more, find better quality men, and form the kind of committed soulmate love that fills the yearning of their hearts. And now you can too!

So read on! I am so excited to be with you on this new journey!

Dr. Diana Kirschner
February 2019

INTRODUCTION

When love beckons to you, follow him, though his ways are
hard and steep. And when his wings enfold you yield to him,
though the sword hidden among his pinions may wound you.
And when he speaks to you, believe in him.—*Kahlil Gibran*

Yes, believe in him.
 Who am I to suggest such a leap of faith? Good question.
 I am a person who knows love: how it works, how it heals,
and how it hurts. I know how it fills hearts, how it fails and empties
them. And how it can return. I study love, talk love, live it and breathe
it. Most importantly, I help it spread and take root in the sweet birth of
new relationships every day. I help love to come, surprise, and delight
people like you.

It most definitely wasn't always this way. I was not born into love or a
joyful welcome. My childhood, adolescence, and early dating life, to use
a technical term, sucked. Loneliness and disappointment were my middle names. But that hard beginning led me to hunger and look for the
secrets of love. And I've been on the mission for a long time.

Here's a flashback from 1986. I was sitting in the sunny spot in my
office at a Philadelphia-based psychotherapy center when Jill, a striking woman with a mane of copper-red, waist-length hair, rushed in. She

threw the latest *Newsweek* on my desk so hard that it went flying over into the trash basket.

"It says a single forty-year-old woman has only a 2.6 percent chance of ever marrying," she blurted out.

Jill was thirty-nine. And single.

"Absolute bull!" I said. "The program you are on is working well for our single clients. Besides that, I feel confident that those stats are all wrong."

Jill flashed me a grin as she settled on the couch. After her session, I checked the files on our single women clients. They were doing quite well, thank you very much. In fact, no matter what their age, they were happily dating and getting married more often than not, if that was what they wanted. The next thing I knew, I was on *Good Morning America* insisting on the good news: The possibility of committed real love was alive and well for women of any age.

Jill was using an early version of the Love in 90 Days Program that I helped develop at our therapy training center. After working the Program she met and married a gifted doctor, and she now has a teenage son who is a budding entrepreneur and a daughter who has the same remarkable copper-red hair. When Jill found out I was writing this book she sent this e-mail: "Thanks to using your approach, I now have love in my life that I once believed only existed for others!" In 2006, on the twentieth anniversary of that controversial article, *Newsweek* recanted its own story. Many of the over-forty women originally interviewed were in fact married.

After that pivotal event, I continued taking a stand for the real relationship possibilities single women could have. More importantly, I spent even more time developing the powerful techniques that helped singles find love.

How did I wind up on this particular mission? I'll tell you more about my family. When I was growing up, a peck on the cheek was the closest thing to love I ever saw between my parents or any of my friends' parents. My father and mother shared a lot of quiet and not-so-quiet resentment with sporadic raging fights that spilled over and terrified me. One time my father ripped a large piece of metal off the stove and threw it at my mother. She fell on the floor crying and calling for help. When I tried to protect her he attacked me. You get the idea.

When I started dating it wasn't pretty; I found myself caught in a web of Deadly Dating Patterns (more on this in Chapter 2). I wanted the guys who didn't want me, partied and tried too hard, settled for crumbs, got dumped in humiliating ways, and hid out with pints and pints of Häagen-Dazs coffee ice cream.

And yet I dreamed about the possibilities of real love, the kind that is so solid and true, one cannot mistake it. As one wise woman described it: "There is no mistaking love. You feel it in your heart. It is…the flame that heats our soul, energizes our spirit and supplies passion to our lives."

I just knew in my gut that somewhere, somehow, someone had figured out how to take the right risks, how to be brave for the right reasons, how to create this flame of passionate yet lasting love. And I wanted to have that kind of fulfillment. So, starting in college where I studied psychology, then in a doctoral program in clinical psychology and beyond, I set out to find the secret lessons that would allow me to live in a state of love. I studied happy couples (hard to find, but I did) and apprenticed with mentors, other psychologists, self-help gurus, and sages. After thousands of hours watching, learning, and studying, I finally "got it"! I discovered the rules, strategies, and personal growth lessons that put people on the path to healing, that transformed low self-esteem and intimacy or abandonment issues into empowerment and in so doing, created the freedom to love and be loved. These principles were the beginnings of the Love in 90 Days Program. Thankfully, I used them to get out of my Deadly Dating Patterns and marry Sam, my rock, my love. I call him my partner in sublime.

I taught these life-altering techniques to professionals at my clinic, the Institute for Comprehensive Family Therapy, and all over the world. After twenty-five years of helping thousands of singles directly and through teaching other therapists, I began to help women find loving relationships *in faster and faster ways.* I put these powerful strategies together, and my Love in 90 Days classes and coaching approach were born. I even created a reality TV pilot, *Love in 90 Days Boot Camp,* which was an Official Selection of the 2006 New York TV Festival. Word of this work spread like wildfire, and it was featured in the *New York Times,* the *Today Show* and in my own PBS Special. E-mails poured in—messages from single women wanting the Program.

I heard your call. And here it is, just for you. I've created this guide to help you get everything you ever dreamed of and more when it comes to love. And I am completely excited about it, and excited to "meet" you, because I know what is possible for you through these powerful strategies. Please give this Program to yourself and really work it—you are more than worth it.

Finally, I want to share a few more personal things. Not because I want to toot horns, but because you and I are about to have an intense relationship and I want you to know who I am.

First, what I am not: I am not divorced four times yet writing books on relationships. I am not a TV personality who has no clue about sustaining a committed relationship. I am not a single, "spiritual" person who's never truly been a partner in a couple.

What I am: I have an MA and a PhD in clinical psychology. I have co-authored books and articles for therapists about singles, couples, and love. I was chosen to have my own PBS Special, *Finding Your Own True Love,* which led to numerous marriages. I've been married—happily—to Sam for over thirty-five years. We've weathered one of our families disowning us and refusing to meet our baby girl because one of us is Jewish while the other is Italian, the devastating death of a child, a life-threatening illness, and deadly boring stretches when we seemed to have absolutely nothing in common. And did I mention fighting like only two competitive PhDs can?

But today we're much stronger, more in love, and sexier than ever together.

I know the road to love personally. And I know it through the countless women whom I've helped to find happy new beginnings. Over the past ten years I have assembled and trained an amazing team of Love Mentor® coaches who have worked with tens of thousands of women around the world using the Love in 90 Days approach. We have gotten phenomenal results, helping our students to have increased self-esteem, deservedness and success in finding love beyond their wildest dreams. This book is based on this extensive clinical experience and my own personal journey, plus the latest research on love relationships. Each chapter contains many references that can be found in the "Notes" at the end of the book. When I give you advice, consider what I've just told you and consider it carefully. Try it on for size before you reject it impulsively. And tailor it to your individual needs so that you make it even better and more effective.

The truth is I'm writing this book because I treasure beyond words what I have experienced with Sam—the best friendship and sexy love that fills the holes in my heart and opens all the possibilities in living my life full out. This gift, this miracle, makes me teary as I write about it. A gift this powerful calls for being shared. With you.

Love
in 90 Days

PART I

The First Month

1

———— ⚭ ————

Your Love in 90 Days Program

Love is everything it's cracked up to be. That's why people are so cynical about it…it really is worth fighting for, being brave for, risking everything for. And the trouble is, if you don't risk anything, you risk even more.—*Erica Jong*

Love is life's golden ticket. It brings in the brightest of colors and the rich high and low notes. There is no mistaking it; you know when you have love. And you definitely know when you don't. The big question is, What are you doing about not having love in your life? Are you going to risk being alone and lonely, missing out on all that love can give?

Imagine if you were losing your job and needed money; looking for one would be your absolute top priority. You would spend hours searching linkedin.com and posting on job sites like monster.com and career builder.com, scanning the want ads and trade journals, calling recruiters, networking through your friends, and jumping on any leads. In contrast, despite being alone, finding love ranks pretty low on your to-do list. You come home from work, run errands, answer some e-mails, text your friends, play with the dog, and watch your favorite show. Maybe you're the type who puts in extra hours at the office, meets the girls out for a drink, notices a couple of interesting guys but figures it's too hard to get their attention, then heads home without giving them another thought. You may be a working single mom who'd like to find a caring, loving partner, but you think, *Who has the time?* At best you spend maybe ten minutes flicking through profiles on Tinder. Sound familiar?

Let's be honest. If you are truthful with yourself, is finding love anywhere near the top of your priority list? You're probably better at planning your weekend or a vacation than planning your dating life. I've helped thousands of women find wonderful relationships, and it all started with one simple shift. Each student made just one decision that changed her priorities and changed her life: the decision to roll out the red carpet for love.

Prioritizing Love

Now, I know what you're thinking: *If it is meant to be, it will just happen. I don't want to be (seem) desperate. Love comes when you let go, when you are not looking.*

But I have critical news for you: Study after study has shown that love relationships have a huge impact on our psychological, economic, and physical well-being. Having a life partner can create a higher sense of self-worth, provide intimacy and emotional support, which fulfills the deepest human need for connection, and lead to greater wealth and economic stability. As a result, married people may be happier, live more satisfying lives, and have fewer psychological problems, including depression. Many researchers say that these factors lead to better physical health, greater health-seeking behavior, and lower rates of alcoholism. Here's the big take-away: For over 100 years studies around the world have shown that married people live longer and enjoy a higher quality of life than those who aren't partnered! With everything a healthy love relationship has going for it, why let anything hold you back from choosing love as a top priority in your life?

Of course, the pro-marriage findings do not necessarily mean that people can't be happy as singles. They can. And they certainly don't mean that women should stay in loveless or abusive relationships. In fact, these days a woman does not even need a man to have a child or build a fulfilling life. But an overwhelming mountain of evidence points to the centrality of a love relationship in creating health and happiness for most people.

Ask yourself: *How do I prioritize love?* Or, more honestly, *Why is it that finding lasting love or working on a love relationship is not my highest priority?* Shouldn't it be, since your long-term quality of life may depend on it?

Okay, I know. You've been on interminable dates where you were bored, annoyed, and couldn't wait to get away. You're sure there are no good men left, and, if by some chance there are, they're certainly not in your town. Sometimes you tell yourself that you really just don't care anymore, especially after your last less-than-satisfactory experience. You may be sick and tired of the whole dating and love merry-go-round. After all, you have been hurt, rejected, and disappointed, big time. I get it.

But those days can all be over. Starting today. Right now, this very minute, you can start your own Love in 90 Days Program and change your life forever. As a wise woman once said, "Love is a fruit in season at all times, and within reach of every hand."

I've helped women who were overweight, shy, older, buried in debt, mega-successful, saddled with problem kids—you name it. Some faced a combo-plate of challenges. Yet these women were able to create real love in their lives. And I can show you exactly how to do it, too.

So buckle up. This course is a fast-forward roller-coaster ride to the love you want, the love that is just right for you. Get ready to be excited, scared, heartbroken, depressed, hopeless, happy, exhilarated, drunk with love, amazed, and surprised—and not necessarily in that order!

I will be sitting next to you through all the twists and turns, the breath-stopping drops, and the dizzying joy-filled heights. As your Love Mentor, I will help you identify and break your self-sabotaging patterns, develop your most lovable and loving self, and work a Dating Program of Three (yes, it means what you think it means; and, yes, even you will be able to do it!). And to show my full support, this is my promise to you:

I guarantee that after three short months of working this Program, you will break out of your Deadly Dating Patterns, make huge gains in self-esteem, date higher-quality men, and be much closer to creating a real, lasting love relationship.

Your Love in 90 Days Basics

WHAT TO EXPECT IN THE NEXT 90 DAYS

You may be thinking, *Ninety days? Dating three men at once? Are you kidding? I don't even flirt!* Or, *This sounds like a lot of work!* I've heard it all. First of all, I'm going to give you all the tools you need to succeed. Second, you can successfully work the program at a slower pace. But, this isn't a set of gimmicks to help you manipulate men; this Program is going to help you find your own true love. Isn't it worth the ninety-day investment?

Here's what to expect: In the first month you'll learn to identify your Deadly Dating Patterns, master the Dating Program of Three, and use the powerhouse secrets of successful online dating. In month two, you'll find a master Love Mentor, someone who helps you discover and express your authentic, charismatic, and beautiful self, and you'll learn how to end your dead-end patterns forever. In the third month I'll share my best prescriptions for healing heartache, show you how to deal with Frenemies (cynics and naysayers in your life), and teach you how to practice the eight habits that healthy couples use to create happily-ever-after relationships.

INNER AND OUTER WORK

Since love is the most delicate and total act of the soul, it will reflect the state and nature of the soul....As one is, so is his love.—José Ortega y Gasset

There are two key elements in this course: the Inner Work and the Outer Work. The Inner Work is assigned as exercises to do as you are reading. You'll examine and journal about your identity, your beliefs, and your self-sabotaging behaviors. The Outer Work is given as homework assignments for the week, to do out in the real world. The homework will help you change your dead-end dating habits; meet new, exciting, and available men; and create a supportive and loving circle of friends and family.

The Outer Work is just as critical as the Inner Work, and vice versa; success in one arena supports success in the other. While you're working through self-sabotaging thoughts and behaviors and turbo-charging your self-esteem, you will be able to get out there more readily, quickly sort through the men you meet, and choose the ones who are more loving and successful.

As you work through the Love in 90 Days course, you'll be able to read what other women* who have completed the course have experienced in their own words. These quotes can help carry you forward emotionally as you learn from and are inspired by other students in our Love Mentor® coaching program.

HOW TO WORK THE PROGRAM

I recommend that you simply read the whole book first, without doing the exercises or homework, to get an initial sense of the powerful Love in

---

* Identifying information has been changed to protect privacy. A few students are composites.

90 Days principles and practices. Then put yourself on the personalized 90 Day Program. The book is divided into three monthly sections with a chapter or two to read each week. At the end of most of the chapters you will find exercises and homework. You know your situation best; use your intuition to choose which exercises and homework assignments you need to do. You can do all of them if you want, following the program right along. You can also work at your own pace, speeding the program up or slowing it down.

As long as you use the principles and strategies, there is no wrong way to work the Program.

We have had thousands of women who have found increased self-love, confidence and dating success and in each case, they used the techniques a little differently!

You can also tailor the course to your unique needs by jumping ahead and then circling back to complete all of the work. Here is a cheat sheet for those with special issues; remember, after reading these chapters please return to the beginning and read through the whole Love in 90 Days Program with an eye to which exercises or homework will be most beneficial to you:

- If you are really shy and haven't been dating at all, go to Chapters 7 and 8 for shyness-busting secrets.
- If you are coming out of a relationship and are suffering, go to Chapter 11 for first aid for your heartache.
- If you are African-American, have kids, are college educated and successful, or are over forty-five, jump ahead to Chapter 13. You will be amazed and freed up as you read compelling research that busts urban legends that have plagued your special group in the quest for love.

TEAM LOVE GROUPS AND COACHING

The Love in 90 Days work can be done solo, with a friend, or in a small "Team Love" group. Running the processes with other women is a very powerful way to give yourself a jump start in the program, increase your accountability to complete the course, as well as to continue the Program after your course is over. Ask around and see who might be interested in having Love in 90 Days meetings weekly or bimonthly. See Appendix A for the ground rules on how to set up a Team Love.

Whether you can find a Team Love group or not, an especially powerful way to do the program is to work with a coach. If that calls to you, consider having one of my professional Love Mentors® work with you. These coaches are part of the handpicked team I assembled in response to requests from women around the world for dating and relationship coaching. They are the best of the best (I even used one personally to coach me when I did my own PBS Special!). Having a Love Mentor® coach is like having a fairy godmother and an incredibly wise wingman! You can go to http://lovein90days.com/dating-coach/ and have a gift session by phone or Skype. Love Mentor® coaching is a unique process of one-on-one support, guidance, caring and uplifting inspiration.

Whether you work with your own Team Love or a dedicated Love Mentor® you can choose to follow the 90-day program and work on one chapter each week or you can have an open format where you work on different Love in 90 Days principles and strategies completely at your own pace. You can follow the readings, discuss the lessons, and share your experiences and field reports with your Team Love or Love Mentor®. Women who have chosen to get direct support find sweet validation, a surprising depth of emotional support, beauty and dating tips, role modeling and encouragement to go for and get love that is surprisingly better than they ever imagined. Sheila, a thirty-nine-year-old makeup artist, wrote this e-mail to her Love Mentor® coach:

When Eric stopped texting me and disappeared into thin air, it was so hard. But you were there for me and I can't thank you enough! For me, our relationship is like magic. I look forward to each of our calls; I get so much more out of them than I can even put into words.

HOW TO CONNECT WITH ME

LOVEIN90DAYS.COM

Go to www.Lovein90Days.com to sign up for free ongoing support through my newsletter. Then I can be with you all the way! The newsletter will also let you know when I am doing my Facebook Live coaching sessions too. At Lovein90Days.com you can also get daily inspirational affirmations, my blog on the latest dating and relationship tips and other helpful resources.

LOVEIN90DAYSUNIVERSITY.COM

There is another powerful option for you that can make all the difference in the world in your love journey: I have developed a Love in 90 Days Certification course, which consists of eight weeks of experiential video trainings at www.Lovein90DaysUniversity.com. The video course is designed to promote your own dating and love success and give you training as a dating and relationship coach using my unique principles. The site also offers other personal growth courses as well. See Appendix C for details.

WHERE TO FIND ME ON SOCIAL MEDIA

You can also connect with me and thousands of my followers at:

https://www.Facebook.com/DrDiana Kirschner/ or search for "Dating
   to True Love Mentor"
Twitter: @DrDiana
Instagram: Lovein90Days
YouTube: Lovein90Days

✎ The Opening Exercises

All you need for the love program is a journal or notebook and we are
ready to start our journey together.

To begin, we will run through several exercises that are designed to
help you look at how you spend your time and discover what's really
important to you. Then you will choose goals for the course and I'll give
you some homework assignments to set you on your way. This first set
of exercises is important. Please do them as they set you up for success.
In later chapters you can pick and choose from the suggested exercises
and homework.

Total Time: 20 Minutes

EXERCISE 1: *THE RIGHT TIME TO BELIEVE IN LOVE*

In your notebook, divide up a blank page; on the left side write *No, Not
Now* and on the right side, write *Yes, Now*. Say the sentence: "This is the
right time to believe in love" over and over. After each time you say it,
alternate writing down reasons why the statement is not true in the left
column and reasons why it is true in the right.

Read over your responses. Interesting, aren't they?

Finish the exercise by writing out *This is the right time to believe in love*,
or another positive affirmation that speaks to you. Post this where you
will see it each day.

EXERCISE 2: *HOW DO YOU SPEND YOUR TIME?*

Make a list of all the major activities you spend time on during the week and the approximate number of hours for each. Do you spend hours texting, Facebooking, e-mailing, gabbing, Net surfing, or shopping on Amazon because you have nothing better to do? Do you let a demanding job swallow your whole life? List your activities in descending order from the ones you spend the most time on (work and sleep) down to the ones you spend the least time on. Remember to put down the number of hours per week you spend on each activity.

Here's how Shareena, a coaching client, who is a twenty-eight-year-old paralegal, broke down her 168-hour week:

Sleep: 56 hours

Work: 50 hours

Watching TV/surfing Net: 12 hours

Shopping/errands: 12 hours

Facebook/Twitter/Instagram: 8 hours

Gaming/Apps: 8 hours

Dinner/drinking/coffee/movies with friends: 6 hours

Gym: 6 hours

Class: 2 hours

I don't know??: 8 hours

If you can't account for all your time, pay attention for one week and do the exercise again. You will be amazed at how much time you squander.

This exercise is designed to confront you with all your time wasters: texting, FaceTiming or talking about the latest gossip, losing yourself in social media or playing addictive games on apps, watching TV and channel surfing, aimlessly shopping on- or off-line, hiding in your head, and/or isolating yourself through work, drinking too much alcohol or other means. What time-wasting activities can you eliminate? To give yourself the gift of love in just 90 days, you will need to open up ten to thirteen hours per week. If you want to go at a slower pace, as few as five or six hours a week focused on working the Program will move you along nicely.

EXERCISE 3: *GOALS*

Following on page 14 is a complete list of the Ten Goals of the course. Pick out the goals you would like to meet and an approximate date for meeting them.

If You Are in a Relationship Already and You Think He's the One

Pick a goal that is farther down the list, like "Declare love for each other." You will skip the Program of Three, online dating, and STUD *(Seriously Terrific, Utterly Devoted Dude)* and DUD *(Definitely Unworkable Dude)* reports, but you must do all the personal and socializing exercises related to these activities, as they will help your self-esteem and self-love, which are crucial to building a solid love relationship. Your program begins with Chapter 6. And when you get to Chapter 14, you will find a road map for making love last and get better over time.

If You Are in a Relationship and You're Not Sure If He's the One

Read Chapter 2 to see if your relationship fits one of the Deadly Dating Patterns. Then read "Choose the One Only After Months on the Program" and "Follow the Guidelines for Graduating from the Program of Three," which are sections 10 and 11 in Chapter 4. These sections will help you decide whether to stick with your guy or go on a Dating Program of Three.

The Ten Love in 90 Days Goals

1. Create an exciting love intention or affirmation.

2. Create greater self-esteem, deservedness, and self-love.

3. Break out of Deadly Dating Patterns and create a successful Dating Program of Three (more on this in Chapter 4).

4. Move up the ladder to better men.

5. Meet someone who has tremendous potential for a love relationship with you and graduate from the Program of Three.

6. Declare love for each other.

7. Talk seriously with your Beloved about what each of you needs and wants in a fulfilling love relationship.

8. Create a loving win-win contract that gives each of you roots (stability and dedication) and wings (fulfilling your dreams).

9. Commit to moving in together or getting engaged to your Beloved.

10. Marry or make a lifetime commitment to live out your dreams together.

EXERCISE 4: *THE CONTRACT*

When students take my Love in 90 Days workshops, they sign a contract that commits them to complete all thirteen weekly sessions. They agree to three hours of class per week and about ten hours of homework assignments during the week. And that is one way to go for you. That might seem like a lot to you, but your week will include fun new activities, sports, shopping, and dating along with your online and app work. If you want to take the fastest route to finding your own true love, you need to give the Program the same level of commitment. You can also choose to work at a slower pace. It is up to you.

Here's what we tell our clients and what I say to you:

- Push yourself beyond your limits. Face your inner saboteurs and the outer behavioral patterns that don't serve you. This means from day one you will be both working on your internal issues and getting out there and meeting lots of men. I know it's scary. But you have to do both in order to be successful.

- I will give you 110 percent and I expect you to give 110 percent. I expect you to cooperate with the assignments you choose to do or modify them so that they work even better for you. I expect you to invest time and/or money in yourself, courses, makeovers, and online dating. Remember, I am your Love Mentor who is 110 percent behind you.

- Don't just read the exercises that you have decided you need to do. Do them. Play full out. Make this the million-dollar course for yourself, the jackpot to end all jackpots. Even if you fall down, keep going and you will win.

- Expect a roller-coaster adventure and hang on for the ride of your life. I'll be there every step of the way. **On the next page you will see a contract to use if you are following the 90-day course schedule. Amend it if you like, but keep its spirit.**

CONTRACT

I, _____, understand that I am undertaking an intensive course in finding love in 90 days. I commit myself to the full thirteen weeks and to doing the exercises and homework assignments that I have agreed to do. I commit to keeping a journal and following the recommended Program to the best of my ability. This work will be Priority One in my life for the next 90 days.

I further realize that this course will raise emotional issues, make me aware of my self-sabotaging patterns, and surface my hopelessness and despair about finding love. I know that at times I will truly want to backtrack, lose my way, and quit. Nonetheless, I hereby commit to taking this course one day at a time and one week at a time. If I falter during a particular week, I will go back and rework those assignments and exercises until I work through the issues.

To this end, I commit to nurturing myself and taking care of my physical needs so that I can do what I and only I can do: deliver the love I long for.

_____   _____

Signature   Date

The contract is designed to help you stay the course. As Anne Morriss, a manager in the strategy consulting group OTF, said, "The irony of commitment is that it's deeply liberating—in work, in play, in love."

Homework

Choose from among the following suggestions, according to your own intuition:

1. Sign up for two ongoing classes or activities that interest you and *that have lots of men in them.* Here are some examples:

   • Finance
   • Investing, business, or leadership at your local college's school of continuing and professional studies
   • Rock climbing
   • Golfing
   • Snowboarding or skiing
   • Hiking
   • Wine or cigar tasting
   • Coed city sports teams (these usually have an even mix of men and women)

Tips:

   ➤ Choose classes or activities that are more advanced, if possible, as these will have greater numbers of men in them. A more specialized wine-tasting course, for example, or a class in investing in hedge funds or commercial real estate.
   ➤ Choose activities with *intense goals*, like triathlons, marathons, and other advanced running, swimming, and cycling

events and training programs, as they will have more men in them. For example, advanced hikes with the Sierra Club can be great for meeting men. If need be, work your way up to these more challenging events. Check your local Learning Annex.

➤ If you have the skills, you can also *teach a course that attracts men* at your local community center, Learning Annex, or school, like "The Inner Game of Baseball," or "Asian Etiquette for Businessmen." You will be in your element, at maximum charisma, and usually surrounded by men who look up to you.

➤ Do some research online to find even more activities to meet men—there are so many out there! Google any activity, class, club, or topic plus the name of a major city near you. Check out www.meetup.com and peruse its groups. Look into volunteering for a local or national political group, Habitat for Humanity, or another non-profit that attracts men. If you like baseball, go to www.sabr.org to find a Society for American Baseball Research chapter you can join in a city near you.

2. Jump in the water: Find and say hello to three new men every day. Assuming you are in a safe or public place, make eye contact, smile, and say "Hi" or ask for some help. This is what I call the Marcia Cross Technique. Actress Marcia Cross was in her forties when she met her husband by chatting with him in a flower shop. She now is the ecstatic mother of twin girls.

If you don't encounter a lot of men in your daily routine, vary it. Try a new grocery store, dry cleaner, pharmacy, or coffee or sandwich shop at lunch. Take the train or bus to work instead of driving. Check out a new gym, bookstore, or dog park. If you are shy, you can start by saying hello to women or less-threatening men and work your way up to the hotties (see Chapter 7 for great exercises that will free you up to connect easily with people).

If someone hits on you and you are not interested, simply say, "I enjoyed chatting but I'm not available."

3. Find or create a fun event for *this week* that exposes you to a whole new network of people, preferably a network with a lot of men. For example, you could throw a pot luck party and invite your friends and their friends, volunteer for a pet adoption day at the park, get yourself invited to your co-worker's party, or attend a Learning Annex class *this week* on how to buy foreclosed property. Remember, find and say hello to three new men at the activities.

4. If you are currently dating online or on an app, continue. If you are not currently dating online, use Google or your browser window to begin looking at a few of these top sites and apps. Most of the larger sites can be used both online and/or on a mobile phone app. The apps listed below are only available for your phone. I want you to begin looking at one or two sites online and one or two apps. Please note: apps tend to attract more singles who are 45 and under.

Top U.S. Online Dating Sites and Apps

SITES

Match.com (*Our coaching clients have great success with Match and BTW we are not affiliated*)

PlentyofFish.com

OKCupid.com

eHarmony.com

Zoosk.com

Chemistry.com

OurTime.com (*Over 50s*)

SeniorPeopleMeet.com (*Over 50s*)

JDate.com

BlackPeopleMeet.com

EliteSingles.com

ChristianMingle.com

APPS

Tinder (*Largest*)   Happn
Dating (*A feature on*   Hinge
    Facebook)   CoffeeMeetsBagel
Bumble   JSwipe
The League (*Requires*
    application)

Top U.K. Online Dating Sites and Apps

SITES

DatingDirect.com   Zoosk.com
Match.com   JDate.com
eHarmony.co.uk   Shaadi.com (*Indian*)
PlentyofFish.com   ChristianConnection.com
Parship.co.uk

APPS

Tinder   Happn
Bumble

Dana, a thirty-three-year-old graphic designer in our Program hadn't dated in four years. She jump-started her Love in 90 Days Program by joining a specialized dating site. Dana was thrilled with her results and wrote me this e-mail:

Thanks to your Program I have a date this weekend and another one in the works!

Congratulations

Here we are at the end of Chapter 1, which is a whole mini-course unto itself. You have set sail on your Love in 90 Days journey and I congratulate you! As the great poet and physician Oliver Wendell Holmes, Sr., wrote:

> To reach the port of heaven, we must sail sometimes with the wind and sometimes against it, but we must sail, and not drift, nor lie at anchor.

2

---–⋈–---

The Deadly Dating Patterns

These patterns pinpoint the exact reasons you don't have the
love you want in your life with an arrow that leads to the
resolution.—*Shelly, a forty-two-year-old accountant who met her
Beloved, a sweetheart Southern gentleman, a few months after completing her Love in 90 Days course*

Let's start with a familiar scene. You're out with a guy and,
suddenly, you get that gut feeling—you're going to get hurt and
lose out the same way you have before. And even though you
insist, *This guy's different*, and you vow, *No, I'm not going to be disappointed
this time*, sadly, it all comes to pass. And there you are, back to the tissue
box and Ben & Jerry's. You've just played out a dating scenario that
creates exactly the loss you've feared. As Edna St. Vincent Millay said,
"It's not true that life is one damn thing after another—it's one damn
thing over and over." She may just as well have been describing what I
call the Deadly Dating Patterns.

We all have bad habits. They may be self-sabotaging ways you think
about yourself, men, or relationships. Others are dysfunctional ways of
dating or of being in a couple. Our negative beliefs and behaviors reinforce each other and together create the Deadly Dating Patterns.

For almost fifty years, psychologists have studied how our negative
beliefs, secret and not-so-secret self-talk, and irrational ideas sabotage

our happiness. They play lead roles in generating our down moods and not-very-fulfilling behavior. They underlie anxiety, depression, phobias of all kinds including social phobia, and conflict with others. And, of course, they are at the root of the Deadly Dating Patterns.

To get at these habitual and sometimes hidden ways of thinking, we will first look at thirteen different Deadly Dating Patterns. As you read about each of the patterns, you will quickly see the underlying self-sabotaging beliefs. To succeed in the Love in 90 Days plan you will have to pinpoint exactly the patterns that have been short-circuiting your love life. If you see that you are stuck in more than one Deadly Dating Pattern, don't fret—this is common.

Then, later in the chapter, you will do a series of exercises designed to change your negative beliefs and self-talk into more positive and empowering affirmations, or what I call love intentions. I'll give you the clinically proven tools you need so that you can smash through your self-sabotage and take your first steps toward freedom.

Jo, a thirty-four-year-old special ed graduate student, who had experienced one "rejection" after another, wrote about her liberating insight in this section of the course:

> I always felt like I was the one who was being dumped. When I learned about my "I'll Make You Love Me" dating pattern, it was so freeing. I finally understood that I was pushing the guys away. I was dumping them. And I was the one who could stop the pattern.

The Thirteen Deadly Dating Patterns

1. THE FLAME-OUT

This is one of the most common and deadliest of the Dating Patterns. You meet a guy, there's lots of sparks, and he says all the right things! You think to yourself, *He's different; he's the One.* You are higher than a 747. You jump into the sack and have urgent, mind-blowing, maybe even unprotected sex. He says he wants to spend the rest of his life with you, or at least that's how you read what he says. You talk for hours and he understands you in a way that no one else does. Some of the texts he sends you are amazing—short love poems (about you) that zap your heart. You spend a glorious weekend together. Then kaput. Finito. Nada. You sit there alone, making excuses for why his text, e-mail, or call never comes.

Ginger, a twenty-eight-year-old artist, described her Flame-Out guy when she first met him:

> *Justin seemed to be almost the opposite of my ex. Very talkative, very expressive and openly sensitive. I got a feeling he might be a little like my brother-in-law, John—just a real good guy. We spent five hours on the phone together the first time we talked. He said he can't stop thinking about me, that he'd never met a woman like me.*

Over the next few weeks Justin started crying about how much he "felt for" Ginger and how he couldn't believe how amazing he felt when he was with her. Just when Ginger started daydreaming about a simple sunset wedding at their favorite beach, Justin disappeared into the dating Netherworlds, never to be heard from again.

FLAME-OUT WARNING SIGN

He is intimate, adoring, and irresistible from day one, and you feel out of control, like an addict who craves her fix: him!

2. THE FANTASY RELATIONSHIP

You are crazy about and intensely focused on a man who really has no romantic interest in you. It could be a guy you used to date, a co-worker, someone you see at the gym, or sometimes even a star, like Brad Pitt.

If he's an old boyfriend, you daydream about what you used to do with him and/or fantasize about what he is doing, how it is "really meant to be," and the amazing "bond" you two have. You fantasize about how he is "maturing" or "fulfilling his potential" and how he'll definitely come back to you.

If it's a guy you're often around, you ignore any signs of his lack of interest and concoct elaborate meanings for whatever he says or does to indicate that he has feelings for you. How he stayed late at the office to help with your overdue project, or how he gave you that special smile and let you skip in front of him in line for a treadmill. It goes on and on like this for months, maybe even years. In the Brad Pitt scenario, you become a raving fan with a shrine in your room—maybe you even start a fan club.

In the Fantasy Relationship this guy takes up all of your romantic attention. You think and talk about him all the time. But he never asks you out or comes on to you. And you certainly don't start anything that shows your real infatuation with him. But you expect something magical to happen that will shift this relationship into a Cinderella happily-ever-after. The magical and irrational thinking that underlie this pattern keep you and your life on "hold" and out of reality.

Jackie, a sloe-eyed brunette, is a massage therapist who is holding out for Ben, a gifted chiropractor whose office she rents. She says:

> I admire his work so much! We had a thing when I first started working there, but he was still getting over his ex. After he broke up with me I went to my psychic and she said that he was definitely my Divine Right Life Partner. It's been three years now… but I just feel in my gut that he is the one for me. I still feel the chemistry every time we talk. Yesterday he gave me a little adjustment and his hands lingered on my back.

Jackie compares every single guy she meets (and there are very few, because she has hit the Hold button on her love life) to the magical Ben. And—big surprise—not one measures up. Yet Jackie often complains that it is hard going it alone.

FANTASY RELATIONSHIP WARNING SIGN

Down deep you feel empty, sad, and—if you are honest—angry, rejected, and heartbroken by your so-called partner.

3. CRUMBS

In this pattern you are involved with a guy (maybe he's married or a hot, irresistible player) who sees you occasionally and *only* when it works in his schedule. If you pay close attention you may see that he is a flaming narcissist who does not seem to know that anyone outside of himself really exists. He may go through the motions, but fundamentally, he's not really interested in anything about your life.

For the most part, he treats you well when he is with you. If he's wealthy, he may buy you Manolos or take you to five-star dinners. He may take you to the Promised Land in bed. But he's never available when you need or want him (Mr. Big played this role, doling out crumbs to Carrie in *Sex and the City*). And he cuts you off if his wife or his "old flame" enters the scene. *The Crumbs scenario is the exact opposite of what happens in a real, loving relationship, where you and your needs come first and foremost.*

This pattern causes you a great deal of sadness and pain, yet you think that overall, it's a good deal. You spend a lot of time thinking and fantasizing about him: how he's going to leave his wife or stop being a player, or cut back on his work schedule and be with you in a rose-covered cottage or on the beach in Maui. Of course, he does make noises or promises in that direction. In the meantime, you may even get involved with a really nice guy who cares for you and wants to be in a serious and committed relationship. But secretly you've given your heart to the fantasy man who gives you crumbs and not to the real man who is prepared to do everything in his power for you. Ultimately, this pattern will destroy the real relationship you have and you will continue to be a beggar at love's feast. You'd never admit it, even to your best friend, but you believe that this second-class status is the very best you'll ever be able to get and you're damn lucky to have it.

Iris, a forty-two-year-old bouncy redhead, says:

Call me Iris the waitress because I've taken crumbs from the table for so much of life. Take Joe. For eight years, I settled for a married guy who was "always going to leave his wife" and accepted the limited ability he had to love me. I broke it off again and again and pined and wept and back he came. I dreamt of him, of how perfect we were together. I had that Oliver Twist mentality, big saucer eyes with my bowl out saying in a whisper, "Please sir, I want some more," but not really expecting to get more than a rap on the ears.

CRUMBS WARNING SIGN

Your partner is always "making it up" to you for time spent away, holidays missed, or being with another woman.

4. THE HERMIT

You're too busy. Between work, the gym, and walking Max, your dog, you don't have any time for a social life. At the end of a long day you need to collapse with Max on the sofa in your apartment, wolf down your dinner, and watch your HBO alter ego, troubled single Issa, on *Insecure*. You signed up on Match.com, but never used it because you were too busy or exhausted whenever you thought of it. You think, *Someday I'll get around to finding a great relationship*, and that takes care of your worries about it. You barely have any sex drive left at all—the darn machinery down there has gotten so rusty. But it's fine. You can take care of yourself. Really.

A Hermit may be very shy or even socially phobic. Being intimate scares her so much that she hides and avoids contact. All of these fears are masked under the guise of being Ms. Independent.

Iris also has the Hermit problem:

My job has been a glorious eight hours a day, but my commute is a killer—three hours round trip. By the time I get home, I have to clean the house for a bit, answer some emails, wind down, pay some bills and make some calls. I spend a lot of time alone. Good thing I like my own company.

HERMIT WARNING SIGN

You get more pleasure out of watching a romantic comedy by yourself or with your friends than actually flirting with guys or going out on dates.

5. I'LL MAKE YOU LOVE ME

You're turned on by the challenge of changing and winning over a guy who has "potential." When you meet a guy you like, you immediately work overtime to get him: hopping right into bed, making exotic dinners, even buying him tickets to the playoffs. You're not yourself with him; you're busy trying to be the image of what you think he wants in a woman. You're his love slave, chef, therapist, and savior. But one thing you are not being is authentic, a real person, with real needs and desires. Those you keep hidden. You may feel that you are not that lovable, or that if you started asking for things, you'd be a drain.

All you want, consciously at least, is for him to stay and never leave you. What you get is a phone that never buzzes to announce a text from him. Ironically, your over-giving may even propel him into the arms of the nearest girly-girl who needs him to take care of her! When you finally get the bad news through the grapevine, you're completely baffled at how stupid men can be.

Sheila, a bone-weary thirty-three-year-old nurse, put it this way:

I've only had a few real long-lasting relationships. The worst part is that in each one I felt like I lost myself, my friends, my whole identity. I would come home and just do what he was doing, or hang out with his friends. I felt like I was being compromised, yet I wanted the relationship and really loved this person. The weird thing is that somehow in each relationship, the guy came to the conclusion that we were very different people, so we broke up and went our separate ways.

I'LL MAKE YOU LOVE ME WARNING SIGN

While you try to hide it, you feel bored, unhappy, or annoyed by something almost all of the time that you spend with your partner.

6. ABUSE RECYCLE

Usually this starts out great: You meet the guy and he is gorgeous, fabulous, to-die-for. Somewhere down the road, maybe even after a trip to the altar, you find out that he is unbelievably controlling, paranoid, or just plain mean. He treats you with contempt, criticism, or even physical attacks, including rape. You may find that you play out the other end of the spectrum and become abusive yourself. But you hang in there, making excuses, trying to change him, and generally lying to yourself about what's going on. Abuse Recycle is common among those who grew up with an alcoholic or drug-addicted parent or who suffered from verbal, physical, or sexual abuse in childhood. This pattern is truly deadly—it will kill off any love that is possible and is dangerous to your well-being.

Underlying this pattern are some common themes, including: thinking that you are damaged goods and worthless, believing that people are not dependable or trustworthy, feeling powerless, and secretly believing that you really can't do anything to change your life.

Bree, a twenty-nine-year-old flame-haired, freckle-faced actress, describes her Abuse Recycle relationship:

I was with Paul for two years. He was very spiritual but also extremely critical. He felt I was "never good enough." Paul would explode if I left dishes in the sink or the light on in the kitchen. He would go into a rant, almost like a trance of rage directed at me. It was very painful, and there were many hellish nights spent fighting with me crying myself to sleep. Of course, there was also wonderful make-up sex. But I never felt like I could do anything right around him. I felt like I was walking on eggshells. When I took the course, I admitted that I felt unworthy of anything better. And once I did that, I left him for good.

ABUSE RECYCLE WARNING SIGN

You are in a downward spiral where you feel worse and worse about yourself the longer you are with this guy.

7. THE SAFETY NET

A guy is crazy about you but you really think he's too: (a) nerdy; (b) ugly; (c) crazy; (d) uneducated; or (e) unsuccessful—and, therefore, beneath you. But you start seeing him because you feel like he'll never leave you. In this pattern the guy is your safety choice—you really don't care for the sucker. If truth be told, you're embarrassed when your besties meet him. But the guy does whatever you want, sees the movies you like, cooks for you, and provides some kind of security and companionship. Deep down you may believe that you're the one who is not good enough and this is the best you're ever going to do. You also may be terrified of commitment.

There are two possible endings in the Safety Net:

1. You finally come face-to-face with the real void in your chemistry and decide you have to let him go. You put it off, agonizing about

not hurting him, but your real worry is that maybe this is the best you're gonna get—why let go of him, only to be crushed out there? Finally you do the nasty deed, feeling guilt ridden and afraid.

2. He turns himself inside out to please you. Maybe he goes to school, gets a makeover, or gets a good job. As he grows, his self-esteem picks up. Then—surprise, surprise—he dumps you for the blonde girl he sat next to in class. All of a sudden he looks good to you, and you're amazed that you feel so upset. Unfortunately, you realize that you're a day late and a euro short.

Rachel, a striking thirty-eight-year-old management consultant, describes her Safety Net:

> *I wasn't even interested in Moshe. He pursued me. He barely spoke English and lived in a crappy apartment. I thought, No girl is going to want this guy, including me. But I let him in and began to like him. What happened is that he grew up and got better looking! All the girls were chasing him. And I treated him like crap. Then he dumped me, saying I wasn't religious enough for him! At that point, I realized that I chose him because he was safe and that in the beginning I didn't want a real relationship. And the crazy thing is, I still have a thing for him!*

SAFETY NET WARNING SIGN

You only notice how hot your Safety Net could be when he is talking or flirting with another girl at a party.

8. NOT PERFECT—I'LL PASS

Your best friend talks you into signing up for online dating. You interact with a number of men and quickly back out of seeing them because of various defects that each one has: this guy is too cynical, that one has bad teeth, the other anxiously spilled his Espresso Macchiato Grande all over his shirt. The reality is that you don't even give them a chance to emerge and be who they are. No one is good enough.

Now you are not going to agree with the next point, but bear with me: You unconsciously project your own feelings of inadequacy onto each guy you meet or date. The flaw in them becomes blinding, completely and totally turning you off. You run. And your reactions are nothing more than defensive maneuvers designed to guard against being rejected yourself. Then you wonder why there are no good guys out there. I know, I know, this last part is not really you, right?

Rachel was stuck in Not Perfect—I'll Pass as well as in Safety Net. Here's how she describes her defensive pattern in a past relationship:

> *I want someone rich and I meet a lot of rich guys, but most seem sleazy to me. In my late twenties, I got very serious with this banker and we had great sex but I held my feelings back. He wasn't what I'd imagined my man would be; he was heavyset and starting to bald. But he was crazy about me. After six months I really let myself fall for him and he proposed to me. And after that I screwed everything up. One day I started a fight over money: he had gotten a small bonus at work and he was very upset. I wasn't sympathetic at all and instead freaked out because we wouldn't be able to rent the perfect apartment I had found. We broke up and I've been sorry ever since.*

Through our work together Rachel realized that she was hiding something from herself: that the desire to be with a rich guy filled her with shame and a feeling that she was sleazy. She inadvertently projected those feelings onto her relationships as criticisms, which ultimately left her feeling turned off. As a sage once said, "Your fellow is your mirror. If your own face is clean, so will be the image you perceive. But should you look upon your fellow and see a blemish, it is your own imperfection that you are encountering—you are being shown what it is that you must correct within yourself."

NOT PERFECT—I'LL PASS WARNING SIGN

You keep wondering why a woman like you who has so much going for her is single and alone.

9. CHASE ME

You meet a guy, have great sex in his king-sized bed, and open up not only sexually but emotionally. Everything is unfolding perfectly. Too perfectly. After the cozy coupling and three-hour confessionals, you get scared to death. Almost against your own will, you find yourself running away while secretly hoping he'll chase after you.

Your fear of commitment surfaces like a Loch Ness monster and starts running the show. You pull back and become unavailable, distant, or quiet—or you act crazy and dump him. Even if he acts loving, you insist that he doesn't really care about you. It happens almost against your own will and for no particular reason.

The Chase Me is all about fear. When you start to fall for someone, you ultimately end up breaking up with him before he can hurt you. This way, you can control the heartbreak. What you really want is for the man you care for to smash through the barricades you've thrown up and ride in on his white horse and claim you, even if you are halfway around the world in Tokyo. *But you never tell him.* You set him up to fail you. Because you've pushed him away, he doesn't chase after you. And you say to yourself and your friends, "I knew it all along."

Shoko, a successful litigation lawyer, describes her Chase Me pattern:

> *John was an up and coming superstar lawyer in a firm we often went up against. I loved to watch him work, even when we were on opposite sides of a case. One day we wound up having dinner, going to my place and hooking up. I think I had about four orgasms (and I had never been multiorgasmic before that time). John and I were on the same*

*wavelength; we got each other without having to say a word. After four
weeks of juicy dating he used the L word and for some reason I felt totally
turned off. I took a three-month assignment in Vegas and he came to visit
me regularly. We talked about living together back in Chicago but I told
him to go out with other women in the meantime just to be sure. I don't
know what possessed me to say that, but when he asked if I was kidding,
I said no. I think I wanted him to sweep me up in his arms and tell me
how ridiculous that was. Instead he got this sad look on his face and left.
I never once told him how I really felt about him and gave him very little
encouragement. I hear that he's gotten married, and meanwhile, I'm still
waiting for Mr. Right.*

CHASE ME WARNING SIGN

**You love him, you hate him, you just don't give a sh*t—and you
can't stop yourself from acting bitchy or distant.**

10. FADE AWAY

You finally force yourself to get out there in the land of men and date.
And you admit that some of the guys have potential. Some you even
like. You're polite, act interested, and are responsive. But for some reason, none of them ever call you back after the initial Starbucks date. You
don't get it.

What's actually happening is that you are driving men away with
subtle verbal or nonverbal signals that come across as "I don't like you"
or "I'm bored" or "I'm boring you." Deep down you may feel as inviting
as a sack of potatoes. You may not be giving out the feminine green
light or "go" signals. Maybe you do not know how to be fully present
and in the moment, and instead you're inside your own head, endlessly
rehashing thoughts and self-talk instead of paying attention outwardly
and to the guy you're with. At the root of all this behavior is low self-
esteem, which leads to shyness, difficulty being real with others, and

perhaps even poor social skills. These tendencies create nonverbal messages that keep men from wanting to get to know you better. Then you complain that the single men in your home base don't really want to have relationships.

Joy, a twenty-nine-year-old Asian-American bank teller, describes her Fade Away pattern:

> I always feel at a loss for words when I go on these dates. So awkward, afraid I am going to bore the guy to death. And then I wind up doing it. I just don't talk a lot. In my gut I know they'll never call me and they never do.

FADE AWAY WARNING SIGN

On dates you are not being spontaneous, quirky, or real, like you are when you hang out with your close friends.

11. JEALOUSY TRAP

Somehow there is always a triangle: when you're interested in a guy, there's some other girl who is drawing his attention and it makes you scared and mad and jealous as heck. In this pattern, you're not the other woman (for that, see "Crumbs"). You could actually have the whole enchilada with this guy, but instead of building a future with him, you drive the whole relationship downhill with your paranoid thinking, sulking, and jabbing accusations. In fact, you drive the guy right into the arms of your competitor.

Here's what you really believe: You think that every man's fundamentally a player and, more to the point, that no one is really going to choose you. At its heart, jealousy is a belief that you are not good enough to be claimed.

Alisha, a thirty-nine-year-old blonde beauty, describes her Jealousy Trap:

This is my most strongly engrained and painful pattern. The example that stands out the most was with Bill. I was on a boat on the Tennessee River where his band was performing. At one point I went to the bathroom and when I came back a groupie was flirting hard with him. He looked at me as I approached, but he didn't respond the way I hoped, i.e., walk away from her and hug me. He was clearly uncomfortable but I never gave him a chance. I started a fight and when he tried to apologize I stormed downstairs to the bar. He tried again and I told him to forget me and go after the blonde; that she was really his type. We broke up a week later.

JEALOUSY TRAP WARNING SIGN

Your thoughts always stray to the other woman and what your guy is really doing or wants to do with her; you feel tense and irritable.

12. JUST BUDDIES

You have no trouble at all meeting men. They treat you like a buddy, watch and play sports with you, or even ask you to play love counselor for them as they pine for another girl. You may have male colleagues with whom you spend a lot of time because you're a workaholic, just like them. You don't flirt or give those female "go" signals, even if you like a guy. But you definitely talk a lot and spend time together. What's wrong with this picture? The men always marry somebody else—and you do not have a good time at the weddings.

Some of the more common beliefs behind the Just Buddies pattern are: "I am not womanly," "I am not attractive, sensual, or sexual," and "No guy would be interested in me."

Dylan, a brilliant, hardworking engineer whose perfect bod was permanently camouflaged in pantsuits or sweats, talks about her Just Buddies pattern:

I work with a lot of guys and I love sports, so we wind up going out after work to sports bars, kicking back a few drinks and doing the guy thing together. I'm the one they tell all their girl problems to. It's all great, except for Rob, who I think I've been in love with for the past year. He just got engaged! During the Love in 90 Days program, I realized that I'm afraid to be more of a woman with a guy. Truth is, I don't really know how to flirt and have never asked anyone for help.

JUST BUDDIES WARNING SIGN

Getting dressed up and beautiful for a date makes you feel truly strange and uncomfortable, like you are not being the real you.

13. THE GRASS IS GREENER

You meet guys with potential, but you always have this nagging feeling that if you choose one of them, you are foreclosing on all your other options. You're sure that the imaginary men you lose out on are much better than the guy you have in hand. You're afraid you will end up settling for an ordinary or boring relationship—the worst possible thing in the world to you. So instead, you end up confused and incapable of choosing anyone.

In this pattern, you may feel more comfortable in long-distance relationships because your options are more open. You are wildly ambivalent about your partner: one moment you feel like he is the One, the next you feel trapped and resentful. As the relationship progresses, you find more and more faults and reasons to leave.

This is classic commitment phobia running your life. Liz, a bright brunette in her twenties, describes her Grass Is Greener pattern:

I do this one all the time. I have a commitment problem and it plays out in all areas, not just dating/relationships. I often think, in the back of my mind, that there could be something better, especially with a guy. It's like I want to be over the moon and just so excited and thrilled to be with someone. I don't want to help someone grow into a person I could fall for.

Take my most serious relationship, Sam. Sam was amazing; he was really loving and such a caring person. He stood by me while I was recovering from a car accident. He was adorable, but over time I felt we didn't have a lot in common as far as things we liked to do or the people we liked to be with. So I left him.

GRASS IS GREENER WARNING SIGN

You are constantly thinking, thinking, thinking—analyzing your boyfriend and comparing him to an imagined or real guy who seems to be so much better.

Deadly Dating Patterns Summary

In order to find your own true love, you need to understand your deeper beliefs, fears, and issues and look closely at the men you are choosing and not choosing. If you've pinpointed your Deadly Dating scenarios, congratulations! By showing the courage to face yourself, you've taken the first step toward change. I am proud of you. It takes cajones!

✎ Facing Your Deadly Dating Patterns: Exercises ___

Choose from among the following suggestions, according to your own intuition.

Total Time for Completing All of Them: About 35 Minutes

EXERCISE 1: *YOUR DEADLY DATING PATTERNS*

Pick out at least one and as many as three of your deadliest Dating Patterns. In your journal write out several real-life examples of a relationship that exemplified the pattern. Tell each story with: (a) a beginning that describes your partner and how you came together; (b) a middle that describes how the relationship worked when you were together; and (c) how it all ended.

EXERCISE 2: *IDENTIFYING SECRET NEGATIVE BELIEFS*

As we've discovered, it is your secret and not-so-secret negative beliefs that lead you to play out your Deadly Dating Patterns. I'm going to help you uncover those beliefs in this exercise. Be brave and honest—I am with you.

Now, imagine that each story from Exercise 1 was written by another woman. Go back and reread them, and at the conclusion of each one write out the following sentence, filling in the blank with whatever comes to mind:

*This woman followed this pattern because she*_____.

Patricia, a forty-three-year-old Web site designer, wrote:

> *This woman followed the I'll Make You Love Me pattern and chose a man who was totally closed to a monogamous relationship, because she believed that if she hung on long enough, was good enough, and proved herself enough, she would magically get the love she so desperately wanted. The bottom line is that she doesn't believe anyone would love her just for being who she is.*

Now take each of your negative beliefs and write about it in the first person, but as you write about it, magnify it over and over again, until the belief seems absurd. Patricia wrote:

I can make a man love me.... I can be so good that I can create a whole
relationship with someone who doesn't want one. I am in total control
no matter what the other person says. I can hang on and force anyone to
love me. I am superwoman.

After Patricia finished writing the last sentence, she laughed and
started to disengage from the distorted thinking that was running her
dating life.

EXERCISE 3: *THE LOVELESS EULOGY*

If you drag these sabotaging beliefs and deadly patterns into your future,
you will be living and reliving your past for the rest of your life.

- Contemplate living with this self-sabotage for the next five years.
  How old will you be?
- Contemplate being stuck in these limiting beliefs and patterns ten
  years from now. How old will you be?
- Contemplate living out those patterns until you die. **Now, write**
  a eulogy for yourself that describes the loveless life you
  have led.
- Do you want to be the person you've just described? You don't have
  to be. Either you can keep the same scripts running your love life, or
  you can change them. It's up to you.

Here's what Julia, a thirty-nine-year-old dentist, wrote as her loveless
eulogy:

Julia lived an overachiever's life. She had reached out, but had hidden
from love. She watched on the sidelines of love, crying and laughing, but
not really participating. Because she was afraid to be vulnerable and
had a habit of isolating herself from romantic relationships under her

many roles of caregiver, mentor, advisor and best friend, she prevented love from fully manifesting or taking root. She had a taste but never a satisfying meal of love. Julia put a lot of effort out, but she always had fear in her heart and the expectation of disappointment and failure. Down deep she believed that she would always be hurt. Julia had a brief marriage that didn't work out and lived out a very long life alone and childless. She died a lonely death in a nursing home at the age of 104.

EXERCISE 4: YOUR OWN PRESCRIPTION FOR LOVE

If you were your own best friend and Love Mentor, what helpful and loving advice would you give yourself regarding men and dating? Write this out and post it in a private place, like your closet, where you will see it every day. Julia wrote:

You have to choose the ones that are into you!!!!! You know you want a baby and there is no time to waste!!

EXERCISE 5: YOUR PERSONAL LOVE INTENTION

What is your intention about creating love in your life? Think about this carefully. I don't want you to write down what you usually spit out when friends ask you what you want in a relationship. I want you to create your real intention, as if there were no limits. State it in one sentence, in the present tense. For example, I give myself a fulfilling relationship with a loving life partner. Or My loving partner and I share a passionate life together including art, children, and service to the world.

Write your love intention out and read it. Does it make you feel good? If not, tinker with it until you feel happy just imagining or thinking it. Once you've created a love intention that's just right for you, post it in your closet or in a place where you will see it every day. What we envision and put our attention on tends to come to us.

Congratulations—creating a love intention that is inspiring and exciting means you have met the first benchmark goal in the Love in 90 Days Program!

EXERCISE 6: *A COMMITMENT TO YOURSELF*

In your journal, I want you to write the following commitment: *I will work on breaking my Deadly Dating Patterns for the next* (90 days or other period of time). *After that, I can go back to them if I so choose.*

Dylan, the engineer who was caught in the Just Buddies pattern, chose to escape it completely during the course. She got a new wardrobe, threw out all her precious sweats, and started wearing dresses that showed her hourglass figure. Dylan says:

> *Putting on the makeup every day was a challenge at first, but then it actually got to be fun, like I was designing a new me. And I am definitely not one of the guys now! I'm dating two different men and I just met a third at the gym.*

 Homework

Choose from among the following suggestions, according to your own intuition:

1. Ask one or two good friends to help you break your Deadly Dating Patterns. Empower her or him to confront you and encourage you to stop taking crumbs, being a hermit, flaming out, or doing whatever your particular self-sabotaging dance is.
2. Continue attending classes or activities with lots of men in them.
3. Continue saying hello to three new guys each day—vary your daily routine, if necessary, to meet them (remember, you can start by saying hi to women first if you're too intimidated to speak to men yet). Every person has a social network of about 200 people, so each

new friend you make gives you that many more possibilities to meet someone. Make smiling and saying hello a habit.

4. If you are dating digitally, continue. As you look through the profiles, make a conscious effort to break your Deadly Dating Patterns. Look at photos and profiles and respond to matches, winks, or messages from people you would ordinarily pass on.

5. Sign on to one of the top online dating sites listed in Chapter 1 as a male looking for a female. Peruse the other women's photos, screen names, and profiles. Jot down ideas for yourself. If possible, have a male friend help you.

You have just completed Chapter 2. No matter how much or how little you have done with the assignments, you are moving ahead and I am proud of you. How did you do in writing down your love intention/affirmation in Exercise 5? Read it again. Does it make you feel good to read or think it? If not, tinker with it until it does make you feel good. When you get to the point where your love intention makes you feel happy just imagining or thinking it, that's a sign that it is just right for you. Congratulations! Creating a love intention that feels good means you have met the first benchmark goal in the Love in 90 Days Program!

Norman Vincent Peale, the father of positive thinking, describes the path so many of us have followed in the realization of any goal, including our love intentions:

> If you want to get somewhere, you must decide definitely where you want to be....Be sure it is a right objective, then photograph this objective on your mind and hold it there. Work hard, believe in it and the thought will become so powerful that it will tend to assure success.

Dating Games Men Play

SIXTEEN DEADLY DATING PATTERNS YOU NEED TO KNOW NOW

You come to love not by finding the perfect person, but by seeing an imperfect person perfectly.—*Sam Keen*

Have you ever asked yourself about guys…
How could he disappear after he was so totally into me? Why hasn't he texted? Why does he pull away every time we get close? Was it just about the sex? How could he not be interested in me? Why doesn't he make a move? *Why did he put his profile back up? Will he ever commit? What the bleep is going on with him? Is it him or is it me?*

Ah, men. Mystifying men.

And we're supposed to be the mysterious ones! Truth is, men are at *least* as hard to figure out as women. Their behavior can be confusing, frustrating, and maddening. They tease us with clever poems, roses, daily texts, and calls, only to turn around in the blink of an eye and completely disappear or disappoint us. Who hasn't fallen for that grand opening game where they lure us with intoxicating conversations, funny dates, a perfect little heart necklace, delicious kisses, and more?

Fortunately, I've logged many therapy hours listening to men as they've opened up and explored their deepest needs and fears. Those private moments have given me a unique window into understanding guys' dating games and issues. And in this chapter, I will take you behind the scenes and share those intimacies with you.

The good news is that they, like us, usually really do want true love, and down deep they realize that they'd be happier, more content, and more sexually satisfied if they had a good relationship. The bad news is they are also scared, and they push real intimacy or commitment away. Men fear being overwhelmed and taken over in an all-consuming couple-ship. Believe it or not, they also fear rejection and abandonment. And all these fears play out in a variety of ways. Men play out unconscious and conscious games that create a maddening push-pull with your heart. That's why dating them can be so confusing and frustrating.

Guys' fears of being vulnerable, of being loved and loving, lead them to enact their dating games or more precisely what I call Men's Deadly Dating Patterns (MDDPs). Like us, they have habitual ways of sabotaging themselves when it comes to romance and love. Unfortunately, men often follow these same self-destructive dead-end patterns over and over again, sinking possibilities of love into the netherworld in the process.

Understanding Men's Deadly Dating Patterns is crucial not only to your success in creating the love you want, but also to your own self-esteem and happiness. When you learn to clearly see whom you are dealing with and understand his patterns, you can free yourself from second-guessing about what you did wrong whenever a relationship falls apart. You will be able to let go of thoughts like *"I should have told him how much I enjoyed the comedy club he picked out and that I would love to go again! That's why he's not calling." "My thighs are so big and I wore that clingy dress. That's what turned him off!" "He broke it off because I am___(old, needy, successful, have kids, am fat.")* (Fill in the blank.) When we don't understand our partner's Deadly Dating Patterns and things blow up, it is ultraeasy to go into knee-jerk negative self-blame: *"It ended because of something I said or did, or something I didn't say or do."*

Being familiar with MDDPs can liberate us from these self-blaming thoughts. Instead, we can more easily say—and understand—*"It is not just about me. It's about him and his issues."* We can view relationships in a more balanced way, examining more objectively who did what to whom.

In order to have this kind of emotional freedom in dating it is important to be like an anthropologist in the world of men—to study them and understand their unique qualities and attributes. You need to suspend judgment about what a man *ought* to be like. We expect a lot based on fairy tales, romantic movies, and the media: the all-perfect prince is supposed to come along and sweep us away to the magic kingdom of love. But real life is not a fairy tale or a movie. There are no perfect guys. Of course, you also need to examine your own Deadly Dating Patterns (see Chapter 2) and be on top of them. Understanding yourself is critical for your own growth. But beyond that, I want you to clearly see men's struggles.

Sometimes a guy is so entrenched in his dating game issues that he will act the same way with most any woman. He is caught in a behavioral loop, an unconscious program he is totally unaware of, that is running in his mind. Chances are he will play out the same scenario with the next six women he dates. If he is truly caught in his own Deadly Dating loop, there is nothing you can do to change this. Not *even you* can succeed—I know what you were just thinking!

You want the guys who are healthier, more normal. There are guys who never had to struggle with Deadly Dating Patterns and they make great partners. There are also thoughtful guys who are aware of their self-sabotaging patterns. They may joke about them or talk about how they have progressed and learned about women or dating. These are the guys who can fall for you in a lasting way. They are the ones who are willing to grow, have the basics, and are crazy about you (see Chapter 4).

The severity of MDDPs varies from person to person. A key question to ask yourself is: How trapped is this guy in the web of his own creation? How consciously and unconsciously determined is he to keep himself high and dry and out of the life-giving water of love? First, look for signs in what he says about the possibility of real love, you, women in general, and his past relationships. Read between the lines: What can you notice that reveals how he thinks about his future in terms of a long-term relationship or marriage? How does he describe other couples? If a friend of his is getting married, is he cynical? Does he describe his married buddies as trapped in some way? Does he say it would take a good three to four years to know if a person is ready to be with someone? Does he say love never lasts? Did his parents stay married, and, if so, how does he describe their relationship? If divorced, did they remarry successfully? Does he have any role models who have shown him what a good marriage is like?

Next, find out if he is willing to grow and work on his issues. If he is self-reflective, willing to take advice, in a growth course, being coached, or in therapy, he is showing signs of working on himself. You may meet an older or more evolved man who has grown beyond his self-sabotage, leaving only traces of it in his current life. If a guy has a few Deadly Dating Patterns, yet he is working on himself and crazy about you, he may become a great partner for you. Once again, no man is perfect. But then, of course, neither are you. The question is how much does this man want to have love—that is, love with you in his life? And what is he willing to do or change to have that special, lasting experience?

Don't be too discouraged if you find as you read through the list in this chapter that the man you are most interested in has a few Deadly Dating Patterns playing out. This is quite normal. Everyone has issues. Men, like us, are works of art in progress.

In the very beginning of a relationship it may be very hard or even impossible to know for sure if a guy is caught in any one Deadly Dating Pattern. Many of the patterns start out with a perfectly great opening phase. This is another important reason why it is a powerful protective step for you to go on the Dating Program of Three. If you see three guys at the same time and compare and contrast their styles, you will see their romantic patterns more easily. Plus by going slowly and avoiding sex with all of them, you will be able to see each one's Deadly Dating Patterns emerge.

By the time you finish this chapter I hope you have many Aha experiences in understanding and being clear about these patterns. Armed with this knowledge you can quickly get away from guys who are DUDs (Definitely Unworkable Dudes) or relationships that are truly dead-end or even destructive. You can see clearly when it is time to stay and work on the relationship or when it's time to cut your losses and go. You can be freer to choose the ones you want, the ones who give you love that is just right for you.

In order to do that, I will arm you with the information you need about the sixteen most common MDDPs based on personality types. Some of them are much more ingrained and difficult than others for the guy to overcome. I rate the degree of difficulty of each pattern, based on my clinical experience, on a scale of 1 to 10, with 10 being the most challenging. I have also divided the MDDPs into three groups: easier to overcome, moderately difficult, and most challenging (these I advise you to stay away from!). So put on your anthropologist hat and identify any Deadly Dating Patterns of the single men you meet.

The Sixteen Men's Deadly Dating Patterns

EASIER TO OVERCOME

1. The Shy Guy

This guy is really into you. He may even be crazy about you. But he cannot show it. He is too fear-bound, afraid he will make the wrong move, turn you off. He may be very handsome, but he has low self-esteem, feels unworthy of love, and, to top it all off, has poor social skills. The Shy Guy is a wallflower who tries to be with you or move toward you but stops short of making intimate contact. Bottom line: he is terrified that he will say the wrong thing, be a poor kisser, or, worse, a poor lover. Because he was very awkward or shy as a teenager and rejected by girls, he may feel he is ugly and just not attractive—in spite of the fact that he is physically a hottie!

A Shy Guy may be attractive to you, but mysterious and totally confusing. You keep flirting, tossing your hair, touching his arm—but he never ever makes a move on you. He's too afraid. The more he likes you, the more afraid he becomes. A Shy Guy makes you wonder whether he is really interested, not interested, or even gay.

With a Shy Guy you need to make the first moves. Flirt, take his hand, and snuggle into him. His response will help you determine whether or not he's truly into you.

Joanie, a willowy blonde who was a graduate of the Love in 90 Days Program, fell hard for a Shy Guy named Jimmy:

> Jimmy is my brother-in-law's friend and I met him at a party. He was totally my type—blond, six foot four, and lean. He was standing against the wall alone, nursing a beer. I just kept talking to him and he nodded. From the beginning, he was so quiet; I had to keep thinking of things to talk about. He did not bring up a single topic. Finally I got Jimmy to laugh about something or other. He went off to get another beer and that was it. I wasn't sure if he was interested at all. Luckily I called my brother-in-law afterward and asked him to scope it all out. He found out that Jimmy was definitely interested and planned to call me. Three weeks went by—no call. So I decided to call him. We met for a beer, had a few laughs. I followed up with a double date with my sister and brother-in-law. Jimmy put his arm around me and showed me a lot of attention and affection. We've been seeing each other for a year now. He's quiet, but I think he's a keeper. To me Jimmy is the strong, silent type. Now that we're together, he comes alive when we are alone.

Shy Guy Warning Signs: *He asks you out but never does so much as take your hand or try to kiss you. Plus, you have to do all the talking.*

Degree of Difficulty: 3. *You have nothing to lose by making the first moves. If he responds positively, you might just bring him out.*

2. *The Geek*

This is the brainiac who doesn't know how to connect or feel comfortable with other people. He has poor social skills, acts nervous, and may do some strange things. He is engrossed in his own unique interests, computer games, or electronics. He might feel ugly, unpolished, and not worthy of a woman's attention or a relationship. He may be physically awkward, avoiding eye contact, or act like he is in awe of a gal he really likes.

The Geek is used to being a loner or hanging out only with his kind. Even if you are geeky, he is usually afraid to put the moves on you. He feels like he can't even kiss worth a darn. Unlike the Shy Guy, our Geek may also be argumentative—taking the opposite perspective on any topic that is brought up. He does this to show how much smarter he is than everyone else. And intellectually he may be, but he can also be obnoxious. However, if he becomes professionally successful, he can blossom socially and become less arrogant.

Often, a Geek is not in shape and may be couch potato fat or very thin. But under this exterior, he often has a wonderful sensitivity and understanding. Unfortunately, those great qualities may be hard to get to because of isolation he suffered in his early years and his history of failure with others. He may distance himself from and reject a woman he cares for. So even though you may like him, you have to understand that he is not used to being liked. You have to be prepared to be pushed away.

Sheila, a twenty-nine-year-old Web site designer, describes her experience with a Geek named Brant:

> We met at the INTEROP, the big tech conference in Las Vegas. Brant
> and I were both interested in virtualization. We spent a few evenings

together hanging out and talking for hours about cloud computing and it was so much fun. He was very geeky looking but absolutely the smartest guy I ever met. I really liked Brant and wanted him to take my hand, kiss me, or come on to me in some way. But I think neither of us was able to make a move on each other. After we left the conference we e-mailed quite a bit, but it was all about cloud computing and never seemed to get personal. I decided to be more forward and invited him to be my guest at a seminar my company was hosting. At the conference lunch break, I took his hand and showed him a quiet place to eat lunch. I know he really appreciated my warmth because he invited me to come and see him speak at a big IT event in New York. Things just progressed from there and even though I've made most of the first moves including the engagement, he was the one who went out and bought me a beautiful ring.

Geek Warning Sign: *He dresses and acts in a decidedly "uncool" way.*

Degree of Difficulty: 4. *Make some moves on him and see if he is interested. He might be able to learn some social skills from you that help him develop into a great partner. Ladies, some of these guys make the best partners because they are loyal and really smart.*

3. The Savior

This is a super-duper caretaker, a Mr. Fix-it. He comes in and repairs your broken pipes, helps you with your work project, runs errands, and is uber-helpful. In fact, he will do just about anything you want him to do. And he tries to be romantic, too. He wants to buy you fancy dinners, maybe even a car or a house. At a deeper level, however, all his caretaking is about buying your attention and affection because at the core he feels like he doesn't really deserve love.

The Savior is insecure and feels not good enough. He comes across with a needy vibe underneath it all, where he is looking to you for approval, asking what you think, what you are drinking or ordering for dinner, before he makes a decision. His feelings depend on what you think and feel. If you are sad, disappointed, afraid, or upset, he is upset. He simply cannot tolerate your being down emotionally. He can't separate out his own feelings.

The helpful Savior can be good for you at first. But if you outgrow him by becoming less needy and more independent, the whole relationship can fall apart. Remember what happens to the Diane Keaton character as she outgrows the Savior played by Woody Allen in the classic *Annie Hall?* On the other hand, if the Savior is willing to grow, he may become flexible enough to handle your independence and things can work out nicely.

Gina, a single mom with two preteen sons, had a relationship with a Savior named Bill, whom she finally married:

> *When I started seeing Bill, I needed a car for my new job. He helped me buy an older model at a very cheap price and did some work on it for me. He was so caring and helpful and bonded with my kids really quickly. He got them a used Xbox game and they loved to play with him! Bill was not the type I usually go for, but I really thought he was perfect for us. But after a while he started getting on my nerves. I had some problems with my boss at work and got depressed. He somehow couldn't tolerate that. He started drinking, I think out of frustration. But my father was an alcoholic and I could not tolerate the drinking. So I called him on it. Bill admitted that he felt useless because he couldn't help my situation. I told him that it wasn't his job to fix everything in my life and that if he continued to drink as a way of calming himself that I would leave him. Strangely, that seemed to turn the trick. We went into couples counseling and he stopped drinking. Six months later we went to Jamaica and got married on the beach.*

Savior Warning Sign: *He is always trying to be helpful and he cannot stand it if he fails and you are still feeling down or upset.*

Degree of Difficulty: 4. *Sometimes the Savior can learn to detach from you and focus on himself and his own needs. Then the relationship can become more balanced and just might work out.*

4. The Coward

It starts out great—he loves you and shows it. But over time he makes you the boss, always asking what you want instead of saying what he wants. He acts submissive and weak and then resents you for taking over. He is afraid of honest straight talk and very afraid of conflict. When the inevitable problems and differences in a relationship come up, he stuffs his feelings and drifts away. He prefers e-mail or texts when dealing with uncomfortable issues. He is a wuss underneath it all who is simply frightened of women. The Coward doesn't have the courage to stand up to his partner, so problems fester and get out of control. And when it comes to the boiling point, he doesn't have the courage to break up. Instead he is passive-aggressive, gently slipping away as his texts and calls fade out. Above all, the Coward fears rejection, a feeling so shameful that it is almost like annihilation, of being completely destroyed. So he slithers and slides around any kind of conflict and may sneak out of the relationship by disappearing, and passively rejecting the woman.

Most men have some degree of this pattern. That is, they try to avoid conflict. This is because guys tend to have much more difficulty in dealing with stress. Research shows that after an argument, men's heart rates and blood pressure readings get more elevated than women's. And they stay higher, too. That's because men have a more difficult time soothing and quieting themselves down after any kind of upset. So they may clam up or try to avoid any kind of charged interaction with you. Some men have a less intense version of the Coward pattern than others—which means you can learn to communicate with them using what I call Positive Shaping Talk. For more on how to use this powerful tool, see Chapter 12.

On the other hand, if the Coward dynamic is extreme, the coupleship simply dies on the vine. While the woman is the one who actively breaks up the relationship, it is the Coward who passively and unconsciously makes it impossible to continue together because he is simply not available for a real conversation.

Shawn, a sloe-eyed brunette in her thirties, had a disappointing experience with a Coward type:

> Jacques was such a dear when we first met for espresso. He was from Belgium and a foodie, just like me. He took me to the best meals I have ever had—and brought me chocolate that was to die for. But he had a real problem with my twin sister, a chef—who happens, I admit, to be a know-it-all. They had some knock-down, drag-out fights. Somehow, I could never talk to him about it. He clammed up and gave me the feeling it was either him or her. Of course he never said that. He just kind of disappeared after scuffling with her. Crawled into a black hole. In the end I e-mailed him to tell him it was all over.

Coward Warning Sign: *When you try to air differences with him, he changes the subject, goes into text communication mode, or otherwise disappears on you.*

Degree of Difficulty: 4+. *The outcome here depends on how willing the Coward is to respond to Positive Shaping Talk, where you present your concerns in a loving, warm way.*

MODERATELY DIFFICULT

5. Burnt Toast

Mr. Burnt Toast was burnt in the past and is living it over and over in the present. He never stops complaining about his ex-wife or ex-girlfriend(s). After all, his wife, naturally, was a "crazy b*tch" or an alcoholic/addict who took him for everything. Or his first girlfriend, the first love of his life, left him to be with his best friend. The Burnt Toast guy is cynical. Mistrusting all women, he vows never to be vulnerable again—because if he is, he will just be hurt. If he took a hit financially in a divorce and/ or is wealthy, he may be afraid that women want him just for his money. But it also means that he feels he doesn't really deserve love. Some of these men had abusive mothers and as a result believe that all women are mean, manipulative, and exploitative.

In spite of his woes, the Burnt Toast guy may be very appealing because he tends to bring out the protector, the caregiver in you. If he spins a really good story about how he was hurt, this trap is easy to fall into. But in the early going, this type of guy is usually after sex and/or sympathy and he is not really interested in having a serious relationship. If he is working on himself and experiences your caring and devotion his attitude may change. But if it does change, it usually takes a few years.

Lina, a client who was a caring and dedicated social worker, is engaged to a Burnt Toast guy:

> I met Larry online. He was a dead ringer for my father, physically and emotionally, as I later found out. At first I really liked him because he seemed so open, talking about his loneliness, missing his kids, and how much his divorce hurt. He told me that he had tried couples counseling with his wife, but that she was an alcoholic. The therapist told him that it was hopeless because his wife was a borderline (crazy). She somehow took all the money and the kids and managed to get Larry fired from his job. At first it all made sense. I even saw him get some nutsy text messages

from his ex. Then I realized that Larry truly had his own issues and hopelessness about women and love. I asked him to take the Landmark Forum (personal growth) course. He finally did after a year of us talking about it. He got an enormous amount out of the course and then started working on his negative beliefs in counseling. It has been five years now and I am very excited to say that he asked me to marry him.

Burnt Toast Warning Sign: *He is endlessly complaining about other women in his past.*

Degree of Difficulty: 5. *Try only if he knows he's got Burnt Toast issues and is working on giving up his cynicism and you are patient!*

6. The Peter Pan

This is a guy who is afraid of growing up, being a man, and taking on the responsibilities of a relationship, children, and family life. This particular Deadly Dating Pattern starts in the guy's early family life. He may have had a father who worked himself into the ground and yet could not provide enough income for a good family life. This was his role model and he identifies and feels doomed to repeat this life script in a serious relationship. Or the Peter Pan may have had a larger-than-life business mogul father whom he felt he couldn't measure up to. If he was repeatedly put down by his parents, told he was stupid, incompetent, or not good enough, he may have internalized that input as part of his self-image. Or he may have had a hyperdemanding mother who criticized his father and/or him for not being good enough. Men in his family may have been put down by the women. The Peter Pan is boyish in his leisure activities. He may be a video game addict who is glued to his game console at all times. Or he may spend many hours watching or playing sports.

Even if he is successful and doing well financially as an adult, the Peter Pan is still afraid he cannot provide the emotional caretaking that is required to make a woman happy. To a Peter Pan, having a relationship means having to take on enormous responsibility.

If the pattern is extreme, he may totally balk at being in a couple. If it is not, he may simply be ambivalent about being in a relationship. If he is in the latter category, he may be won over as he eases into a win-win relationship with you and sees that it can be a true partnership.

One variation of the Peter Pan Deadly Dating Pattern is the Mama's Peter Pan. In this variation, the guy is smitten with you in the beginning. Even though there are some alarm bells, you are charmed. After all, he has such a great relationship with his mother! He seems to really appreciate women. He is self-confident and a little cocky and thinks he is hot stuff. You find that all very appealing. Plus, he is a loyal guy who is close to his whole family. He may live at home or near his relatives. Or he may visit his family at least once a week. He may even be a great caregiver who looks after a sick or impaired family member.

Little by little, the other shoe drops. You find out that he talks to his mother on the phone *every day*. As the relationship unfolds you come to understand that his family only tolerates you and may not like you very much. You find out that you may be the wrong color or ethnicity or just not good enough in his mother's eyes. Even though he says he is truly crazy about you, the bottom line is that his life is all about loyalty to his mother, his family, and his ethnic roots—all of which somehow turn out to be in opposition to what you need and want.

His mother's/family's wishes come first. He can't take you away to that Caribbean resort on your birthday because his family reunion is that weekend. The mama's boy is torn in half between his feelings for you and his loyalty to the clan. In the extreme case he can't seem to separate from his family and can't/won't stand up to them to claim what he says he really wants: you. On the other hand, there are mama's boys who are less emotionally entangled with their mothers. If you are willing to be patient, it is possible to help this type of guy grow away from his childlike enmeshment and into a relationship with you.

My client, Karimah, succeeded after a number of years with a Mama's Peter Pan type:

> *Biagio and I totally hit it off after meeting on a large online site. We would amuse each other, talking and laughing for hours. We were totally on the same wavelength and even used to finish each other's sentences. Even our bodies seemed to fit together. It was quite magical. We dated furiously for six weeks and then he told his mother about me. She was a supercontrolling Italian mama (mind you, I love Italian families!) who did not take kindly to the idea of her son dating an African-American woman. Biagio swore up and down that he didn't care and he was going to choose me. But I noticed that after every visit with his mom, he was withdrawn, depressed. It made me very uncomfortable. After two years of battling about it, I told Biagio I was leaving and I meant it. He came after me and actually cut things off with his mom for a while, which I think was good for him! It has been four years now and we have just gotten married.*

Peter Pan Warning Signs: *He comes right out and says that marriage and family life would be too much of a burden for him. Or he has to consult with family members every time he makes a decision more important than what socks to wear.*

Degree of Difficulty: 6. *Move on unless (1) he is working on his separation issues and fear-bound thinking and becoming more mature, and (2) you are the patient type.*

7. *The New Ager*

You meet him at yoga, at a retreat, or through your spiritually minded friends. Sweet and sensitive—the New Ager is a dream come true: he looks deeply into your soul, giving you the best eye contact you've ever had. He gets five stars for being cute, in great shape, a listener, very spiritual, and possibly on your very own path. Maybe he even teaches at the yoga studio you go to frequently.

Yes, he is soft, sensitive, conscious, and gentle...too gentle. Try as you might, there is never that masculine spark, that sexy-aggressive come-on, that cocky walk and talk that gets your pulse racing. You have a serious crush and wait and wait in vain for it to happen. But it never does. Bottom line: this guy is more into his spiritual path than into dating. And, while he is seductive and asks you to meet him for carrot juice, he is definitely not into you.

A variation of this theme, which is very confusing, is the guy who uses his spiritual platform to sleep around with as many women as possible. Usually he convinces you that he is not really interested in sex, but only what it can do for the two of you spiritually. This type of New Ager is actually a closet Player!

Jorga was a spiritual raw foodist who experienced a round of "dating" with a New Ager:

Ray-El was giving a lecture on green living at the local health food store. I couldn't take my eyes off him—his face was so healthy and radiant! There was this cleanness, this innocence about him, that I fell in love with immediately. I signed up for a lecture series he was giving and hung around with him after every meeting. When he asked me to teach him how to go raw, I was thrilled—after all, my last boyfriend had broken up with me over the whole raw food thing! Ray-El came over to my apartment. I made him my best feast, from uncooked soup to dessert nuts. He told me he was studying tantric yoga—and I was a goner. He was the gentlest lover ever and I was in heaven. That is until I found out this was Ray-El's standard MO with every woman under the age of thirty in our whole green community.

New Ager Warning Sign: *He is very spiritual and there is either no chemistry whatsoever or he's in a hurry to explore tantra and other sexual practices.*

Degree of Difficulty: 7. *Ladies, stop wasting your time unless he becomes "enlightened' and decides to make room for a relationship!*

8. The Trophy Seeker

This is a narcissistic guy, a prince or king in his own mind who is successful and used to getting his way. He shows off his power by spending wildly on you with grand gestures calculated to blow you away. He loves to dress you up and parade you around. $650 Manolos? No problem! Showing you off just enhances his personal power and prestige. In the extreme pattern the Trophy Seeker may feel perfectly entitled to see other women—after all, he has paid his way with you. You are one of his beautiful possessions.

As you continue along in a relationship with an extreme Trophy Seeker, you come to realize that his gestures of love toward you are simply part and parcel of the typical caretaking and polishing he gives to his other possessions. Buying you a dress is like putting a marble facade on the front of the entrance to his business. It is hard for a Trophy Seeker to love a woman with true empathy, compassion, with all his heart. He often believes that his lover is with him just for money. Of course, like all the patterns there are different degrees of narcissism. In the less extreme case a Trophy Seeker may be aware that something is missing from his emotional life and he may be willing to work on developing empathy and compassion.

Demi, a stunning brunette model and actress, dated Rich, a very successful CEO and Trophy Seeker:

> *Rich and I met at a children's charity event where I came with another guy who was a friend. I could feel him eyeing me from across the room.*

He bid for more auction items than anyone else and put out big bucks for the kids. I was impressed. When I left my date to go to the ladies' room Rich cornered me and asked me out. Wowed by him and his generosity, I immediately accepted. What followed was a series of dates where he picked me up in his chauffeured limo and took me to the best restaurants, celebrity-laced parties, and fund-raisers. Both of Rich's homes—the gentleman's farm in Bucks County and his penthouse in the city—were filled with art and antiques. Only later, after the wow factor wore off, did I realize that both places were like museums, in every sense of the word. Rigid was Rich's middle name. He even had the food in his refrigerators in color-coded Tupperware and screamed at me if I moved them out of their prescribed order. Rich loved to talk—about himself. The sex was great but I never felt like I could share intimate thoughts with him. If I seemed upset, he would want to buy me something. I never really trusted him. After discussing the whole situation with Diana, I decided to break things off. I need someone who I can connect with emotionally.

Trophy Seeker Warning Sign: *He is very into himself, his possessions, and his status or appearance to others.*

Degree of Difficulty: 7. *This depends on how into himself the Trophy Seeker is and how important it is for you to have a close, emotionally intimate relationship. If money and security are most important to you, it can work out with him.*

9. The Commitment Phobe

It all starts out perfectly enough. At first the Commitment Phobe comes across as a super or at least interesting guy who is totally into you. Months pass and you draw closer, happily thinking he is the One. Then the "F word" rears its ugly head. Not that "F word"—I mean "F" as in "future." If you even mention having a future together, he changes the subject and slithers out of the conversation. If you come back to the topic he gets quiet, nervous, upset, or angry. The Commitment Phobe may be reluctant to act like he's in a couple when you are with friends or out in public. He may talk only in the first person, saying "I" instead of "we" or "me" instead of "us." He may keep you away from meeting his friends and family. You may be in an on-again, off-again relationship with a Commitment Phobe for years—where he always seems to want you when he can't have you, yet he just cannot pull the trigger and commit when you are together.

If the relationship has progressed to having sex, he may need to make an escape and go home instead of spending the night in your bed. He may feel emotionally unavailable to you. Usually the Commitment Phobe is unable to use the "L word," as in being "in love" with you, even though you have been seeing him steadily for many months or even years. He may say he is not sure what love really is or that he is incapable of experiencing love. Or that he doesn't have to say it, he just has to show it. He may come right out and say that he does not believe in love, marriage, or getting serious and settling down with one person.

This is a guy who is terrified of jumping fully into a long-term relationship because he believes he can't be himself and fully be with a woman. In his view he has to give up the lead role in his own life if he is stuck in a supporting role with you and/or the children. It seems like his golf, buddies, bar days, sports, even the Super Bowl are going to be ripped away by the all-powerful, all-controlling vortex of the couple. For this man commitment, love, and marriage mean being trapped in a cage from which there is no escape.

Sheri, a graduate of the Love in 90 Days Program, spent three years trying to work it out with Jason, a Commitment Phobe type:

> *Jason always said he didn't really believe in marriage. Somehow I blocked out the truth of that statement. Deep down I believed he was my soulmate, the One, and it was our destiny to be together. Several psychics even told me that. I made many affirmations about us being together and happy. But the truth was, we fought like crazy about*

getting married and broke up a few times. He would always come back, with promises—promises he couldn't keep. Now I am turning forty-one and worried about ever having the kids I want more than anything. That relationship may have cost me my dream.

Commitment Phobe Warning Signs: *When you mention commitment, moving in together, getting engaged, or married, he (a) clams up, (b) changes the subject, (c) gets nervous, (d) picks a fight, or (e) all of the above. Another Warning Sign: the guy is forty-five-plus and has never been in a long-term relationship or married.*

Degree of Difficulty: 8. *Intensive therapy is required. Be prepared to wait five years or longer. If you are thirty-five-plus and you want to have kids, be prepared to adopt.*

MOST CHALLENGING

10. The Grass Is Greener

Online and app dating has made this Deadly Dating Pattern VERY common. Because there is such a smorgasbord of women out there, many men are ready to stop seeing you at a moment's notice to see what new chickie is appearing on his screen. The Grass Is Greener guy may sweep into your life and start a perfect romance. Being superattentive, he brings you your favorite cupcakes with little heart-shaped sprinkles, acts like your best friend, and seems as if he is generally smitten. You notice that he has a very hard time making up his mind or trusting his own judgment. When he orders one dish at a restaurant, he immediately regrets not having another. He is not sure that the law firm he works at is really the best one for him. This guy is afraid of making a decision that forecloses on his other options.

Then you have sex with him and/or you start to come together as a couple. All of a sudden he texts less, and starts pulling back. Everything goes into second and then third gear in the relationship. Once-a-week dates turn into once-every-other-week meetings. He mentions getting together on Saturday and yet never makes the arrangements. You may even find his profile back up on an online dating site that brought you two together. Bottom line: he is pursuing or looking for his next Grass Is Greener hit.

Michelle, a twenty-nine-year-old nurse, tangled with a Grass Is Greener guy named George:

> I met George on a boutique dating site. George came on strong, brought my favorite lilies to our first date, which was dinner at a little Italian place that had romance written all over it. He was shorter than he said on his profile and balder than his photo, but he grew on me. George was the type of person who would take what seemed like hours to pick out an entrée or choose a movie. We talked and texted every day for two months, not to mention going out at least once a week. Then I decided to go almost all the way with him. Big mistake! He didn't contact me for five days after that. On a hunch I checked the site where we met and saw his profile right back up there. I moved on.

Grass Is Greener Warning Sign: *He's the calculating type who can't make up his mind. He's either never been in a long-term relationship or hasn't been in one for years.*

Degree of Difficulty: 8. *Usually this guy is not really into you because he is mortally terrified of settling and missing out on "somebody better." This is FOMO in action, a fear of missing out that is pandemic these days because of choice overload on dating apps!*

11. The Flame-Out

It begins with a bang, literally and figuratively! This guy is different, entirely different, or so you think at first as you fall headlong into the crucible of fiery infatuation. And he's right in there with you! The dopamine madly-in-love chemicals ignite fireworks in your brain and his. You have found him, the One, and this is the real deal! You are sure of it! After all, there is a profound connection. You spend five-hour dates kissing, canoodling, and going further than you planned. You are hooked and so is he. He professes undying, overwhelming love at first sight…sometimes at the first viewing of your online profile! He calls, texts all the time with adorable and adoring messages. He nicknames you "Freckles," takes you to see the tulips in bloom, teases you in a cocky, irresistible way! You see a princess wedding gown on a wedding show and start fantasizing about you, him, and who's doing the ceremony. Almost against your will you wind up having the most intoxicating, most incredible sex of your life with him one fateful night. He swears he wants to spend the rest of his life with you in the ultimate happily ever after. Then it quickly starts to unravel.

Suddenly and without warning, he "gets busy," becomes less attentive, cancels dates, or is a no-show. You feel like your heart is ripped out as he disappears and sinks slowly away from you, like Leonardo DiCaprio falling away from Kate Winslet after the *Titanic* goes down. This guy is a serial monogamist who has very brief periods of being in love—mad, passionate love with you, then the next, and the next, and the next one. He follows the path of chemistry, wherever it may lead.

Patty had a whirlwind romance with a Flame-Out guy named Terry:

> *I am in my fifties and should have known better. But Terry was irresistible. He was in his sixties but he was a cyclist with the body of a hunk. A retired exec from a* Fortune 100 *firm, he was bright, caring, and a crazy romantic who bought me a diamond necklace after knowing me for only a week! I am a VP at a firm very much like the one he left and he spent*

hours mentoring me about a job issue. Somehow this made him even hotter to me. One night Terry took me to see a superromantic play and we went to his penthouse afterward to open some Cristal. Next thing you know, we were having sex on his couch. The next day I found out that his adult daughter (who could never hold a job) was in town. It just seemed like all his attention switched over to her. And when I tried to discuss the situation he simply stopped calling me.

Flame-Out Warning Sign: *He catches you up in a whirlwind of romance and passion that spins you out of control and into bed before you can even think about what is happening.*

Degree of Difficulty: 8. *Stay on the Program of Three and resist the temptation to be a moth to his flame.*

12. The Slacker

The Slacker is a guy who is lazy in most every aspect of life. He doesn't finish anything—not his degree, his remodeling job, his new Internet marketing Web site, his new song, book, project, or the very deal that will get him ahead. He does not own his own place or even a car. He may live with his parents or in a run-down apartment. He may have a low-level or no job. He usually has big dreams and plans for himself that somehow never ever materialize. Even though it looks like he is working on his goals, he almost never takes the most important action or pulls the trigger that will make it all happen. He is so unconsciously afraid of failure that he does not really try.

The Slacker may be very cute, like an irresistible puppy in a pet store window. He has poor self-esteem, but he is sweet and you want to rescue him. He never catches a break and/or has been victimized by most everyone in his life. The Slacker has many excuses for why things are not working, including how much he's in debt, that he has no money, and suffers endless problems with bosses. The Slacker may be unreliable about keeping dates or appointments or calling when he says he will. This reflects a general disorganization in his life. Long-term mature relationships do not fit in with his lifestyle. At his core, the Slacker is terrified that he can't give a woman what she deserves or needs. This anxiety can be magnified if he is really smitten with her—so the more he is into you, the faster he will fail you in some irretrievable way. Slackers are often into recreational drugs like pot for which they always seem to have money.

Of course, there are Slackers who have hit some kind of bottom in their lives and have begun to work on themselves. If a Slacker is moving in this direction and in therapy or going to growth courses, there may be a chance that the relationship can work out.

Jillian, a twenty-nine-year-old administrator, fell for a Slacker named Bud who lived a few doors down the hallway of her apartment building:

Bud was exactly my type—a muscular guy with a soft crown of wavy hair. He was twenty-four and lived with his parents, which he told me was a temporary arrangement so he could save money and go to helicopter maintenance school. I kept saying hello to him in the hallway and he invited me over to play his new Wii game. We started hanging out at his place, playing Guitar Hero and other cool games. When his mom was out we would smoke pot and fool around. After a while I realized that he had no intention of improving his life and that becoming a responsible adult was not important to him. In fact, he looked down on his brother "the drone" who had a regular job. Dating Bud was like being stuck in high school. Definitely fun but going nowhere.

Slacker Warning Sign: *He is not getting anywhere in life and not trying anything new to get around that central problem.*

Degree of Difficulty: 8. *Unless he has clearly started to do some meaningful growth work, you cannot rescue this guy. No, not even you.*

13. Not Perfect—I'll Pass

This guy is supercritical and judgmental and looking for your fatal flaw. He has extremely low self-esteem and feels like he doesn't want to be with anyone who would be in a club that would have him. But all this is unconscious. What he would tell you is that there are no great women out there. The Not Perfect—I'll Pass guy always finds fault with any woman he dates, her nose is too big, she is not a size two, she is too needy, etc. So he is quick to jump in and out of your life. This is a nit-picky hypercritical guy who is looking for the perfect woman. Chances are he has never been in a long-term relationship or marriage because "no one is good enough." He's even failed at being matched through a pricey, "elite" matchmaker. Surprise, surprise!

Joan, a client, was a Realtor who dated a Not Perfect—I'll Pass type of guy named Brandon:

> *I met Brandon online. His photo was amazing—he was one gorgeous guy. We hit it off at first because we were both into sci-fi movies. We had a great time together. Then Brandon showed me an ad for Smart Liposuction. He said he thought I might be interested in it. He told me that he knew a lot about plastic surgery and that he helped his last girlfriend get a nose job. I was getting turned off to him pretty fast. Luckily he just disappeared anyway.*

Not Perfect—I'll Pass Warning Sign: *When it comes to describing his ex, you can hear how picky he really is.*

Degree of Difficulty: 9. *Pass on this type.*

14. The Alcoholic

You may meet him at a bar or a party or online. He is a fun guy and you hit it off. He may turn you on to the latest and greatest mojito. He does great at work and may be in a high-stress profession, like sales, financial services, consulting, or anything that requires lots of travel. You discover that in order to unwind or relax he needs to have some drinks and he definitely does not want to have dinner at any restaurant that doesn't serve liquor. As the months go by you notice that he and most all his friends have alcohol as a central part of their get-togethers. He parties at home, in clubs, sports bars, or even bowling alleys that serve booze. He needs to drink. Usually every day. When he gets going he often becomes sloppy, snippy, and mean or even falls asleep midsentence. He is not aware that he has drunk too much to drive and takes the keys anyway, putting both his and your life at risk. Over time all these problems become extremely annoying. You try, at first subtly and then loudly, to suggest he drink one less glass tonight. But he fights you. You begin to argue a great deal about his drinking. He tries to hide it. He swears that he has control, is absolutely not an alcoholic, and can stop at any time.

Just how do you tell if a guy is an alcoholic? It is not about the quantity being consumed. The most useful way is to ask one simple question: Does the person's drinking get him into trouble in his personal relationships? If the answer is yes, chances are the guy is an alcoholic.

Ella, a forty-one-year-old nurse, had a go-round with an alcoholic:

> Ned was as Irish as they come, with impish humor, red ringlets, and an adorable accent. We met at a party and talked together for hours. He was in pharmaceutical sales and traveled quite a bit, but kept in touch via text. As soon as he got back into town he would make a beeline over to my place with a six-pack and we would have dinner. He actually liked my cooking. Then we would spend weekends together. It was great for about four months. But his job situation went south and the drinking really got out of hand. It got to the point where he would just fall asleep

*in my apartment. He wasn't even that interested in having sex. Whenever
I confronted him and suggested that he go to AA, he would blow me off. I
had to go to Al-Anon to work up the strength to leave him.*

Alcoholic Warning Sign: *He needs his booze to relax and he insists
on eating only at places that serve alcohol.*

Degree of Difficulty: 9. *You will not win the war against booze.
Best to move on unless he is firmly in recovery and has been for
years.*

15. The Player

The Player thinks with his lower head and just wants to score, period. He
may be handsome off the charts. Or he may be a gaudily dressed geek
who is a card-carrying member of the seduction community. This group
of guys plays a very deliberate and conscious game with women: they
have studied pickup lines, body language, alpha male behavior, and even
magic or ESP tricks for the sole purpose of seducing as many women as
possible.

Whether handsome or not, the Player is an expert when it comes
to bedding women and is definitely accomplished at being cocky and
funny. He knows just how to use his bad-boy aura to send you on tilt
and going gaga as you wait desperately for his next text, e-mail, or sound
of his voice. A seasoned and fantastic kisser, canoodler, lover, he knows
how to play you and your body like the proverbial viola. This guy knows
exactly how to stimulate you to produce dopamine, the rocket fuel of
mad, passionate, insane love—the brain chemical that makes your body
crave him like an addict craves a fix. He is smooth, erotic, pressing you
sexually for more and more. And you find it hard if not impossible to
resist.

The Player appears in your life and then disappears, explaining that he has to visit with out-of-town family or work overtime (he is with another woman). He makes up excuses—especially about not being available on a weekend. He may disappear for stretches where you don't quite know where he is. You find yourself desperately wanting to believe him when he says you're the only one—even though deep down you know that it is not true. If the Player is married he is willing to talk or meet only at odd hours and possibly only at your place. He may lie a lot, is evasive and not forthcoming about personal information.

This is a guy whom you catch flirting or even cheating and yet he is so smooth he can talk you out of what you have just witnessed. For the Player, you represent simply another notch on his belt. He may talk love like the greatest poet, but the Player is all about scoring and sex. And what he delivers is heartbreak. Plus something much worse! Watch out for sexually transmitted diseases with this one!

Ferrah, a bright, thirty-year-old superstar lawyer, had a dating go-round with a Player:

I cannot believe I fell for Salim. He was a graduate student studying music at Juilliard, or so he said. Later I found out that, like most every-thing else he told me, this was a lie. He was actually dealing pot and God knows what else. Yet, the real truth is that I wanted to believe Salim. He had a physicality, a touch that was electric. He made me feel more alive, more sexy, more beautiful than I have ever felt in my life. I had an orgasm for the first time in my life with him. Yet, as soon as I got to know Salim, I did not respect or like him as a person. He had no integrity to speak of. The consummate Casanova. I am embarrassed to say that I still slept with him a few times after I discovered the truth. It was that good. I am just thankful I made him wear a condom!

Player Warning Sign: *Even though he talks love to you, it somehow feels like a politician's spin.*

Degree of Difficulty: 10. *You know what to do with this one. Get out ASAP.*

16. The Pr*ck

It all starts out great at first. The Pr*ck seems powerful, sure of himself, and cocky. He may be quite big-time and successful. And in the early stages he is also gaga about you. You find yourself unbelievably attracted to him. He takes you out to charming restaurants, buys you a cute summer dress, and your dates are straight out of one of your favorite romance movies. But as you get to know the Pr*ck you come to realize that he is quick-tempered and mean, especially when he can get away with it—as in barking at waiters or other drivers on the road. You see that he is superdemanding. He is extremely judgmental about you, or your background, and one-ups you all the time. He acts like he is much smarter than you and/or that you are lucky to be with him. In fact, when you are with him you feel inferior and bad about yourself.

The Pr*ck may treat you with disrespect when he cancels, comes late, or no-shows for dates. He may swear at you or call you names. If you are in a longer-term relationship, the Pr*ck may threaten you physically or even hit you. Usually he is a control freak who deep down does not feel very lovable. So he controls you by putting you down or threatening you so that your wings are clipped and you can't leave and reject him. You feel like you are always walking on eggshells, waiting for the ax to fall. If he is deeply ingrained in this pattern and is physically wild (throws stuff, pounds walls, or strikes you), you may be truly afraid of him. In this case, you must consider your own safety first and foremost. It is at the very moment of leaving an out-of-control impulsive Pr*ck that he is most dangerous. If you are with a guy who is/could be physically abusive, you must make a safe exit. (If you feel caught in this kind of relationship, see the "Abuse Recycle" Deadly Dating Pattern in Chapter 2 and "The Abuse Recycle Fix" in Chapter 10.)

One variation on the Pr*ck Deadly Dating Pattern is the guy who is overly possessive. This guy, the Possessive Pr*ck, is jealous and insecure. He is paranoid and controlling with you because he is (a) afraid that all women cheat and/or (b) that some other guy will come and steal you away. At the bottom of it all is the Possessive Pr*ck's low self-esteem and lack of trust. He will tend to see you as cheating on him if you so much as look at another guy. Having a close male friend is out of the question. Talking or dancing with another man may drive him bananas. If you get dressed up to go out with him, he may insist you put on clothes that cover you up. He is afraid you are really dressing to get attention from other men. The Possessive Pr*ck tends to track you and what you are doing. He wants a report about your whereabouts and activities. He may actually push you into the arms of another guy through his smothering behavior, which is sometimes punctuated by blowing up in jealous angry fits. The Possessive Pr*ck often unwittingly creates the very thing he fears most: losing you.

Li, a stunning thirty-three-year-old Korean woman, struggled with a Pr*ck named Rod:

Rod was as charming as they come when I first met him. We had been dating for five weeks, I was looking for a place to live, and he invited me to move in with him. Big mistake! He was superjealous, crazy jealous. He wouldn't let me wear short skirts to work and would blow up at me if I was ten minutes late getting home. Usually after a bout of rage he was so sorry and worked overtime to make it up to me. But when he slapped me in the face after we came home from a party I finally realized I had to get away from him. He claimed I was flirting with a guy there—who was actually gay!

Pr*ck Warning Signs: *He is very judgmental and puts other people down, including you. Plus he has a bad temper.*

Possessive Pr*ck Warning Sign: *He thinks you are having an affair with a friend in your social circle who is completely unattractive to you.*

Degree of Difficulty: 10. *Don't take chances with your emotional and physical well-being! Make a clever and safe exit as soon as possible.*

So there you have it: sixteen of the most common Men's Deadly Dating Patterns based on personality types. Please don't think that you can overhaul, inspire, ground, or otherwise cajole a guy out of a firmly entrenched Deadly Dating Pattern! Even if you are a therapist, great with people, or the "best woman" he has ever been with! If this guy is showing serious signs of one or more of these patterns and unwilling to work on himself, move on and save yourself a great deal of pain and aggravation. Even if you are crazy about him. Even if you feel that he is truly the One. Even if you crave him like a coke addict craves her dear fix. That is just the love-addicting dopamine talking! If a guy is hanging on to one of these self-sabotaging patterns and making no moves to break through his dating games and fears, go cold turkey, cut off all contact, and move on to dating other guys quickly. As in right now! There are good guys out there. Repeat: there are good guys out there. And I mean good matches for you, no matter what baggage you are carrying.

So if you have to, move on. Remember that many of the guys who are caught in these Deadly Dating Patterns are perfectly willing to endure a difficult or on-again, off-again relationship for years. Years! If this is not what you want—if you want true, lasting love, be smart and act quickly to protect yourself. Otherwise you could be stuck in a dead-end relationship for the next decade.

If you are several months into the relationship, think about what you want and have some straight talk with the guy. See if he is interested in working toward the same goal with you. If this kind of talk creates a fight, or he distances or sulks—you may need to reevaluate. If you yearn for engagement, marriage, and/or children and he firmly does not, get out now. By the way, cutting the relationship off completely is often the most powerful thing you can do to help the guy grow. It is when your partner experiences loss that he may be willing to examine his own behavior, go into therapy, or take growth courses in order to get out of his Deadly Dating Patterns. Then he may come back to you as a sincerely changed man, ready to commit, to marry, and to create the life of love you truly want.

Therefore, the most important question to ask yourself is if he is willing to grow. Is he working his way out of his Deadly Dating Patterns? The process starts with step one—his being aware of how he is sabotaging himself. If he refers to the trap he's in, even jokingly, this is a good sign. If he is in therapy, counseling, or coaching or taking a growth course in order to work on transforming his life, it is even better. See Chapter 4 for more on assessing a guy's willingness to grow. If he is actively into it, give him some time and space to work things out for himself.

Research shows that there are clear differences between the "marrying kind" of men and those who don't want to marry. These differences include having good parental role models and a religious or spiritual background, among other things and are reviewed in Chapter 9. If you want a long-term relationship or marriage, don't waste time with DUDs who are entrenched in their dead-end dating games and patterns and not into these goals. Move on. You will save yourself a lot of time, frustration, disappointment, and heartbreak.

Look for a guy who is comfortable around you, who feels like he could be a solid, caring friend. One who does not try too hard, but shows that he is totally into you. A good person with whom you share chemistry that is brewing, but not over the top and out of control. He just may turn out to be a STUD (Seriously Terrific, Utterly Devoted Dude) who will help you make your wishes and dreams come true.

It doesn't matter if the guy is perfect, or the girl is perfect, as long as they are perfect for each other.—Good Will Hunting

4

—◆—

Dating Three to Find the One

Love moderately: long love doth so;
Too swift arrives as tardy as too slow.

—*William Shakespeare*

When it comes to dating, the Bard got it right. Moderation is key. It keeps you from moving too fast or too slow when you're getting to know new men and what they bring to your table. And the most powerful way to achieve moderation is by using the Dating Program of Three.

The Program of Three is exactly the opposite of the urban legend "three-date rule," which dictates that you must decide by the third date if a guy is potentially the One and have sex or lose him forever. On this dating program, you avoid that pressured decision and its aftermath: a Flame-Out that usually kills the relationship. Instead you date three men at the same time without having sex with any of them. By not seeing any one man too often, you find the men who are really into you and who will stay the course. Plus, you break out of your prison of Deadly Dating Patterns and maneuver more skillfully in the dating world. By following this program, you build your self-esteem and find men who are much more fulfilling.

Although the idea of finding, much less juggling, three guys may sound challenging—if not downright impossible at this point—let me reassure you: It won't be once you begin using all the tools you'll learn in this Program.

Why It Works

There are sound *biological* reasons why the Dating Program of Three rocks!

First of all, it helps you avoid the *number one mistake* that single women make: the addictive moth-to-a-flame overinvolvement with some new guy who is supposedly the "One," which you now know as the Flame-Out Deadly Dating Pattern. As Helen Fisher, the renowned anthropologist, describes in her fascinating book *Why We Love, romantic love is a real addiction.* It is like shooting up cocaine or heroin, which means reason often goes out the window. When we "fall in love," our brains make large quantities of dopamine and norepinephrine, which also happens when you take speed! These brain chemicals create the excited, exhilarated, and focused state that allows us to have eight-hour dates and remember every detail about what our new hottie did and said. These speed-like chemicals can also drive up our levels of testosterone, which increases sexual desire.

Second, when we fall in love, serotonin levels fall and resemble the levels found in people with obsessive-compulsive disorders. We tend to ruminate, fantasize, and obsess about our new (drug-like) boyfriends. The new love is in our thoughts all day and in our dreams at night. Your brain says, *Focus on him, focus on him, focus on him.*

Once this process takes you over, you become like a craving coke addict. You lose touch with reality, seeing only the positives in the hottie. You lose self-control. Instead you are locked on the target, the fix—hot-wired and ready to do outrageous things, sometimes self-destructive things, whatever it takes to be with him. One look, one sweet word, is all it takes. Even if you don't really know him. Even if it is not in your best interests. And as you continue to spend more time together, the addiction intensifies. As Homer wrote, you fall prey to "the heat of Love, the pulsing rush of Longing, the lover's whisper, irresistible—magic to make the sanest [wo]man go mad."

If you move too quickly into the pulsing rush of love, you put yourself at risk for an agonizing withdrawal if this man rejects you. Then sleeplessness, crying jags, over- or undereating, obsessive and upsetting thoughts, all mess with your brain chemistry even further.

The Dating Program of Three safeguards you against all these dangers of love addiction. On this program you will see the new hottie less often and have a measured coming together. You will be less likely to lock on to him with a singular focus that puts you at risk. In this way you elegantly avoid getting physiologically and emotionally devastated if it turns out that he is a player or all wrong for you.

The Program of Three also stops you from having sex prematurely. Why is this so important? Simple biology. When you have sex with someone, your body drives up the levels of oxytocin both during the whole sexual act and after you leave the scene. Oxytocin, which has been called the cuddle, bonding, or tend-and-befriend hormone, creates a strong biological attachment. This means that your *body* may automatically start the attachment process with almost anyone you bed, whether or not you want to be in a relationship with him! Add that chemical to any dopamine surges and you're desperately waiting for his text, e-mail, or phone call. Jumping into bed too soon means you open yourself to premature infatuation, dependency, and a kind of pseudo-intimacy that almost always backfires. Then, caught in the chemical soup of dopamine and oxytocin, you will likely lose yourself.

Another benefit of the Program is that dating multiple men usually gets the guys' juices flowing. Some men (especially achievers) are wired to compete and win in the courtship game, so competitiveness gets them aroused. When his reward (you) is not easily gained, his brain will pump out more and more of the rapturous chemical dopamine. Extra dopamine intensifies his feelings of being swept away by love. As one love researcher puts it, "Those who want to trigger romance in a would-be lover might artfully create some mystery, barriers and uncertainty in the relationship." When you are on the Dating Program of Three, you do not have to fake this quality of not being so available; the program automatically accomplishes this desirable state. As one student in our coaching program discovered, "Now I don't have to pretend. I *am* hard to get."

Dating three guys helps clarify what you want and need in a man, because you can easily and instantly compare and contrast. So, for example, Friday rolls around and "Sean" is cheap and miserly, Saturday's date with "Randy" will more clearly showcase his giving nature. When you come from abundance in the land of men, you can give yourself many possibilities rather than just one.

> *The world is full of abundance and opportunity, but far too many people come to the fountain of life with a sieve instead of a tank car...a teaspoon instead of a steam shovel. They expect little and as a result they get little.*—Ben Sweetland

Program of Three dating is challenging, but it's truly empowering. It allows you to be long-sighted and keep your eye on the prize: a lasting, fulfilling relationship that's just right for you. It helps you end your Deadly Dating Patterns, frees you from the "three-date rule," and keeps you protected from all the scenarios designed to break your heart. Of course, there are definitely obstacles to creating a Program of Three, but I've helped thousands of women do this already, and you can do it, too! Here are all the secrets to get you started on your own Program of Three.

How to Work the Program of Three

I can hear you already. *Dr. Diana*, you might be thinking, *I'm still trying to find* one *man to date. How can I find three?* First of all, listen up, ladies:

There are more than 51 *million* single men just in the U.S. right now, and different ones are coming on the market all the time! And every year there are new online dating sites that bring in whole new crops to choose from. There *are* men out there—no matter what your age, weight, or "problem" is.

What if you have special challenges because you are African-American, over forty-five, a single mom, or so highly successful that you scare men away? Skip over to Chapter 13 to get the latest research on the real truths about these issues that will show you just how great the possibility of finding love is for you. It is here. Right now.

In fact, *every* student we have ever had who was willing to work the principles consistently, no matter what her challenges or Deadly Dating Patterns were, has been able to create a successful Dating Program of Three. *"Where do I meet the men?"* you ask. Good news: you're already meeting them if you've been doing your homework, going to places where there are lots of men and saying hello. Oh, you say you're really shy and haven't done any of those activities so far? Well, there's a special surprise in this chapter's homework that is going to get you talking to men in the next few days!

You will also be putting out the word to your family, friends, and co-workers that you are looking, starting this week. And you will work two digital dating sites. In the next chapter you will learn powerful online secrets that bring the better guys to you. One coaching client had 200 responses on one online site alone! And in Chapter 7 you will learn to discover and connect to people with what I call your Diamond Self. This is the authentic, not-shy, real you who is loving and lovable. You will learn how to be at your best, which means you will be attracting even more men!

It's not as hard as it seems. Drew, a forty-two-year-old single executive with weight issues, was the highest bidder at a charity auction where a mentoring session with me over lunch was the prize. Here's what she e-mailed me about a year later:

I particularly thought the point of "dating three guys at once" was amusing at first, but then you know . . . it worked. Even though at times I knew some guy wasn't going to be the love of my life, it was still a diversion from getting involved with another guy too fast before I knew it was the right thing. I think this is the best advice ever and have passed it on to several of my friends. Last summer, I joined eHarmony and ended up meeting a really nice guy, although at first not necessarily what I thought I was looking for. We get along great, have tons in common, and it's by far the most mature and healthy relationship I think I have ever been in. We got engaged this past October while on vacation in Florence. He proposed in front of the Fountain of Neptune in the Piazza della Signoria. We are planning a wedding for next June on Martha's Vineyard.

GET RID OF STINKING THINKING

In order to work the program, you must cut back on the negative self-talk. *I'm too fat, too old, too shy, I have too much cellulite*—blah blah blah. Most women also carry around negative self-talk based on scarcity. This kind of stinking thinking compels them to grab the one they're with. They think, *I might as well jump in because there are no good men out there. There are too many women and too few men!* or *I have to hang on to him because I have to take whatever I can get!* and other depressing, self-defeating thoughts. Committing to the Dating Program of Three banishes this stinking thinking.

There is nothing like having three men interested in you to boost your self-esteem. Being on the Program helps you practice the kind of self-loving inner dialogue that is an important key to creating a love relationship that lasts.

Here's how Joan, a thirty-two-year-old Realtor who had emerged from an empty marriage a year before she started the course, describes working the Program:

It has been daunting to date three men as I never had dated that many at a time. But it is helping me to stay less attached to who I think is "the one." And with so much attention, it's strange, but I'm just beginning to feel, "I deserve to be courted. I'm worth it for guys to hang in there and work for me."

BEING SELECTIVE

As you use two online dating sites as well as social networking to meet a lot of men, you'll begin to sort through and select men for yourself based on what you want and need. It's like looking at and interviewing a lot of different companies to see if a job is right for you. This sometimes brings up faithfulness and guilt issues that need to be worked through. Just remember: you are simply turning the tables. Many men have been in this role for years; they have been following a patriarchal tradition of dating more than one woman at a time. In other words, they did the sorting and selecting.

Not anymore. When you begin dating three men at once, you're shifting the balance of power to be more equitable. Starting now, take a stand for yourself, a stand that says you deserve a great partner. Take your time, learn what is possible in a relationship, and start playing an active role in choosing who you're with. Don't wait to be chosen. Now, with all the online and offline possibilities, you have an abundance of men at arm's reach; you have the ability to pick and choose for yourself.

If you need or want an empowerment boost, have a gift coaching session now at http://www.Lovein90Days.com/dating-coach/.

The Dating Program of Three Rules

1. USE THE THREE-QUESTION DUD/STUD TEST

Use the test below to determine whether a guy is worth putting into your Dating Program of Three. These three questions separate a DUD

(Definitely Unworkable Dude) from a STUD (Seriously Terrific, Utterly Devoted Dude) and weed out those who are heartbreakers or not good love matches. There is no perfect guy. But you can find a wonderful guy who is willing to grow into an almost perfect STUD!

When you meet someone, ask yourself the following questions.

Is this guy:

I. Crazy About Me?

- Eager to see me
- Reluctant to leave me
- Interested in me and my life
- Wants to be helpful
- Is verbally and physically affectionate
- Wants to be sexual with me
- Acts like I am very special; doesn't really want to date others
- Willing to hang in there as I work the Program of Three

Program of Three Contender = Yes on at least 4 of the above

II. Willing to Grow?

- Takes suggestions or advice
- Is self-reflective
- Is willing to go to therapy or life coaching
- Takes growth courses
- Meditates or prays
- Is in a 12-step program or men's group

Program of Three Contender = Yes on at least 2 of the above

III. Meeting the Basics?

- Is a good guy—reliable, tells the truth, cares about others

- Wants a real, committed relationship
- Willing to have children if I want them
- Is successful—has a good income
- Is a member of my religious faith
- Is not in a relationship with anyone else
- Comes from a stable family of origin
- Is geographically desirable

Program of Three Contender = Yes on at least 4 of the above

You will read more about these criteria in the next chapter, but for now I want you just to get an overview of the three critical questions. A guy has to meet the standards in each of the categories to date you on an ongoing basis. Choosing from this pool of men will save you a lot of wasted time with men who are not into you, scoundrels who betray you, or narcissists who blame you for any and every problem. Using the DUD/STUD screening sets you up to have a solid, long-lasting love relationship. This means that your partner is your best friend, but with great sex.

I know, I know—you can't even get *one* good guy to date. Yes, you can, and you will. The Program of Three will get you there.

2. DON'T PASS ON THE ONES THAT ARE NOT YOUR TYPE

If a guy passes the three-question test, give him a real chance, even if he is balding, paunchy, nerdy, or is not particularly attractive. In fact, you *want* to date against type. Even if you are not exactly blown away by a person on the first date, remember to stay open. *If he passes the DUD/STUD Test, go for at least a second or third date.* You cannot know what secret goodies are hidden in someone just by meeting him once. You have to let a potential partner unfold and show you his different sides. If there is any connection with this person at all, give it another chance. Even if you feel there is no chemistry. Chemistry can happen in a heartbeat.

Remember, you are breaking your Deadly Dating Patterns, which have led you to be attracted to guys who were not right for you. Love almost always comes in a surprise package; most people do not end up with the kind of person they imagine for themselves. The woman who dates starving artists marries a rich, balding lawyer. One client who was deeply infatuated with a hot George Clooney look-alike later created a gem of a marriage with a short, plain guy who was her champion and a healing force of nature in her life.

3. USE THE OPEN (OPENING POSSIBILITY EXERCISES NOW) TECHNIQUES WITH GUYS WHO ARE NOT YOUR TYPE

If a guy passes the DUD/STUD Test—he seems crazy about you, is willing to grow, and is a good guy—use my OPEN Techniques to see what may be there. First, think of him as a present wrapped in nested boxes. As you interact with him, you are unwrapping the present and finding out more and more things about him that may open surprisingly marvelous chemistry and connection!

Try using one or two of these affirmations before each date: *I have fun with this man. I see the hidden possibilities in (his name). This man is a present for my enjoyment. More will be revealed about this person. I uncover and enjoy the wonderful aspects of this man. I find chemistry with (his name). This guy is a hottie! (His name) turns me on!*

Second, go on dates that are exciting, novel, and get the adrenaline pumping. This simulates the speedy brain chemistry of love. Go on a roller coaster at the amusement park, rock climbing at your gym, take a helicopter ride, try hiking on a high, winding trail or windsurfing, make a mad dash to catch the sunset at the beach, scream yourselves silly at a football game or the racetrack. Studies show that people who are emotionally aroused, whether by joy, fear, or any feeling, fall in love more easily. As two love researchers once wrote, "Adrenaline makes the heart grow fonder."

Third, see him in his element. Plan a date around skiing, a performance of his rock band, a wine-tasting event, or whatever he excels at. You will catch sides of him you haven't seen before. His personal power and charisma will be at their height and just may open up a host of juicy feelings.

Fourth, to open up chemistry, try turning yourself on first. Go on a date wearing your sexiest lingerie under your clothes. Flirt with him, get touchy-feely, whisper in his ear, and maybe kiss him. If he suddenly comes back with some sensual, sweet, mind-blowing moves, your "chemistry experiment" may prove to be a sparkling success!

4. WORK THE PROGRAM WHEN YOU MEET A GUY WHO IS SPECIAL

When you meet someone who is very special, that is when you *must* do the Program of Three. This will keep you from being overly focused on the new hottie and falling into a painful Flame-Out. Iris, whom we met in Chapter 2, puts it this way:

> *When you really like someone, that is when you MUST do the Program of Three. I said to some of the gals when I met Bob that it all flies out the window when you finally meet someone you really, really like. In my last meeting with him I wish I had said, "No problem if you're too busy next week. I'll look forward to hearing from you when you're in town." Now he hasn't contacted me and I am unearthing my inner voices that tell me I screwed up....I really think I believed I didn't deserve him, he was too cute, too accomplished, too everything for little overweight me.*

Iris fell prey to her neediness and inner sabotage more easily because she did not have other guys in place to shift her focus away from her new "find." If you do find yourself quickly becoming addicted to a hottie, use these tips to avoid an out-of-control Flame-Out:

- *Take it slow.* No five-hour dates. Less frequent and shorter dates will slow down the addictive love process and allow you to assess whether this is a good guy who is truly interested in being with you.
- *Write up a list of his negative qualities.* The addictive brain chemistry blinds you to his faults. This process will help you to become more realistic.
- *Ground your mind with meditation, yoga, or other mind/body practices.* These activities calm the mind and offset the speedy quality of the love addiction.
- *Distract yourself.* Take on a major project at work, go on a trip, or engage in other activities to take your focus off the new guy and slow things down.

5. BE UP FRONT ABOUT DATING OTHERS

On the second date let each of the guys know you are dating others. Do this casually by saying something like, "I'm having the best time with dating this go-round," or "It's been really good for me to get back into dating." Don't make a big declaration about it. The second date is a good time to put it out there because it's too soon for him to feel betrayed or wounded. If you let a guy know you are dating others after many dates, he may be more emotionally reactive because he assumed an unspoken contract about being exclusive.

If somehow your date misses this info and it comes up in conversation later, don't lie. Let the guy know you are dating more than one person right now, but that you are looking to develop a special relationship. Tell him that the time with him is extra special. You can also communicate this by what you don't say. For example, if he says he wants to be exclusive and is taking down his online dating profile, you can simply smile and nod and say, "I'm really enjoying this, too." If he presses you to see just him, you can refuse by saying something like, "I made a commitment to myself not to slide quickly into one relationship. I can't imagine liking anyone else as much as I like you, but right now I need to keep to this plan for myself." If he meets the DUD/STUD criteria, he will hang in there and fight to win you. You have to have faith.

Joely, an artist who was vigorously working a Program of Three, e-mailed me about how her STUD handled seeing her out at dinner with another guy:

> I thought I did it this time. Spencer called me and asked if I was out to dinner last night at Otto's. I said yes. I was actually out with John, who was reaching the bottom of the list fast. Spencer and I talked about the food, and when I got off the phone, I felt like something was wrong. A little while later, I emailed him, "I want you to know that you are my number one squeeze and I would rather spend more time with you than anyone else." He called and said he really appreciated my email. He told me that a week ago he took his profile off Match, for me.

Of course, there is one caveat here: If you are dealing with a man who turns out to be violent, get away from him quietly, quickly, and safely and *do not* share the truth about dating others with him.

6. ALLOCATE TIME FOR EACH GUY

Spend time with each guy so that you can see who he really is. Consider yourself an anthropologist in the world of men. This means you can't be all wrapped up in one creature right away. Make sure you give time to each of the guys—in the beginning, about one date a week each.

Ask yourself: What are the personalities of these natives? What are they really into? I know it can be daunting to keep track of both the men you are dating and those in the pipeline whom you are e-mailing, so keep a record of contacts, dates, and reactions to each guy in your dating program. This way, you don't get them confused. In Chapter 9, I will give you a DUD/STUD report form that will help you determine which guys teeter on the edge of your Deadly Dating Patterns and which ones fulfill some of your deeper needs.

As you're getting to know the men, ask yourself: Who works better with me? Do I need a lot of physical affection? Is it important to have an adventurous time together? What about humor? Who can give me the kind of companionship, teamwork, nurturance, and encouragement I need to be my best self? Notice what qualities feel like a good fit.

7. IN THE BEGINNING, MAKE ONLY A FEW PROACTIVE MOVES

In this Program, you are looking for guys who are crazy about you. This means in the beginning, even if you have initiated things, you want men to pursue you. Limit yourself to *only* a few Proactive Moves that either initiate or take the relationship to a new level—e.g., flirting, winking online, sending the first message, or suggesting the first phone contact or date. Then let the guy carry the ball. If, for example, you are texting back and forth but he is not moving to the next step of phoning or meeting, then you can suggest it. But that's it. You must step back and let him do some heavy lifting.

Saying thank you via text for a date is not a Proactive Move. It is part of the normal give-and-take of making friends and getting to know someone. In fact, if you do meet someone and have a really good time, do send a *short* text the next morning; this will let the person know that the door is open to getting together again. Write something specific about the date that points to the connection between the two of you or refers to something you both loved. For example, if you went to a comedy show, write a message that refers to a particular joke you both enjoyed. (Do not directly suggest the next date.) Chances are, your date will be very happy to get your message. A *Cosmo* poll showed that 86 percent of guys stress after a date about whether the woman had fun.

If the guy drops the ball in the midst of the give-and-take of communication and *doesn't respond to your message within three days or so* (assuming he is not traveling out of the country or tied up in some short-term crazy work project that needs attention 24/7), then you are in the Proactive Move realm. At that point, contacting him and/or suggesting a date-like activity either indirectly (sounds like fun!) or directly (let's go sometime) is a possible Proactive Move.

All of the above applies only to the early stages of a relationship. Once you're dating regularly, have established a dating rhythm, and/or have talked about a future together, you can be more free about making Proactive Moves.

The Shy Guy Exception

The Proactive Move rule is a guideline, and ultimately you have to use your intuition. If you meet a seriously shy guy who seems to be into you, is willing to grow, and is a good guy, the Proactive Move rule goes out the window. With a shy guy you have to be more available and flirty, take the lead more often, and maybe even give him the first kiss. Keep in mind, however, that he needs to be responding very positively to each of your moves. If he doesn't, you need to end the relationship. Otherwise you will be getting into the I'll Make You Love Me Deadly Dating Pattern and wasting a lot of your very valuable time and energy.

8. NO SEX

Kissing and canoodling are okay, but avoid having sex with any of the men so that you can take your time getting to know them. Remember, men typically view sex very differently from women. In a recent University of Texas study, two thousand people were canvassed about the reasons they had sex. While women often reported that they had sex because "I wanted to express my love for the person," guys were more likely to say they did it because they wanted to boost their social status, were slumming, or because the opportunity presented itself.

Again, forget about the three-date rule, which is a belief that women have to put out by the third date or it's all over. You won't be the only person ignoring this urban legend. An anonymous poll of 5,237 singles conducted by Match.com showed that over 34 percent of the group said they took four or more dates to have sex and almost 7 percent reported that they would not have sex until they had a ring.

Remember that having sex also releases oxytocin, which initially heightens attachment feelings in both men and women. While it's true that he gets a blast of oxytocin during sex and after his orgasm, unfortunately the upsurge falls back down to Earth within *thirty minutes*, to its original level. So biologically, he might say the "L word" during sex and immediately after climaxing, but have no interest in pursuing you later. This is why holding off on sex is important.

9. RANK ORDER THE GUYS

When you find three guys whom you are interested in dating, rank order them from most to least fulfilling. Think about who is a better match for you. Who's more compatible? More fulfilling? More fun? Who has similar values and goals? With whom do you feel more yourself?

Also, keep refreshing your Dating Program of Three until you find the One you want to choose. Look for replacements if one of the relationships ends, and look for replacements for your lowest-ranked guy. When you find a replacement, you can handle the change gracefully by giving the unlucky candidate three real, heartfelt compliments and then telling him it is just not working out between you. If you are so inclined, invite him to be a friend. The great thing is, as you work the Program, less-compatible, -stimulating, or -enjoyable partners are replaced with higher-level ones. Your guys will get better and better over time until you find that certain person who fits you like a glove.

Joely writes about letting John, her number three, go after the dinner incident with her number one:

I can't get over how well John took the news. He said he wasn't surprised.
I guess all my silence after he kept talking about being exclusive from the
second date on added up. In thinking about our time together, we did
have some idyllic dates and created some nice memories.

10. CHOOSE THE ONE ONLY AFTER MONTHS ON THE PROGRAM

You will be meeting men who are better matches and more exciting to
you over time. After you meet someone who seems to be the One, continue with your Program of Three for at least two months. *During that*
time there should be regular, consistent contact with him that gets better over
time. As the relationship unfolds he should be more physically and emotionally available and more committed to you. This includes the following behavior:

- He should grow more attentive and loving.
- He should become more open to sharing his feelings, his social life
  with friends and family members, and his space.
- You should feel able to be yourself with him.
- You should find yourself continually surprised at how he fills your
  needs to be understood, appreciated, romanced, and celebrated for
  who you are.

Warning: If you are already in a relationship and are not sure if he
is the One, you may be sensing that he is afraid of commitment. After
several months of exclusivity and talk of love, it is a bad sign if he is
ambivalent or does not want you to: (a) sleep over; or (b) leave some of
your things at his apartment. This may indicate that he will pull out of
the relationship. To further assess him and your possible future together,
skip forward to "The Marrying Kind: What the Research Shows" at the
end of Chapter 9.

11. FOLLOW THE GUIDELINES FOR GRADUATING FROM THE PROGRAM OF THREE

After there is a clear coming together with some talk of exclusivity and a future together, you can stop the Program of Three. Here are four guidelines:

1. Read about the Eight Habits of Living Love in Chapter 14. They provide a model of a healthy relationship, which is grounded in intimacy, appreciation, devotion, respect, and good collaboration. Make sure that you are experiencing most of these habits now with your chosen STUD. Remember, the beginning of a relationship should be a very fulfilling time.
2. You can have sex. But make sure it is safe sex until you are both tested for STDs.
3. Don't jump in too quickly with your Beloved; do not go on ten-day trips or move in together right away. Take several months to continue getting to know each other. Exciting as it is, you still want to let your new love relationship deepen and unfold naturally. Then if you have a fight or a downtick you will have enough of an ongoing bond to weather it.
4. Let your other two contenders know that it is not going to work out with them. Give each one three sincere compliments and tell him what you have learned or gained from the relationship. Expressing gratitude will help you to end in a win-win way where you and they can feel as good as possible, given the circumstances.

Joely writes about graduating from the Program of Three:

Spencer told me that the most beautiful thing is sharing your life with someone you love. It's official. We are going steady. I told Spencer that I only had 10 more guys to contact. He said 15 or 16, he might have been

jealous, but 10 he could handle...he knew I was kidding. My assistant,
Carla, says we are like teenagers texting and talking on the phone. I am
floating and beaming.

✎ Dating Three to Find the One: Exercises_____

Choose from among the following suggestions, according to your own
intuition.

Total Time for Completing All of Them: About 35 Minutes

EXERCISE 1: *REASONS WHY IT CAN'T/CAN WORK FOR ME*

In your journal, alternate writing out positive and negative statements.
First, write down one reason why conducting a Dating Program of Three
is impossible for you, followed by a reason it might be possible for you.

EXERCISE 2: *YOUR LOVE INTENTION REVISITED*

Rewrite the love intention you created in Chapter 2. List any doubts you
have about fulfilling that intention.

Iris's love intention is: *I have a genuinely wonderful, loving, and commit-*
ted relationship with an exciting, authentic life partner.

Her doubts: *It hasn't happened yet and I'm a pretty powerful gal. Things just*
keep on staying the same. Every Christmas I am hanging just my stocking and one
for a nameless other. My apartment is cluttered. I haven't lost the weight I wanted.

EXERCISE 3: *YOUR LOVE INTENTION MEDITATION*

Sit upright in a comfortable position with a clock nearby. For ten minutes listen to your favorite uplifting music or meditate. Then for the next

ten minutes, sit quietly, close your eyes, and use the love intention you created in Exercise 5 in Chapter 2 over and over again as a mantra. That is, softly say it in your mind without forcing. Pause for about fifteen seconds between repetitions of your love intention. When nagging doubts, negative self-talk, and other distractions intrude, simply observe them. Do not fight or resist them. Instead, just notice these passing clouds and gently return to the love mantra. Occasionally eye the clock to time yourself.

Note: If need be, shorten the love intention statement so that it is under ten words.

Mantra-based meditative processes have been repeatedly proven to de-stress and promote self-actualization in those who practice them. Give yourself an even better gift: practice your love meditation every day.

EXERCISE 4: *YOUR LOVE SCENES*

Listen to a love song that inspires you. Imagine that you have found your life partner and the love you really want. Think about three different scenes or interactions between you and your partner in which you feel incredibly loved, grounded, or peaceful.

These are the three scenes Iris created as love scripts:

First scene: We're having a lazy morning, snuggling on white sheets and white pillows. We're giggling, talking—really talking—laughing and he says so genuinely, "I could look at you forever." He's lovely, brown hair parted down the center, a little grey mixed in, a kind and handsome face. He's tallish, broad-shouldered, cares about the world. He's a good solid guy with a heart as big as they come but an uncommon wisdom; his default setting is to do the right thing even when it is hard.

Second scene: We're standing talking and I tell him I'm pregnant. He scoops me up in his arms, lovingly, protectively. With my head against the hair on his chest, he says he's so happy. Tears roll down my face. I tell him I'm so happy that he's happy, and that I was worried. He looks at me and says, "I hate all those other men who led you to feel that way."

Third scene: We're in a village in Africa; we're so happy working together for UNESCO or some other organization. He's speaking to a villager in his native tongue. The man mentions that my heart is as large as my lovely bottom in a language I don't understand yet. My man diplomatically says something to him that I'm his—and to back off in a good natured way. Whatever he does apparently defuses the situation and everyone has a good laugh.

 ## Homework

Choose from among the following suggestions, according to your own intuition:

1. Make sure you're attending classes or activities that interest you and that have a lot of men in them.

2. Continue saying hello to new guys—work up to the hotties.

3. If you are shy, sign up for speed dating (just Google "speed dating," or Pre-Dating.com and the name of your town) to get used to talking to guys. This is simply for practice, practice, practice. Expect *not* to be chosen by any of them. Social conversation for a shy person is like learning to play the violin—you'll squeak and squawk before you sound like Itzhak Perlman. I know—I used to be extremely shy. Also, see Chapters 7 and 8 for exercises to help you.

4. Put the word out to your family, friends, and co-workers that you are looking to meet a good guy and you're not fussy about the particulars. Tell them the gist of your love intention, e.g., "I am looking to get married to a great guy." Saying it aloud is a form of anchoring it in your mind. Initially it may be embarrassing or hard, but then it will get easier. Ask them who they know. Get at least three of them to promise to set you up. Follow up to make sure it happens.

5. Ask each of your two best friends to write up a one-paragraph description of you, highlighting your unique and wonderful qualities. You will use these descriptions in your online profile.

6. If you are dating digitally, continue, but look through the profiles with an eye to breaking your Deadly Dating Patterns. Look at photos and profiles and respond to matches, winks, or messages from people you would ordinarily pass on.

7. If you have not been dating digitally, get your friends to help you enroll on one of the sites or apps listed in Chapter 1. Explore the new territory!

This is the end of Chapter 4. Doing the exercises has helped you to feel more deserving and to envision more clearly the love you want. And learning about the Program of Three has given you the road map to get there. Remember, as Thomas Merton says, "The biggest human temptation is to settle for too little."

Jane, a fifty-one-year-old consultant, describes what happened to her after she stopped settling for too little:

I was single and looking in the wrong places for love, not seeing what was possible in my life for 15 years. Now I'm in a positive, loving and committed relationship, one that I thought I would never have. Because of the Program of Three and Dr. Diana's other teachings, I have been able to sustain it for two years. Brian is a lawyer and a serious athlete, has actually taken personal empowerment classes with me and we talk things out. He even cooks! I just had my special birthday weekend and Brian had the den painted in orange and gold, the colors I love. As we celebrated in there, it hit me—this is the happiest I have ever been in my life.

———— ◇ ————

Secrets of Rapid Online and App Dating Success

I sit at the computer in my pajamas at 2 AM reading a sweet note from my new friend, a connection, a wonder, perhaps the one I am waiting for.—*Joanne, a night-owl writer*

Do you want to learn how to leverage the technology that has resulted in more than 600,000 marriages on one site alone? Online dating on sites and apps has created a new age of romance that makes it entirely possible to find a great partner in just 90 days. I call it the Age of Abundant Love! An estimated 200 million singles globally now use digital dating services each month. And they are succeeding in finding soulmate love! Recent research has found that one in three marriages in the U.S. now begin online. Online relationships progress to marriage faster. And they are happier marriages! And they last longer!

Apps have exploded our dating possibilities. A 2016 study by the Pew Research Center found that 59 percent of Americans think dating apps are a good way to meet someone. And our Love Mentor® coaching results in working with tens of thousands of single women suggest they are right! This is because dating is a numbers game. And apps are a super numbers game!

For example, as of late 2014, an estimated 50 million people around the world use Tinder every month with an average of 12 million matches a day. And apps are great because with most of them you have to indicate interest in a guy who is matched with you in order to communicate. There are fewer unwelcome messages from unsuitable DUDs who can randomly say Hi to their heart's content, like there are on dating sites. Plus, things move a whole lot faster on apps, so you can sort out many DUDs very quickly.

But there is a downside to using this crowded digital bar. Spam and bot profiles are also common, where you are just being lured to a spammy link; and these bots are programmed to come across as real humans. In fact, 49% who message a match never even get a response. Also, apps started to facilitate hookups. While they are now used to find relationships for the most part, men can still wind up sending or requesting sexually explicit photos.

App users have become fickler, as they face match after match to swipe on. Dating apps can be like an addictive online game for guys, where they are just seeing how many women like them or using apps for a mindless diversion. Lack of engagement and ghosting, where people abruptly disappear on you without warning and for no apparent reason, is common with app meet markets. Plus, our brains are only wired to handle around 8 or 9 choices—so facing all the myriads of choices offered from an app can be paralyzing to you and to the matches you are interested in. And finally, texting is the new way of communicating with a match and can go on endlessly without ever leading to an actual meeting. If you don't know what you are doing, you can spend 10 to 14 hours to get one date.

But, the good news is that all these obstacles can be dealt with and overcome, so that you reap all the tremendous benefits in the Age of Abundant Love! And you will learn exactly how to do that in this chapter!

You are no longer constricted by time and space in terms of meeting interesting men; you now have a smorgasbord available right at your own laptop or phone. And you can sample the different dishes at this spread any time, day or night. Online dating and apps are formidable tools that give you power and control. They provide a practice ground for figuring out what you want, for always having a field of men to filter through, or for knowing you can always have a flirty encounter or a date during a dry spell.

But, Dr. D., is online or app dating right for me? you ask. The answer is a resounding *Yes!—if you know how to work them.* I'm going to show you how to make the most of your digital dating experience, coaching you through potential pitfalls and giving you the Seven Secrets of Online Dating Success on Sites and Apps that have helped tens of thousands of clients and students. You'll learn how to:

- create the kind of photos that draw men in droves
- craft a unique screen name and profile that represent the real you and act as men magnets
- describe your ideal match so that you maximize your prospects
- choose two different sites for better results
- optimize your search-engine ranking so that many more guys see your profile
- use the Love in 90 Days Online Dating Report to judge the productivity at each site or app
- pinpoint Red Flag DUD signs to weed out the liars, con artists, bots, and other disappointing guys quickly, both on- and offline, in order to find the STUDS

Many students in our Program who have followed through on these techniques and exercises have been amazed at how many responses they've gotten. Here's what Susan, a thirty-three-year-old nurse, wrote:

> *I was against dating online until I participated in the course. Then after really working on my profile and photo, I was overwhelmed with 150 responses on JDate. I've met some amazing men this way and within a month I was dating three interesting guys.*

When you wade through all the men out there, you can truly find some great STUDs. Here's an e-mail from a graduate who found the One who happened to be living right in her small hometown!

Had we not done online dating, we never would have crossed paths, even though we shared similar interests and lived so close to each other. I can't get over how physically and spiritually compatible we are. We both feel so comfortable with each other. Joe says he almost feels like I'm a part of his body. Me too! We both feel so "at home" with each other. Even doing something as simple as just holding each other close.

Before you log on, let's bust the most common myths people have about dating online.

Debunking the Myths

MYTH #1: *DATING ON APPS OR SITES IS ALWAYS AN UNPLEASANT EXPERIENCE*

While there are articles in the media focused on how much dating apps suck and lead to frustration and burnout, the proof is in the pudding: In the Match Group's 2018 Singles in America Survey, which polls more than 5,000 people who are not Match users, the company found that the number one place where singles meet is online. In 2016, the Pew Research Center reported that 27 percent of people aged 18 to 24 had used a dating app or site, up from 10 percent in 2013. The proportion of 55- to 64-year-olds doubled. While dating apps can be frustrating and take some time and effort, the truth is that they can lead to some great dating experiences and long-term relationships. And they are gaining in popularity! The key is knowing how to work them—which you will by the end of this book!

MYTH #2: *DATING ON APPS AND SITES IS ONLY FOR DUDS AND THEIR FEMALE COUNTERPARTS*

According to a 2013 study by U.S. researchers in the *Proceedings of the National Academy of Sciences* more than one-third of U.S. marriages begin with online dating, and those couples may be slightly happier than couples who meet offline. In the past ten years dating through sites and apps has increased tenfold. And research shows that people who meet online progress to marriage faster. Forty million single Americans now use online dating and there are definitely STUDs among them! Clients in our Program have met rap stars, successful writers, and guys worth $20 million online! Wonderful, successful, and available people are dating online in droves. You just need to know how to find them.

MYTH #3: *THERE AREN'T ANY MATCHES FOR ME*

Online daters' high expectations get them into trouble. For example, you might believe that the personality tests touted on a site will help you find a mate, but after you take the test, the site can't find you any matches. Research has shown that many of the online sites' personality tests do not work in their ability to match you with your soulmate. Don't let it discourage you! There are plenty of sites; you just need to find the right one for you. Change your site or app until you're getting the results you want. Even if (you think) you are: shy, too fat, too thin, too small, too large, not pretty, too pretty (I've heard that one, believe or not!), not successful enough, have too much debt, are in the wrong ethnic group, saddled with kids, over the hill, or have assorted cellulite, warts, and pimples, there is a match for you—if you work at it. I have seen it happen time and time again. There is a male yang to every female yin. As Richard Bach puts it, "You are never given a dream without also being given the power to make it true. You may have to work for it, however."

The Seven Secrets of Dating Success on Sites and Apps

To get the most out of your online dating experience, you'll need to generate a lot of matches and expect to go through a number of DUDs before you get to the STUDs. These secrets will teach you how to sort through a large number of guys quickly, with minimal emotional reactivity or burnout, in order to meet the good prospects.

1. LOWER YOUR EXPECTATIONS!

Yes, you read that right! To lay the groundwork and prevent burnout and frustration you need to do one thing: *Lower your expectations*. This may sound like I am contradicting what I said about the STUDs being out there. But I'm not. Remember, this is a numbers game. You'll probably need to sort through many guys quickly in order to find the good matches. Many of the men will simply disappear, as they are also sorting quickly. Ghosting is common. Remember, on apps, 49% who message a match never even get a response. This will take some time. At this point I really want you to avoid suffering by EXPECTING NOTHING. Then when the good ones come along and stick around you will be pleasantly surprised.

Please write down this statement and post it near your computer where you can see it out of the corner of your eye:

I am playfully looking at guys and they are playfully looking at me. I EXPECT NOTHING.

Now let's get you set up to meet lots of guys.

2. YOUR PHOTO IS EVERYTHING

Men are visual creatures. When they scan women's profiles, they sort based on photos. According to Match.com, men are fourteen times more likely to look at a profile that has a photo. They can't help it—this visual scanning behavior is based in their biology. When men look at the faces of beautiful women, the part of the brain associated with dopamine, the all-too-powerful falling-in-love chemical of love we described in the last chapter, actually increases in activity. Men consciously and unconsciously choose beauty because it gives them a better chance at healthy reproduction. Beautiful women are often healthier women with the right amount of estrogen. I know this may offend you, but you can't fight biology.

You can make it work in your favor, however. First and foremost, you must put time and energy into getting your best photo for your profile. You want a *great* head shot of you, with *no one else in the photo.*

If you're thinking, *I'm not exactly Angelina Jolie—there go my chances,* think about all those makeovers you've seen in magazines and on TV shows: everyone is beautiful; it just needs to be brought out. You have to find your signature look: the hair, makeup, and clothing that make you pop. That's where Beauty Mentors come in, as you will see below and read about in Chapter 6.

Creating Your Look

- Optimize your hair and get your makeup done or do it yourself so that you look and feel your best. Most men like soft, longish, touchable hair and makeup that is not too obvious or overdone. Splurge on getting an updated haircut from a trendy salon. Get your makeup done for free at a high-end department store. (You don't need to buy their high-priced products—duplicate the colors with drugstore brands if your budget is tight.) Make sure you are surprised and happy about how good you look.

- No matter whether you have A cups or DD—buy or find a flattering top that has a scoop neckline. You want to show skin up there, although not too much. You want to look beautiful, with a touch of sexiness, as men like a hint of sexuality in a serious partner. However, avoid looking slutty.

- If beautifying does not come naturally to you, read about "Beauty, Advice, and Matchmaker Mentors" in the next chapter. If you have played out the Hermit or Just Buddies Deadly Dating Patterns, definitely do some work with Beauty Mentors before your photo shoot. While you're readying yourself for your photo, learn how to re-create your look for your dates.

Taking the Photo

- Have a friend who is a fabulous photographer take over a hundred head shots of you to find one that is so good it surprises you. Make sure you take at least one hundred; although it sounds like a lot, the whole process will get you over the hump of holding back or being shy on camera. You can also have your photo done by a professional photographer who knows how to interact playfully and help his or her subject to be real. If you take this route, *make sure your photo looks casual.*

- If you are having trouble loosening up, deliberately take some "bad" photos where you are overly serious or silly. This technique, used by professional models to warm up for a shoot, will get you into play mode and guarantee that some good pics will be snapped.

- Make your photo warm and inviting. As you look into the camera think about your love intention, something like *I give myself a warm, loving life partner.* Or imagine that a man you really love is giving you the biggest compliment! Think about whatever brings a twinkle to your eyes and gives you a real smile. Men rate women who make eye contact and smile in photos as more beautiful. For example, on an app, a smile increases your chances of being right-swiped by 14%. Finally, try heightening the contrast to make your photo pop.

- Take a second or third picture that shows you in your element—whether that is at the top of a mountain or with your beloved pooches. Again, *do not include photos with others.*

- Take some full-body shots that are flattering to your figure. Experimentally add the best one to your profile to see how that affects your responses.

Okay, I know putting all this work into photos or profiles may make you annoyed or squeamish about having to sell yourself. *But this is what it takes to go for it.* You need to shine and distinguish yourself from others. You did it to get into college or grad school. You did it to get the job you wanted. Now do it to get the love of your life. If you want to ditch your single days you have to put your best self out there. Period.

The truth is, when our clients do this process, they can become quite smitten—with themselves! Liz puts it this way:

> *I worked on my hair, makeup and got a gorgeous outfit to have my photo done by a professional. When I saw it I was blown away! I'm a hottie now! Still go back and forth sometimes, but the hottie comes out more and more and is here to stay forever (at least until I'm 90)!*

3. YOUR SCREEN NAME AND PROFILE NEED TO POP AND PROMOTE ENGAGEMENT

To differentiate yourself from all the other women out there, your screen name and profile have to be real, upbeat, engaging, and clever representations of who you are. By now, if you have been doing your homework, you have signed on to one of the top online dating sites listed in Chapter 1 as a male looking for a female and jotted down ideas for yourself. Ideally this was done with a male friend to help you see what men are looking for. Per your homework, you have also asked each of your two best friends to write up a one-paragraph description of you, highlighting your unique and wonderful qualities. If you have not done this homework, please do it now. You will work off these assignments and put together an optimal screen name and profile that is 100 percent you and stands out.

Do it now. You become successful the moment you start moving toward a worthwhile goal.—Anonymous

Sizzlin' Screen Names

Dos: Screen names like *BubblyBrit, RioGirlinNYC, RareYetWellDone, LovingSmartNFun* all pop. They give guys a vivid picture of your personality. Try variations on these examples, or other positive and creative examples you can see by logging on to a major site as a guy looking for a woman. You can also appeal to men's interests in a clever way. *FoxyFootballFan, ILuvGolferss,* or *MatchPointMatch* will catch the eye of a guy who shares your interests. Similarly, you can create screen names that appeal to baseball enthusiasts, lawyers, doctors, Sudoku players, or those with any other hobby or interest.

Don'ts: Avoid defensive, kooky, or negative monikers, like *IHaveaKidIWillAlwaysLove, OrangePolkaDots,* or *LuckyLies.*

The Perfect Profile

For the profile, start by working off your friends' write-ups. Be honest and lead with your most inviting and wonderful qualities. Are you funny? A people person? Do you have a quick mind? Are you creative? Write about it. Then throw in some quirky, endearing, or funny *specifics.* For example, you can say that you are a Sunday *New York Times* crossword puzzle person or you love music from the eighties. List your interests that men would be likely to share. For example, you might mention hiking with the Sierra Club, wine dinners, or your favorite sports team. Ask a question about these interests to invite a conversation. Barbara, a people-person Realtor, writes:

> *I have that approachable quality where people think I'm someone they know. I'm a fiercely loyal friend and a good listener who loves storytellers. I also love the thrill of the deal, am pretty handy in the kitchen and a great speller. I love peanut butter & jelly sandwiches, baseball games,*

stand-up comics, kissing and spur-of-the-moment road trips, especially to Big Sur. Love adventures, large or small. What adventures call to you?

LESS IS MORE WHEN IT COMES TO DESCRIBING YOUR IDEAL MATCH

When you write about an ideal match, make it short and general. Less is more—you don't want the man feeling like he can't measure up to a long list of qualities. Also, remember that you are going to be filling your Dating Program of Three dance card, which will include guys who at first are "not really your type." End this section with a beautiful vision of the love future you are creating for yourself and your special guy. Something like the following works fine:

> *Looking for a good-hearted, successful man who wants an extraordinary, committed, joy-filled relationship with his best friend and lover. We will make each other happy, we won't be bored, we will create & discover things. Being with you will feel like home.*

You want to cast a wide net to capture men who are interested and then do the picking and choosing. And you want to see who vibes with your vision of love. When you do start sorting through your responses, you can then choose men whose profiles indicate that they are in the correct age range, successful, and are looking for your kind of long-term relationship and children, if you want them.

END WITH A CALL TO ACTION

You want to come across as inviting and suggest connection at the end of your profile. This helps a guy take action. For example: *Does this resonate? Message me. I'm looking forward to seeing the twinkle in your eyes.* Or if you have just described an amazing vision of love, you can refer to that.

For example: *Our relationship will be full of laughter, full of love and full of understanding. It is going to be a great life! "Yes?" Let's get started.*

IF YOU ARE USING AN APP, USE THESE KEY TIPS TO BOND WITH GUYS AND CREATE CONVERSATIONS

Because there are so many choices and you can only put a brief profile on an app (for example, Tinder only allows 500 characters), your profile needs to stand out so you catch a guy's attention and engage him immediately. You want to invite conversation from the get-go. Playfulness, a bit of silliness, or revealing your own little quirks and details about your life work well. In addition, be sure to ask a question to get things going between you. For example, you can ask, *What's your hidden talent?* Or, *So here I am. What are your other 2 wishes?* Or, *Excited about scuba diving in the Bahamas. If you have any tips let me know!*

Hinge reports that answering the question *Most Spontaneous Thing I've Done* increases your likelihood of getting a response by 61%. For example, you might say, *Most Spontaneous Thing I've Done: Took off for Burning Man the day after I realized I could!*

Also, *First, Last* or *I've Never* lists can work well. If you use these, make sure you put in any male-oriented interest you may have and something that indicates how genuinely caring you are with others—both of which are very attractive to guys. Always end with a vision of the relationship you want. Do not waste time because you feel you need to be cool or chill about not asking for what you really want on an app profile (which is a common myth in the 35 and under crowd). For example:

Last:

Sports event I watched: NBA Playoffs.
Friend I helped: My Little Sister Anisha.
Movie I loved: The Shape of Water.

Place I hiked: around my building on 34th Street.
Pet: Sady the ferret.
Time I Swipe Right: we'll have to see, won't we ... ☺

I'm ready for a magical, lasting relationship with an out-and-about
geek who uses his powers for good. Is that you?
What's on your "Last" list?

Or,

I've Never:

Met a Maroon 5 fan I didn't like.
Not been there when a friend needed me.
Passed a beach without stopping.
Gone skiing without a big smile on my face.
Passed up a Starbucks S'mores Frappuccino, Yum ☺

I'm looking for a guy who, like me, is able to laugh at silly things, and
communicate about the hard stuff. Someone who has my back as I've got
his. Someone to be my partner as we create our life as an adventure filled
with wonder, lots of play and delight.
What's on your "Never" list?

Another option that works well, especially with the 35 and over crowd
on apps, is to just go with the general guidelines I gave earlier for longer
site profiles, but in an abbreviated way. Here is an example of an app
profile that attracts real STUDs:

Profession: Nursing and loving it
What I bring to the table is caring, girl-next-door charm, smarts & a
sense of humor that catches you off guard!

I'm all about following my heart. Always root for the underdog. Can get freaked out by heights but still leap. Make bucket lists & love crossing things off. Love travel & working out.

You're looking for an amazing relationship with a true partner in sublime & you're up for slow dancing in the living room once in a while. So here I am. What are your other 2 wishes? ☺

Note: These first three tips for your digital dating photo and profile creation are pivotal keys to you finding a wonderful soulmate match. Feel free to copy a phrase or two from the sample profiles if they describe you. There are so many people in the digital dating world that it won't matter! If after working on your materials you find that you are still having trouble deciding on which photo to use or crafting just the right screenname and profile, one of my expert Love Mentors® can help you. Just go to http://lovein90days.com/dating-coach and sign up on the coaching form for a free session.

4. WORK A LARGER SITE AND ONE APP OR BOUTIQUE SITE

Following are the top online U.S. and U.K. dating sites and apps. By now I hope you are on a site already, per your homework. I would like you to be a paid subscriber on two: one large site, such as Match or eHarmony, and one app like Tinder or a specialized site like JDate, Christianmin gle.com, or Elitesingles.com. Browse through different sites, reading the profiles. Go with your intuition in picking a site.

Top Online U.S. Dating Sites and Apps

SITES

Match.com (*Our coaching students have great success with Match and BTW we are not affiliated*)
PlentyofFish.com
OKCupid.com
eHarmony.com
Zoosk.com

Chemistry.com
OurTime.com (*Over 50s*)
SeniorPeopleMeet.com (*Over 50s*)
JDate.com
BlackPeopleMeet.com
EliteSingles.com
ChristianMingle.com

APPS

Tinder (*Largest*)
Dating (*A feature on Facebook*)
Bumble (*Women message first*)
The League (*Requires application*)

Happn
Hinge
CoffeeMeetsBagel
JSwipe

In Europe, the leading site is DatingDirect.com, which currently features 13 different languages and hosts 160 live events/month.

Top Online U.K. and European Dating Sites and Apps

SITES

DatingDirect.com	Zoosk.com
Match.com	JDate.com
eHarmony.co.uk	Shaadi.com (Indian)
PlentyofFish.com	ChristianConnection.com
Parship.co.uk	

APPS

Tinder	Happn
Bumble (Women message first)	

5. MASTER THE SEARCH-ENGINE SECRETS THAT GET MORE RESULTS

A highly ranked profile can increase your visibility and generate more responses. When men run a search for women and you meet the criteria, you will land at the top of their search results, ahead of other women, just by following a few simple rules. Some sites allow you to pay a bit extra to boost your profile. Definitely take advantage of this feature. On a number of sites, recently updated profiles are ranked higher. You don't have to do much to qualify. You can just tweak your info, changing your ideal first date or hobby frequently. On some sites, you will come up as "New" all over again if you simply delete a sentence in your profile and then replace it. Though these are easy ways to update your profile, it's also a good idea to experiment with your photo, screen name, and profile to see if making some changes pulls in better guys.

On some sites like JDate.com, you have to log on repeatedly to show up in the most active searches list. Logging on in the morning and leaving the computer on all day will net you more men by the evening. On those sites, trade e-mails with friends to boost your activity level. On others, including eHarmony, if you don't like your yield, complain to customer service and they will send you more matches.

Note: Experiment with these techniques when you log on to other sites as well.

6. RIGHT-SWIPE AND REACH OUT A LOT

You want to increase your numbers, right? Try something different. Respond to those who are not your type. Love almost always comes in a surprise package. The woman who says she wants a tall dark businessman can be entirely smitten with a short, blond motorcycle dude. We usually don't understand all the soulmate factors that will turn us on mentally, physically, and emotionally. Even in popular fiction we can see this kind of love story. For example, in the *Fifty Shades of Grey* trilogy, heroine Ana is intimidated and turned off at first by Christian Grey's power, wealth, and S&M control freakishness. Meanwhile, at the beginning of their relationship Christian is thinking that all he wants is a submissive woman to have kinky sex with. By the third book, they are enjoying a great marriage. They come together because he takes in her caring validation and becomes more loving, while she takes in his strength and becomes empowered and sexually alive. This is what soulmates actually do in the real world. Researchers call it the *Michelangelo Effect.*

7. USE THE LOVE IN 90 DAYS ONLINE DATING REPORT

On page 116 you will find the Online Dating Report. Make copies and fill out a report for each week that you are on the Program. This will help you track how each site or app is performing in terms of producing men who are really connecting with you, evaluate whether it is time to experiment with your photo or profile or change sites, and reflect on your love intention while you are using the sites. It is perfectly normal for a site to go stale after a few weeks or months, so don't worry about switching to a new site or app. However, you should do this only after you have experimented with your info and have sent out a number of winks, likes, right-swipes, and other flirty messages.

On the Online Dating Report, your love intention rating is the most critical item. You have to be honest here. If you are just mindlessly swiping at people for entertainment, or have a knee-jerk rejection toward all the guys, this is a waste of your time. It is imperative to work up the self-assessment scale using more and more positive thinking and being truly *mindful of looking for love while you are online or on an app*. Deanne, a forty-year-old clothing designer, ended one of her reports by giving herself a 1 on the love intention rating and writing:

> *If I am honest with myself, I go on Tinder expecting to be disappointed.*
> *It's all part of my glass is three-quarters empty mentality.*

This was a courageous reflection on her part and led to her going back to Chapter 2 and doing the Inner Work on her self-sabotaging beliefs.

LOVE IN 90 DAYS ONLINE DATING REPORT

List the online dating services you are currently using and fill out the following information for each one every week:

Date:

1. Name of the site or app:
   Number of promising inquiries: _____
   Number of new site or app message-only relationships: _____
   Number of new phone relationships: _____
   Number of first dates: _____

Is the trend up or down?

Rate appropriateness and quality of men on a three-point scale:
A. *Several have possibilities* B. *One or two have possibilities*
C. *Poor matches*

2. Name of the site or app:
   Number of promising inquiries: _____
   Number of new site or app message-only relationships: _____
   Number of new phone relationships: _____
   Number of first dates: _____

Is the trend up or down?

Rate appropriateness and quality of men on a three-point scale:
A. *Several have possibilities* B. *One or two have possibilities*
C. *Poor matches*

♦ Do you need to change your photo, screen name, or profile on any of the sites?

♦ Do you need to try a new site or app?

Most important: Rate your love intention while using these sites on a scale of 1 to 5, where 1 = Knee-jerk nitpicking and rejecting; 2 = Distracted; 3 = Somewhat serious; 4 = Trying to work it; 5 = Focused, clear, strong intent to find a partner: _____

Making Contact

MESSAGING TIPS THAT MAKE HIM BEG TO MEET YOU

For an initial message reaching out to a new match, share a specific experience you enjoyed related to an activity he mentions in his profile and add a question about it. For example, if he mentions Chaco Canyon, you might write, *I love Chaco Canyon! I got a very cool piece of Anasazi pottery from the Heritage Center that I keep in my office to remember that sunset. Did you go on that crazy pink jeep tour?*

Or give him a sincere compliment. Something like, *I just started running myself and noticed you did half of the NYC marathon. Not too shabby!*

After a hottie has responded to your initial message, follow these tips for keeping the bonding and energy growing between you two.

- **Use his name if you have it and flirt by throwing in a bit of a challenge.** Using his name is another awesome way to create a feeling of connection between you. If he's into baseball, something like, *Well, Jason, what about a Red Sox-Cubs World Series? How cool would that be?* This kind of flirting, coupled with your Diamond Self photo, is a one-two punch that is TOTALLY IRRESISTIBLE.

- **Be upbeat and fun.** For example, you could say, *I just had a breakthrough in my lasagna recipe! One taste and you'll be hooked (fair warning).*

- **Be honest but no confessionals or overly personal info.** You don't want to message him about how you drank all last night and are sick at work now.

- **Make your messages about the same length as his.** This is a fantastic and subtle way to bond.

- **Be careful with spelling and grammar.** Since all he has to go on are these messages, grammar at this point will affect the way he sees you. It can come across as hurried, disinterested, sloppy, or uneducated.

Ideally you want about 3 to 4 fun, flirty messages on the app, 2 to 6 text exchanges, 2 phone calls, and then to meet for coffee. Don't get stuck in a fantasy messaging relationship with the "perfect" guy whom you never talk to or meet—try to hasten phone contact. Even though you may feel intimidated about talking to him, it will give you so much more info about your match—so that you don't waste time. You can feel a guy's energy, his mood, and whether he is a good conversational match for you. Remember, we want to be weeding out the DUDs, and a phone call is a very efficient way to do that! In fact, in our coaching program we have found that STUDs will often call in the beginning without the woman asking to talk. They are more successful and don't want to waste time, so they are more interested and willing to connect via phone. A guy's availability for talking with you is very telling! On the other hand, if he doesn't meet with you after two or three weeks after matching on a site, or a week or so after an app match, move on.

Keep a journal with notes about conversations and dates for each guy.

TIPS FOR INITIAL PHONE AND IN-PERSON CONVERSATIONS

Your first contact with someone you've met online can be awkward, especially if you are used to texting as your preferred communication mode. But here are some easy ways to make sure you put your best foot forward and bond with a guy:

- Smile and give the person your full attention (even on the phone, this will come across!).
- Imagine you are meeting an old best friend and give the guy a warm hello as if he is someone who is in your inner circle.

- Ask general, casual, open-ended questions like *How did your day go? Where did you grow up? Do you enjoy living here? How did you get interested in X? What drew you to my profile?*
- Ask questions about the interests he mentioned in his profile.
- Have topics ready to discuss around movies or TV shows, books, and news that you both may find interesting (nothing political or heavy).
- Prepare your answers to the questions, *What's new? What have you been up to?*
- Share what you are enjoying, i.e., something like, *I'm having a fantastic day playing hooky at the beach! What about you?*
- Avoid discussing old boyfriends or relationships (the number one conversation killer on a first date); talking about marriage, kids, or sex; or discussing debt or health problems.
- If you are meeting in person, make yourself as beautiful as your photo and dress down or up so you fit in at the meeting place.
- If there was any connection at all, at the end tell the guy how much you enjoyed talking with him and that you would like to continue it sometime. In your journal, make a note to ask him about the topic you were discussing in your next conversation. If you don't feel much chemistry but he seems like a good guy, remember that you are still going to try a second date and use the tips I gave you in the last chapter to help bring out chemistry.

Remember, safety comes first whenever you're meeting someone in person. Google the guy and check him out on LinkedIn.com. Arrange to meet in a public place, tell a friend where and with whom you are meeting, and take your phone.

Red Flag DUD Warning Signs

As you work your on- and offline Love in 90 Days Program, watch for these Red Flag DUD warning signs and be ready to terminate a budding relationship immediately:

- He is only willing to communicate by text and his texts are often flirty or witty but never authentic.
- As he is texting you, he asks for more photos, or sexier photos, or he sends you a sexually explicit photo (67% of women on Tinder have gotten explicit photos).
- He asks you lots of questions, but provides very few details about himself (he may be a realistic spam bot who is angling to get you to buy a game or go to a spammy link. To check, message him with random alphabet letters or spell words backwards. If he is a bot, he will reply as if you sent a real message. A human will say, *What?*).
- He is willing to talk or meet only at odd hours and never on a weekend (married!).
- He is evasive and not forthcoming with his phone number, where he lives, or other personal information.
- He answers a question with another question.
- He outright lies to you about his profession, marital status, etc.
- He pressures you for your personal information, more meetings, money, or sexual contact.
- He is quick tempered.
- He has been victimized by most everyone in his life.
- He can't stop complaining about his ex.
- He professes undying, overwhelming love at first sight (see next section).

Romance Scam Red Flags

In 2016, singles (mostly women) lost more than $230 million through online dating romance scams. These scammers are very clever professionals who know how to get women to fall in love with them, without ever meeting in person! And there are organized romance scam rings that use strategic protocols. I have seen this firsthand when two women in different cities, who had just started our Program, were asked to send money to their matches and the requests were worded the same and came in on the same day! One of the women was seriously considering sending the scammer her money—that is, until she talked with me, thank goodness!

But the good news is that you can easily avoid these criminals. Just be on the lookout for these red flags:

- **Lives or works outside of the country**—while this doesn't necessarily mean the guy is a con, it is important to know that romance scams are often committed by rings that operate abroad.
- **Appears to be too wonderful**—he is self-employed, rich, has a master's degree plus, he loves you madly and may refer to you as a soulmate immediately.
- **Quickly wants to email outside of the online dating site**—this is because he is using a fake name and email address that make it hard to catch him.
- **Comes armed with a sob story**—he has a dear family member in need of help, or had a tragic accident out of the country without access to needed cash, and/or just lost his wife, etc.
- **Suggests secrecy**—says no one could understand the extraordinary soulmate love you share, so it is best not to talk about it. This is so your family and friends will not stop the scam.
- **Wants your FINANCIAL INFORMATION** (social security number, credit card number, or bank info)—these cons are so

clever that they can make this insane request seem entirely reasonable. **This is a true scam marker. Block him and bow out immediately.**

- **ASKS FOR MONEY**—because he needs help with the sob story mess you learned about earlier. **Another true scam maker— block him and head for the hills.**

If you suspect a romance scam, conduct a search. Copy the photos from his profile and run them through a reverse-image search engine, such as TinEye or Google Images. If the images come up associated with a person who has another name or lives in a different city, you may have good reason to suspect they were stolen. And if you've been communicating with someone by email, check their address at a site such as RomanceScamsNow.com, which compiles lists of email addresses belonging to known scammers. The website Scamalytics maintains a blacklist of scammers who use false pictures.

In general, when you find a new prospect who interests you, type the name of the person you met online into Google or Bing and see what comes up. From their social media profiles, LinkedIn page, and other information you find, you should be able to get a sense of whether they are who they say they are!

Feel free to terminate a relationship and block or cut off contact with any guy who is questionable. You don't want to waste your valuable time. And there are plenty of decent guys who would love to be with you. If you feel guilty or squeamish about doing this, give him three real compliments and then say it's not working between you. The compliments will help you feel better doing the deed.

Remember, we expect to wade through a lot of DUDs. *Very often* they are the kind who don't respond or disappear on you for no apparent reason. In this fast-paced age of swiping at love the vast majority of the guys will not hang in there, even after you are matched. Even on the large online sites as few as one in five guys will actually continue to respond to your messages. It is to be expected that men will disappear; *never take this as a personal rejection.* This is ghosting—with no forewarning; where a guy abruptly stops communicating or making contact, no matter how much you reach out to re-engage him. The hook-up culture prevalent in the early version of apps, coupled with the relative anonymity and isolation have made it easier for many guys to behave poorly. If he disappears on you, it is about him and shows that the guy is a poor match. I repeat, it is not about you!

You have to view online dating and apps as a form of play, and sometimes it's pretend role play. If you get no response or a rejection, do not waste energy and time feeling hurt. He may have thought you were a goddess, but unfortunately his wife or old flame just reappeared on the scene. Guys who disappear are doing you a favor. They are helping you wade through the DUDs as quickly as possible to get to the STUDs, the good guys who are crazy about you and willing to grow.

Here's what one graduate, who had a history of simply falling into relationships with players and commitment-phobes, said about her online experience at the end of her first month on the Program:

> *During the first couple of weeks I was against online dating. Now I've shifted significantly because I understand that this is a numbers game. I'm understanding my patterns, forgiving myself for mistakes I've made and putting my attention on what is desired. I have been seeing better quality guys. One is a world-class photographer who brings me little gifts from Tahiti and South Africa. I am having a lot of fun with dating. It feels completely different now.*

✎ Secrets to Rapid Online and App Success: Exercises _____

Choose from among the following suggestions, according to your own intuition.

Total Time for Completing All of Them: 20 Minutes

EXERCISE 1: *ONLINE/APP DATING ISSUES*

Alternate positive and negative endings to this sentence:

    Online/App dating is _____.

As you can see, online dating can be viewed from many different viewpoints. Write an affirmation that states the way you would like to experience online dating going forward, e.g., *Online dating is a fun game that helps me sort through lots of DUDs to find STUDs.*

EXERCISE 2: *ISSUES ABOUT SELF-MARKETING*

"It makes me feel uncomfortable. Like I shouldn't have to do it—it's all wrong," one thirty-year-old insisted.

What are your issues? End this sentence over and over again with whatever comes to mind:

    Self-marketing means I am _____.

This exercise usually opens up our deeper fears about ourselves, especially about accepting and showcasing how great we are. Every person has the most exquisite, amazing parts: shining gifts, loving warmth, funny quirks, special beauty. Accept these great parts of you. Celebrate them. Put them out there online.

EXERCISE 3: *LEARNING TO HANDLE "REJECTION"*

End this sentence over and over again with whatever comes to mind:

    If a guy doesn't respond to me it means I _____.

Now circle the most problematic answer. Then write it out using "and that means" and make it stronger and stronger until it becomes totally absurd.

For example, Ayanna, a green-eyed beauty who struggled with her weight, wrote:

*If a guy doesn't respond to me it means he's dumping me and that means
I'm a fat loser and that means that I'm totally unlovable and that means
that I'm definitely going to wind up being a bag lady on the street.*

The bag-lady image finally made Ayanna laugh.

EXERCISE 4: *UPDATING YOUR GOALS*

It has been a month since you started the Love in 90 Days Program. On
page 126 you will find the program goals repeated from Chapter 1. Do
you want to modify your goals? Does the Dating Program of Three or
moving up the ladder to better men seem more obtainable now?

Write down any new goal and a timeline for achieving it. Post this
where you will see it every day.

 # Homework

Choose from among the following suggestions, according to your own
intuition:

1. Work on your photo prep, photo shoot, screen name, headline, profile and ideal match. Have your friends help you.
2. Sign up for one large dating site, in addition to an app or boutique
   online site.
3. Begin working the two digital dating sites using all the search-
   engine optimization secrets *for at least one-half hour every day
   (including weekends).*
4. Begin filling out your Love in 90 Days Online Dating Reports each
   week.

The Ten Love in 90 Days Goals

1. Create an exciting love intention or affirmation.

2. Create greater self-esteem, deservedness, and self-love.

3. Break out of Deadly Dating Patterns and create a successful Dating Program of Three.

4. Move up the ladder to better men.

5. Meet someone who has tremendous potential for a love relationship with you and graduate from the Program of Three.

6. Declare love for each other.

7. Talk seriously with your Beloved about what each of you needs and wants in a fulfilling love relationship.

8. Create a loving win-win contract that gives each of you roots (stability and dedication) and wings (fulfilling your dreams).

9. Commit to moving in together or getting engaged to your Beloved.

10. Marry or make a lifetime commitment to live out your dreams together.

5. Make sure you're attending classes and activities that interest you and that have a lot of men in them.
6. Continue finding and saying hello to three new guys every day.
7. Continue working your network to meet new prospects. Make sure that your three friends follow through on setting you up with dates. Continue to speak your love intention aloud and ask to be set up when you find new people who may have prospects (which is pretty much anybody!).
8. Get yourself two to three good dates this week.

You've made it to the end of the first month of the program! I am proud of you because you've learned a lot about yourself, even if you have just been reading along and not doing the exercises. Congratulations! How are you doing on breaking your Deadly Dating Patterns? Even if you make one small change or say something different that frees you from a pattern, you are on your way to love. One small step leads to the next. This insight by Jack Canfield and Mark Victor Hansen, the co-authors of the wildly successful *Chicken Soup for the Soul* series, has always inspired me:

> *Don't wait until everything is just right. It will never be perfect. There will always be challenges, obstacles and less than perfect conditions. So what. Get started now. With each step you take, you will grow stronger and stronger, more and more skilled, more and more self-confident and more and more successful.*

PART II

The Second Month

———— ❧ ————

Finding Love Mentors

Some people come into our lives and quickly go. Some stay for a while and leave footprints on our heart and we are never, ever the same.—Anonymous

What is the most important thing you can do to create love? Get yourself Love Mentors. These are people who are crazy about you, cheer you on, confront you as needed, boost your self-esteem, and assist you in becoming your most lovely and lovable self. Sometimes they will even introduce you to good men and help make sure it all works out to a happily-ever-after ending.

You've got one already: me. But you may need others. In this chapter I'll show you how to find mentors who can help you with your Inner Work—that is, developing self-love and positive self-talk, and with your Outer Work, shaping how you look and act to create personal empowerment in action. As I've said all along, the Inner Work and Outer Work reciprocally support each other. When you feel great you look great; when you look hot, you have more self-esteem and feel freer and more engaging. Your mentors will be a crucial support system as you make yourself over, inside and out.

Over the years, women have told me that they also wanted the option of having professional Master Love Mentors who are trained by me. So I handpicked and assembled a team of awesome Love Mentor® coaches. Just go to http://Lovein90Days.com/dating-coach and you will be talking to a wise helpful ally in a complimentary session very soon!

The Importance of Mentors

Study after study has shown that adults who have mentors are more successful in their careers and in school. Women, in particular, have greatly benefited from mentoring; they have greater self-esteem and a heightened ability to break through the "glass ceiling." They do even better when they have multiple mentors. Besides serving as a Love Mentor to many women, I've also played the role of a business mentor to women in large companies here and in Europe. In my experience, having a Love Mentor leads to greater success with men in much the same way as having work mentors helps career advancement. Remember, Cinderella had her Fairy Godmother.

For your crucial Inner Work, you will first learn how to find a master Love Mentor who will be a healing force in your emotional life. She or he gives deep emotional support, honest feedback, and advice that works based on your unique needs and wants. Most importantly, a master Love Mentor helps you become what I call your Diamond Self—the identity in which you feel most loving, empowered, and lovable. We'll learn more about becoming and using your Diamond Self in the next chapter.

Here is how Tamara Green, LCSW, one of my senior Love Mentor® coaches, describes the Inner Work mentoring process:

> *We carry the qualities of the Divine Feminine: caring, empathy, wisdom, healing, peace, love, kindness and nurturing, all of which are very powerful. Each of these qualities can transform hard into soft, dissolve walls, and heal battered, untrusting and broken hearts.*

Just like the woman's womb, we are entrusted with the great mysteries of the universe... The nurturing cave in which a baby's new life grows into safety; the enriching soil where seeds alchemize and sprout; the therapeutic cocoon in which caterpillars morph into butterflies.

We see past the defenses, resistances, excuses and procrastinations of the wounded heart. We experience who you really are, a brilliant light... that over the years has been dimmed by hurt, pain and loss. We witness your dimmed light, but only focus on the radiant Diamond that is YOU, your True Self. This is the YOU that is overflowing with joy, awareness and possibility, the YOU that awakens to your visions of true love. This is where the magic happens!

In addition to Inner Work Mentors, your Outer Work Love Mentors will give you the gift of making yourself beautiful in your own eyes (and in the eyes of others!) and educate you or introduce you to possible matches. They will help you construct yourself as the star of your own life, and show you how to cultivate your unique beauty and dormant vibrancy. These mentors will teach you how to develop pizzazz and work the red carpet leading to the premiere of the most important love story ever told: yours.

Finding Your Master Love Mentor

Let's start with getting a master Love Mentor. This is a person you look up to, who is like a good parent or loving benefactor. Like a good mother, she sees the perfection in you.

Most self-help books talk endlessly about how you can't rely on others to give you what you need. Well, on one level that's true—ultimately you have to do it for yourself. But it's an awfully long road, pulling yourself up by your own bootstraps. In the end, you won't succeed anyway by trying to be Ms. Independent. So give yourself the gift of a mentor.

You are the only one who can, and as Oprah once wrote: "You must be fearless enough to give yourself the love you didn't receive."

Finding a master Love Mentor will open the door to love. This is a person who provides a kind of reparenting for you. And this process is the secret, the strategy that has totally transformed my life and the lives of thousands of others.

A personal story first: I was the fifth daughter born to a Sicilian family that only valued boys. My mother was less than thrilled to have me. When my father found out I was a girl, a throwaway, he did not bother to come to the hospital to see me. The rest of our relationship flowed from there. Basically, the only attention I got from him was a hard smack on the back of my head while he called me *stronzo* (a turd). Growing up, I was disconnected from myself, shy with outsiders, and pretty much mute. These wounds did not exactly set the stage for love with a man. Instead they landed me in the Abuse Recycle Deadly Dating Pattern, among others, throughout my early dating life. I dated bad boys who treated me like crap. I hungered for more. There was no amount of rejection I seemingly couldn't handle. At one low point I was lost in the throes of sex with one of the bad hotties and another girl called him. He jumped away from me, threw on his clothes, and ran out the door. And, like a fool, I actually agreed to see him again. That's a Deadly Dating Pattern for you.

But in my early twenties I got into a PhD program in clinical psychology and my life changed forever. I lucked out and got into therapy with an innovative psychologist who was a validating and prizing coach. He told me that I had great potential and that I was smart and beautiful—all the things I needed to hear from a parent. I thought he was either insane or just lying to build up my self-esteem, but in a secret compartment of my heart, I slowly took it in and began to feel lovable. This therapist never crossed any boundaries and was not sexual with me in any way. He was, however, my surrogate father and a master Love Mentor, because he helped me love myself. Out of that experience, I was eventually able to accept the love of a good guy who was crazy about me and willing to grow. That man is my husband, Sam.

So, even if you come from a very difficult family background, have suffered emotional setbacks in your early love relationships, and don't exactly have the highest levels of self-esteem, you still can create love in your life. *If I can, you can.*

How do you find a Love Mentor? One could be right there in your social circle. A simple five-step process can lead you to the person who will help your self-esteem, deservedness, and self-love blossom.

1. IDENTIFYING TENDER AND TOUGH LOVING CARE (TTLC) NEEDS

Tender and Tough Loving Care (TTLC) needs are your deep emotional needs. When you were growing up you needed to be chosen, nurtured, valued, taught, and disciplined so that you felt loved, empowered, and safe. You wanted to be told how adorable you were, taught how to sing your own songs, and stopped from playing with fire or getting into trouble. Your parenting figures either met or didn't fulfill these needs. Their failures in providing TTLC created gaps in your inner model of yourself, your feelings of lovability, and the way you relate in intimate relationships. The more dysfunctional your inner blueprint, the more impossible love seems to be for you now.

For example, if you were an unwanted child, you are likely to feel unwanted by men. You may choose to date men who don't want you, provoke any partner who does want you so that he rejects you, or project being unwanted onto a partner who really does want you. Deep down, your TTLC need is to feel wanted. When you allow yourself to accept this fundamental need without judgment and self-criticism you will begin to feel more whole and empowered.

One way to hasten accepting and fulfilling your TTLC need is to work with a master Love Mentor, who provides you with the experiences you missed or gives you other kinds of reparenting, without all the complications that a romantic relationship brings. A master Love Mentor sets up a model of being loved that you can then duplicate with a partner.

The first step in this process is easy: Read through this list and see which items tug at your heart. Which ones bring up a little sadness, emptiness, a touch of anxiety, or a feeling of longing?

- Being chosen and wanted as the special one
- Being helped to feel safe
- Being loved unconditionally
- Getting a commitment
- Getting hugs and physical affection
- Being understood
- Being prized
- Being told I'm attractive
- Being treated as if I'm desirable
- Being encouraged to live my dreams
- Getting constructive and helpful critiques
- Being helped to explore the world and my place in it
- Getting recognition for my accomplishments
- Being told to "suck it up" when I have to do something difficult or scary
- Getting teaching, advice, or guidance
- Believing in my unique potential and talent
- Getting a "swift kick in the butt" to help me get motivated
- Being praised and rewarded for accomplishments
- Being supported when failing or feeling vulnerable
- Being treated with respect
- Getting constructive limits on my behavior
- Being encouraged to be real
- Being encouraged to play, to find my bliss
- Being forgiven
- Being treated fairly

- Being given to
- Being confronted when I'm out of line
- Being treated as if my wants and needs are very important

You deserve to have all these things. We all do.

Most people automatically react to nurturing or tender love but may be undisciplined, unsuccessful, or lacking in guidance or limit-setting. Nurturing love is only half of the equation in every person's life. We all need tough love—coaching, guidance, and, sometimes, confrontation— to achieve our dreams.

2. FINDING YOUR MASTER LOVE MENTOR

Your master Love Mentor is someone who knows about your warts or pimples yet sees the beauty, the poetry, the soul in you. This is some-one who believes in you and sees your attractiveness and your unique lovable qualities—a person who gives you advice and encouragement to go beyond your fears. This is a person who already experiences you as deserving and successful at love. The master Love Mentor holds the future vision of you fulfilled as if it is happening right now.

Think through your social network. Pick out three women or men who might be able to meet your needs. Candidates can include good aunts, stepparents, 12-step sponsors, life coaches, therapists, ministers, rabbis, growth course leaders, and married work mentors, among others. Think carefully—I know you have at least one person who has the poten-tial to be your Love Mentor, even if you don't feel like you deserve it.

Important: Pick a person for your master Love Mentor who is more successful at love than you. If you can, ideally use someone who has the kind of love relationship you would ultimately like to have or a person who is an informal and successful matchmaker. They know the road. Don't keep asking your friends who are at the same level in their rela-tionships, or lack thereof, as you. That tends to get you nowhere. Suc-cessful graduate Shelly puts it this way:

For many years I tried to navigate relationships using my single men and women friends as guides but I learned after all this time that it was a journey I had to take on my own with the help of my love mentor. I realized it was OK to not share every detail and keep people closely apprised of my relationship, welcoming all opinions and sometimes ending up in the middle of drama that didn't need to be created. I usually ended up giving up on love and going it alone. I learned with a wise and experienced love mentor your patterns can change. I feel such gratitude that you have helped me find love.

Ask people who are happily married, ones who make you jealous, to be your master Love Mentor. That's right. Swallow your pride and admit to them that you want what they have. Nothing is more exciting to a caring married friend than helping her buddy get hitched. And the good news is that a master Love Mentor who is in your life will often continue to help you navigate the inevitable twists and turns that happen after you are happily ensconced with the One.

Now, select one person who is or could be like a good parent or loving benefactor to you.

Rachel, whom we met in Chapter 2, had a rejecting mother and needed an experience of being chosen and prized. She describes this experience:

I thought I had dating and men down pat, but was just stuck on one guy. In reality, I had a lot to learn about myself and how to get what I wanted. There are so many wonderful things I could say about this course but most of it comes down to having a master Love Mentor. It was a mothering experience I never had. You helped me to see that it is possible to find love and that I deserve so much more than I believed. And now I'm dating a guy who really cares for me.

Later on, when you are in a committed relationship, your partner will act as a master Love Mentor and you will be his. Creating a healing partnership where you help one another to feel more grounded, safe, special, and empowered to live your dreams is the ultimate experience. In Chapter 14 you will learn and practice the habits of healthy couples, which will take you even farther on the road to creating this kind of partnership for yourself.

3. CULTIVATING A RELATIONSHIP WITH YOUR MASTER LOVE MENTOR

Begin to spend more time with your master Love Mentor. Being generous will set the stage for a win-win relationship. Offer to help your mentor based on his or her needs—with shopping, cleaning out closets, watching the kids, doing an errand, researching some project, whatever it takes. Take your mentor out to lunch, dinner, a great museum exhibit, or a show. Send fun or helpful e-mails or texts. Buy thoughtful little gifts. In short, cultivate a relationship by giving. The goal is to see or at least have some contact with your master Love Mentor once a week.

4. ASKING FOR THE TTLC YOU NEED

Tell your master Love Mentor your love intention. Come right out and ask for the loving input you need. Be specific. Talk about the gaps and wounds from your past. It is always more powerful to have straight talk— that is, to speak the truth to those who are closest to you. So if you grew up with a critical mother and an absent father and have been repeatedly deserted by the guys you are really into, talk about it with your master Love Mentor. If you are prone to diva-like fits of anger or are terminally shy, share that. If you need the experience of being valued, prized, and chosen, ask for it. You should be on solid ground because you have chosen a person you admire and who thinks highly of you.

Malika was a twenty-nine-year-old graduate student who was raised by a single workaholic mom given to rants of anger. As much as she hated it, Malika herself was very much like her mom—she always had her head down in school or internship assignments. Malika had only two serious relationships, both ending in a Chase Me Deadly Dating Pattern. When figuring out her TTLC needs, Malika felt that she needed to be chosen and have unconditional prizing and love advice, but she also needed a swift kick in the butt regarding the anger that fueled her Chase Me dating. As Malika thought through potential master Love Mentors, she flashed on Linda, who used to be her Overeaters Anonymous sponsor. Linda was a soft-spoken artist whose warmth, caring, and compassion lit up her face. She had a solid, fifteen-year marriage to another 12-stepper. Malika remembered how Linda told her that her African name meant "princess" and always called her Princess Malika.

Malika e-mailed Linda and made arrangements to help Linda sell her artwork. Linda was delighted. Malika told Linda she was working a Love in 90 Days Program, shared about her parents and men problems, and explained what she needed now—a Love Mentor who could help her feel special, give her advice, and call her on the carpet about her anger-management issues. Linda told Malika that she was already like a daughter to her and that she "had the whole package, everything any guy would want." Malika tears up when she talks about this moment.

Linda started mothering Malika in a way that was new and helpful, spending time with her through texting, on the phone, and in person. Malika started feeling better about herself and even used the nickname Princess Malika with her closest friends. In return for all Linda's help, Malika found a gallery connection for Linda so that she could exhibit her art. Eventually Malika met someone online who was "like Linda, only a man! And really sexy." He even calls her Princess Malika.

5. TAKING IN HEALING INPUT

Just as Malika took in the princess identity and other loving input from Linda, the last step in the process is for you to internalize the loving messages that you receive. This means you become a master Love Mentor for yourself. This is the final, yet absolutely crucial step.

You can have the most perfect, most adoring, most giving master Love Mentor in the world, but if you argue with her loving words, fight her advice, and generally block the love by defining it as not real or useless, it will do you no good at all. Often it takes internal discipline to correct yourself and accept the caring that is coming your way. Do not discount and throw away the love that is being given to you.

As Tagore says, "Love's gift cannot be given; it waits to be accepted."

Pay attention, listen carefully, and echo in your mind the loving statements your mentor says to you. You are learning to think positively about yourself, regardless of your life experiences, your disappointments, heartbreaks, and betrayals. Focus on your mentor's loving intention. Actively imagine seeing yourself the way she or he sees you, in all your glory. This process will increase your self-esteem and bring out your realness, which is your charisma. (Everybody has it, thank goodness!)

When I first tell our students this particular technique, they sometimes fight me, saying, "Come on! You're talking about deluding yourself!" If this is what you're thinking right now, this is what I tell our students, and this is what I say to you: Your whole bit about being unlovable or whatever is a delusion. You are a diamond; maybe a dull, uncut, or crazy one, but a diamond, nonetheless. So take in the light and shine on.

Master Love Mentor Training

Another option that may call to you is to enroll in a course to learn how to become a Master Love Mentor®. At http://www.Lovein90DaysUni versity.com/ you can take a Love in 90 Days Coaching Certification course that helps you experientially understand how the love process unfolds. I personally teach this video course. It is designed to give you powerful support in your love journey as well as training as a coach using my unique principles. See Appendix C for details.

Beauty, Advice, and Matchmaker Mentors

To really shine through all your facets, you also need Outer Work Mentors. Even if you feel you have the beauty angle covered, it is always good to evolve and move to the next level. It gives you a shot of adrenaline where you feel hot, renewed, and ready to go. Of course, most of us do not feel like we have the physical angle covered! But here is the truth: Every single one of us is beautiful. This means you. It just needs to be brought out. Assets highlighted. Flaws minimized. Personal style and pizzazz developed. As Tagore, the mystic poet, says, "Beauty is truth's smile when she beholds her own face in a perfect mirror."

You can see what Tagore and I mean if you think about new celebrities. No matter how nondescript, overweight, or unattractive they are in the beginning, they become more and more attractive as they shoot their way to stardom. They nurture and develop their outward appearance. They sculpt their bodies in the gym, eat right, get clothes that showcase their bods and hairstyles that make them hot. Many of these up-and-comers also use personal trainers, nutritionists, stylists, and other consultants to help them create their own perfect mirror.

Now I want you to construct yourself as the emerging star of your life. I know, you can't afford the people who work in Hollywood. But you can find exercise classes and gym trainers, clothing saleswomen, free department-store makeup makeovers, hairstylists, and yentas who can become your Beauty, Advice, and Matchmaker Love Mentors. Ask them for help. They will show you how to eat, exercise, dress, style your hair, and put on makeup in a way that may be strange or hard at first, but turns out to be fun and, amazingly, just right for you. They will teach you about the power of push-up bras, décolletage, the right heels and skirts, feminine, touchable hair, and subtle, fresh, natural makeup (sorry if this offends you, but once again, there is no getting around male biology!). They will help you emerge in the world of men, bringing more men— better men—into your orbit.

This transformative magic can occur at *any* age. Here's an e-mail from Roz, a fifty-five-year-old woman who was a dedicated equestrian. She was hiding out in the Hermit pattern in horsey outfits with no makeup and her hair tied back with a rubber band. Then she took a Love in 90 Days workshop. A month later she e-mailed me this:

> *I was snatched off the streets of Back Bay by a Clothing Expert. Having left a work interview in my new "let's look great outfit" complete with my version of make-up and jewelry, I passed two women sitting at an out-side table. We all smiled and they commented on my beautiful outfit. I stopped to talk and in time I told them about my dating plan. One of the women was the manager at a trendy clothing store. The clothing is very bright and colorful. The fabrics are soft. The styles are very inviting. She begged me to come in to her store with the intention of dressing me up.*
>
> *I put on the most amazing red/magenta and orange dress that defi-nitely accented all my best features: boobs, waist and hips. Then she put this sexy hat on my head and gave me one of those fortune cookie purses in magenta. She added red to my lipstick, retouched my make-up, and called her friend in to see me. Wow, I looked really hot. We had so much fun. She sent me off with the request that I get back to her with my success stories and the promise to call me when a new outfit comes in that she thinks will work for my figure. I walked down the street to my car with my head high. Of course, the only people around were the contractors, repairmen, etc. But, I've been invited to a party next week to try out my new outfit. What fun!!! A new Clothing Love Mentor.*

All this beauty stuff is especially imperative if you have been caught in the Hermit or Just Buddies Deadly Dating Pattern. You have to learn to give the guys "go" signals, and a feminine appearance with a touch of sexiness is the most basic green light of all. Focusing on your physical appearance is not superficial. It is an act of self-love, a way to honor yourself. Jewelry, clothes, and a crowning knock-out hair color and cut are ways to respect the body that houses you. These things do not foreclose on spiritual and psychological development, but can actually augment them. As Tagore writes, "Love adorns itself; it seeks to prove inward joy by outward beauty."

Do not go out of the house without making yourself look and feel fabulous. It will make it easier for you to do your hello assignments. You never know whom you are going to meet and where you're going to meet him. Remember the Marcia Cross story in Chapter 1?

Note: If you miss a day and do find yourself out of the house in your ratty jeans and no makeup when a hottie shows up, just remember, a big smile is the most powerful beauty accessory.

Now about Matchmaker Mentors. My experience has not been a positive one with the professional kind. But there are natural-born matchmakers who do a great job setting people up just because it is their mission in life. If you can find such a person, let her introduce you to guys even if you think you are being set up with dorks. If your aunt Gerdie wants to set you up with the nerd next door, go for it. Remember, you are experimentally dating against type.

Loving friends can be helpful Beauty, Advice, or Matchmaker Mentors. It is great to surround yourself with caring people who uplift you with their positive thinking. Conversely, detaching from entrenched naysayers, cynics, pessimists, and whiners who echo your own self-sabotaging thoughts is definitely a must. In Chapter 12 we will deal with Frenemies and other non-supportive types. One powerful way to set up a supportive circle is to form a Team Love, or group of students who are working the Love in 90 Days Program together.

Team Love Groups as Mentors

You can create a Team Love group with your single friends that meets weekly or bimonthly (see Appendix A). As you work the Love in 90 Days Program together, the whole group or individual members can take on Beauty, Advice, and Matchmaker Mentoring roles. The team can be a tremendous resource for you where you will learn about hot shopping, hairstylists, exercise classes, networking opportunities, and more in your local area. You can come to your Team Love group for solace when you are hurt, be inspired by others' wins, and have a whole team of women who can set you up with guys. You can either create a Team Love Group with your friends or join one led by one of my professional coaches at http://www.Lovein90Days.com/dating-coach/. I have been completely blown away with how generous, caring, and empowering the women in these groups have been toward each other. Here is a series of supportive, educational, and inspirational e-mails going out to a Team Love group run by one of my coaches.

Roz hits a down cycle as she starts to come out of a Hermit Deadly Dating Pattern and writes:

I am a dead mouse. I have had NO SECOND DATES at all. All my first dates seemed fun and enjoyable and I found things in common with each person. I must appear to have two heads instead of one or something like that.

Several supportive messages come back to her, including this one from Dyanne:

You're NOT a dead mouse!!!! You are Ravishing Roz! You've got to BELIEVE in yourself—So, you didn't get a second date, no big deal because there will be more! You've got to look on the positive side of things, you had first dates. You are moving! And I haven't even been meeting men.

Roz writes two weeks later:

Hello Team Love, Just wanted you to know that I am meeting men!!! I had a chance meeting with an amazing trader earlier this week and he called me today to make sure I was coming to his meeting Friday. And

I met another walking down 46th St. at Madison Ave. We chatted for a few blocks and had a drink at O'Rourke's. He is a lawyer from Memphis and asked if he could take me to the Opera when he comes back in a few months. The vibe is on. Ravishing Roz ☺

Drew responds:

Your beauty is irresistible!
I experienced some serendipity on Friday night that inspired me. I went to a talk on spiritual partnerships at the Lotus Buddhist Center. During the break I noticed Tommy, a surf instructor who I met last June at a surf-yoga retreat. Keep in mind that this is the type of man I've been including in my visualizations of a husband. He's a surfer, but his main work is engineering solar-powered buildings. He and I talked for a while. It's a sign that I'm starting to resonate at the level I want to be at and attracting men who are in alignment with me on a number of levels…
spiritually, intellectually, artistically, physically, etc.
Here's to resonating at higher levels!
Let's keep it going, TL:)
Sending love to all of you!!!
Drew

Layla responds:

You go girls! My luck turned this weekend at the co-ed softball game. There were so many great guys but one in particular caught my eye. We went for coffee and set a date to go out for real. I couldn't have done it without your encouragement.

Sneak preview: You will read about "Dead Mouse" Roz's sexy happy ending in Chapter 13.

Now on to the Inner Work exercises that will help you find Love Mentors.

✎ Finding Love Mentors: Exercises_____

Choose from among the following suggestions, according to your own intuition.

Total Time for Completing All of Them: About 30 Minutes

EXERCISE 1: *FIGURING OUT YOUR TTLC NEEDS*

Review the list of unfulfilled TTLC needs that we covered earlier. Which ones would give you the most healing? Which would most help you to become a happier and more generative human being? More deserving of love? Which inputs do you intuitively feel or know you need?

Think through each need on the list, imagining how each one feels. Write down the five most important ones to you. These are the needs you will work on with your master Love Mentor.

EXERCISE 2: *TURNING YOUR NEEDS INTO AFFIRMATIONS*

Make each need into an affirmation by writing out, *I need and claim* (need). For instance, you might write, *I need and claim being understood,* or *I need and claim being chosen and wanted as the special one.* Use your own words. If you feel weepy it is okay. This is heavy stuff. Allow yourself to experience whatever you are feeling, and then it will pass through like a storm cloud.

Write out your affirmations on separate pieces of paper and put them around the house. When you see one, close your eyes and meditate on it for a few minutes. Putting attention on your affirmation is like putting Miracle-Gro on your plants.

EXERCISE 3: *LETTERS FROM PERFECTLY LOVING PARENTS*

Listen to uplifting music or meditate for ten minutes. Prepare to write a letter to yourself as if you were your own perfectly loving mother. Feel free to let your imagination go and do not tie your thoughts in any way to your real mother. Simply imagine that you gave birth to a perfect, innocent little being—who is you. Then write the letter to yourself. Talk about how unique, beautiful, loving, and special you really are. Write about those qualities that make you especially attractive as a woman and loving partner for some lucky guy. If you get stuck, imagine that it is me writing the letter to you. This is an emotionally powerful exercise and many students cry while doing it.

Next, follow the same process but write the letter from a perfectly loving father.

If you are forming a Team Love, one powerful exercise is to break up into dyads in which each person gets her own letter read to her. Here is an excerpt of a mother letter written by Myrna, who had a lifelong estrangement from her narcissistic mother:

Dear Myrnalee,

We were waiting for you and now that you are here, you are more perfect than we could have dreamed. We name you Tziviah, the female deer (dear) because you will walk the earth with grace, gentleness and the lithe of a deer. You are a very special soul that the rabbis tell us is kadosh, kadosh, kadosh (holy, holy, holy). There will be many who want to love you and be in your presence. Choose wisely because you deserve to have a man beside you who fawns on you, stands behind you, walks with you and carries you when you need it. You are endearing and easy, understanding and breezy.

Your legs are long and slender, your fingers are gentle and graceful. Your walk is determined and your smile inviting. When you enter a room, so follow light and hope. Your strength gives strength to others, your touch comforts every child and melts even the toughest man. Your beauty is mirrored in the universe and so beautiful souls appear on your way.

EXERCISE 4: *CHOOSE A MASTER LOVE MENTOR*

Make a list of all the people who have been most loving or validating toward you in your life. Pick out ones who are still living whom you look up to and admire. Circle ones who could become your master Love Mentor. If there are none in your immediate circle, consider engaging a warm and validating life coach or therapist. Make sure that the person is in a successful loving relationship. Don't be afraid to ask about this. When it feels appropriate, show the letters from Exercise 3 to your master Love Mentor. Then have her or him read them back to you.

EXERCISE 5: *YOUR TO-DO LIST*

Write out your beauty to-do list. Expense is not such an issue now: with high-end designers creating lines for inexpensive stores like H&M, Target, and Walmart, you can get up-to-the-minute looks for very little. At the more-upscale department stores, you can get made up for free in the cosmetics section. Then, following the palette the beautician has used, buy drugstore cosmetics, which are often very close in quality and color to expensive makeup lines. Get a fab haircut by going to a pricey salon one time and then go to less-expensive hairdressers and have them follow the lines. Maybe you want to buy a wild-looking faux fur or try hair extensions. Go for it.

For your to-do list, also consider eating a healthier diet, and going to a gym or yoga class. Self-discipline ultimately leads to self-love, which is the first step in getting the love you want.

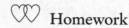 **Homework**

Choose from among the following suggestions, according to your own intuition:

1. Cultivate a relationship with a master Love Mentor. You can do it and you deserve it!
2. Find Beauty, Advice, or Matchmaker Mentors as needed.
3. Create yourself as the star of your life each day. Go out looking and feeling fabulous! Give yourself thought compliments throughout the day.
4. Work your two online dating sites/apps using all the search-engine optimization secrets *for at least one-half hour every day (including weekends)*.
5. Fill out your Love in 90 Days Online Dating Report.
6. Make sure you're attending classes and activities that interest you and that have a lot of men in them. If you find that you are not meeting men at the regular events, shift over to two *singles events* each week. Simply Google your city plus "singles" to find activities.
7. Continue finding and saying hello to new guys.
8. Continue working your network to introduce you to new prospects.
9. Remember, this is a *numbers game*. By getting a bunch of men in the pipeline you ensure that you meet the right number of good guys and that will allow you to end up with top-level prospects. Quickly work your way through the DUDs and get yourself two to three possible STUD dates.

This chapter contained deep work and I am so proud of you for whatever piece of it you did! I celebrate you. The bottom line with Love Mentoring is the decision to allow others to prize and adore you and ultimately to celebrate yourself. This begins and ends with positive self-talk. Be compassionate, kind, and validating to yourself. And consider creating a Team Love to support you in your work. It can be a loving gift for yourself and your friends. Let's end this chapter with a poem that Iris wrote for Dawn, her Team Love sister, who married an incredible STUD in a heartfelt and simple ceremony:

> *Celebrating the end of your courting and dating,*
> *Here we are assembled... your ladies-in-waiting.*
> *Thank you for proving the prince is for real,*
> *From the light in your eyes,*
> *to the way that you feel.*
> *My eternal wish as one of your magical coven*
> *"A life filled with grace and a lotta good lovin'!"*

Discovering and Using Your Diamond Self

Most of the shadows of this life are caused by standing in our own sunshine.—Ralph Waldo Emerson

The overwhelming majority—that is, about 66 percent—of U.S. marriages come from meeting partners at work, school, or through family or friends. Building your social network opens up new possibilities in every arena of your life, including the love department. So how do you make networking happen like magic? How can you comfortably meet lots of people, make strong allies, and flirt with the hotties? The secret is to find and develop what I call your Diamond Self: your most connected, lovable, and loving identity.

Networking is hard and I'm shy, you protest. You're right—it does take courage, but by working the ultimate shyness-buster techniques I'll teach you in the Inner Work and Outer Work of this chapter, you will soon be able to bring out your charisma at will. I'll show you the most powerful ways to introduce yourself, make memorable impressions, and create instant friendships with new people. These tools will help build a posse who wants to help you! You're also going to learn what your mother never taught you: how to flirt. Guess what? Men are very often insecure and need clear "go" signals from women. Flirting not only boosts your self-esteem, but it boosts men's as well. The Key Flirting Moves module teaches you just how to give the kind of green light that opens up fun, new connections.

Your Diamond Self

The Diamond Self is your most dynamic, self-loving, and passionate identity. It builds on all of your prior successes in love and at work. This is the self that you are most proud of—the self you believe in. It's the "you" that acts in ways you like, enjoy, and respect, the "you" that is your own beloved warrior. It's ultimately the real you, who acts freely without fear and doubt, who is at home in your body and true to your passions, and who attracts people into the orbit of your charisma.

Hard to relate to, right? I know. You think your "real" self is nervous, uncomfortable in her body, and lacking confidence with attractive men. You're convinced that your own mysterious Diamond Self is either impossible to muster up or dead and buried.

Well, here's a news flash: You are suffering from a serious delusion about your real self. You are confusing the wounded, fear-bound, and scarred-over you, the one who is constrained by delimiting cultural and familial labels, with the beautiful and perfectly okay self you were born with. As Marianne Williamson puts it, "Love is what we are born with. Fear is what we learn." Here are four steps to help you rediscover and build on that original loving and lovable self.

Four Steps to Creating Your Diamond Self

1. REDISCOVER YOUR AUTHENTIC NATURE

Think back to when you were an infant, toddler, or young child. Look at photos where you were all smiles, alive, and in the moment. You were born with innocence, natural curiosity, and joy in the world. The original you was a fully present, adorable little being, in touch with all of her blissful feelings and naturally assertive and self-expressed.

When you were that sweet child running around, what did you enjoy? Was it the running around, or cooking on your Fisher-Price play stove? Maybe it was sitting still staring at a bumble bee. Were you a big talker or a chubby witness who sat on your potty throne and took it all in? Did you love to finger paint? Think back and remember that early time when you were free to play and explore the world. What were you like? This is a time before you were boxed in by your parents' and society's expectations, fears, and neuroses. Before you were ignored, shamed, or told you were bad. Before the limitations and fears set in.

Chances are, all those early traits are still with you, in their grown-up manifestations. And they are all utterly you and okay. In fact, they are charming, even captivating. But they may be entirely hidden.

I have an old photo of myself from that innocent first era, before I closed down my heart and got shy to the point of being mute. It shows a cherubic three-year-old in a beloved park where I used to love to race around and climb all the rocks. I am sitting in the dirt, grinning wide-eyed at the camera, posing with joy and confidence, an impish tomboy in my dirty polka-dot dress. I keep the picture by my computer and look at it with great appreciation almost every day. That is me. In fact, when I watched myself on the *Today Show* recently, I giggled outright because I caught the tomboy imp in a dress staring back at me from the TV set.

We are all born with unique temperaments and biological predispositions and gifts. Know and celebrate yours. As you get in touch with and create a life from that "real self," you'll begin to tap into your unique charisma. Here is a mantra I learned from the brilliant acting teacher Jack Plotnick: *Every person is interesting when they are real.* When you are your authentic self without social facade or pretense, none of your energy is bound up in monitoring yourself and how you are coming off to others. Instead your full energy and attention are available in the moment. You are able to pay attention to the person you are with. You are free to act and speak from your whole self, based on real needs, impulses, and desires. Voilà! Your natural liveliness, inquisitiveness, quirkiness, and funniness emerge. You can still be polite and socially appropriate but in a real way that is grounded in natural feelings of loving connection and compassion. This is true happiness and beauty.

Here's how Margery Williams describes the Velveteen Rabbit becoming real in her classic allegory:

> *He was Real.... That night he was almost too happy to sleep, and so much love stirred in his little sawdust heart that it almost burst. And into his boot-button eyes, that had long ago lost their polish, there came a look of wisdom and beauty.*

Being real means you become grounded in knowing that you are beautifully okay just as you are. You regain your basic wisdom, which is grounded in the ability to know what you really want and need. You are free to feel your feelings and be in love with life, just as you were when you were first discovering the world.

Build on that early identity so that you open the beautiful facets of yourself like a well-cut diamond. Take chances. Be different. Have fun. Dance on a table, be silly, sing off-key. Don't do anything self-destructive, but catch the impulse, follow it, and see what you say or do. Play and let yourself be you. If you break free like this you will fall in love—with yourself—in a way that helps others feel good and free to be real, too.

2. PRACTICE BEING GRATEFUL

Gratitude is the recognition that we have gained something of value in our lives and not necessarily through our own efforts. Regularly practicing gratitude has been linked with creating happiness, contentment, pride, and hope. To be grateful is to look at your life regularly as a beneficiary of random and premeditated acts of kindness. In a Gallup survey, 90 percent of Americans reported that when they expressed gratitude or thankfulness it helped them feel either "extremely happy" or "happy."

In the previous section, I asked you to reconnect with your authentic self, the innocent self of childhood. This process may arouse painful memories of abandonment, abuse, or betrayal. If you hit any new waves of painful memories, talk about them and work through the issues with your master Love Mentor coach, Team Love, or a therapist.

Ultimately, you want to let go and create more happiness for yourself by living in a state of gratitude. To live in this state, you must learn to look at the past very differently. The past no longer exists; only your stories about it exist. And there are always many different viewpoints one can have about any event. If you allow yourself to stay with the old negative stories in your head you are actually revictimizing yourself. You are creating pain for yourself right now.

In order to stop hurting yourself, begin reframing your past more positively—starting with childhood and adolescence and then moving on to old love relationships. Remember successes and times you felt lovable and loved. Even relationships that had horribly negative aspects or ended badly had wonderful or good parts.

Like glasses of water, past relationships can be remembered as half full or half empty. Or all the way empty. Holding them in our memory as empty, useless, shameful, or bad keeps us down and feeling like failures. If we hold them as learning and growing experiences, we can begin to feel better about ourselves. It is important to understand that all shared love is forever. The good experiences you had in past relationships live on in your memory and have been part and parcel of learning about what it means to be chosen and loved. It is important to understand that all parties in your past relationships did the best they could. And that you learned very important things about how wonderful you truly are, key aspects of your Diamond Self identity. For example, if you cleverly handled a guy who cheated on you in terms of finding out the truth, you can deeply appreciate how smart, courageous, strong and amazing you truly are.

This positive way of thinking leads to constructive self-talk and personal happiness. In fact, gratitude research suggests that if you take the stance of counting the blessings in each and every relationship you've ever had, and noticing what you did that gained your own respect and admiration, chances are you will be happier and more optimistic about the future. This is a gift you can give yourself, starting now.

In order to choose happiness, practice appreciating and being grateful for whatever you do have right now. In three different studies, researchers randomly assigned people into a "gratitude," "hassle," or "control" group. Every morning the participants in the first group simply wrote a list of up to five things in their lives, both large and small, that they were thankful for. The hassle group did the same for problems. The controls wrote only about daily events. All the groups were matched so there were no other differences between them. The gratitude group had much greater satisfaction with their lives as a whole and more optimism about the future. They also felt more connected with others! This one process alone sets you up to be happy and have networking success. When you feel more connected, you will be warmer and more relaxed with people, which will help you deepen your friendships and forge new ones.

I want you to practice the following mini-exercise every day. At the end of each day, think about what went right at work, with your date, with your love life. What wonderful things did you do to make these things go right? This sets the stage for Diamond Self gratitude to appear. The question always to be asking is, What is going right? Notice, appreciate, and get your Diamond Self glow going.

Next, we will build on all the positives you have noticed about yourself in the first two steps and create your own special, unique, self-loving Diamond Self identity.

3. DO THE LIFE-CHANGING DIAMOND SELF EXERCISE

This is one of the most important exercises in this whole book! It has helped thousands of women all over the world become more self-loving, self-confident and naturally charismatic so that they were able to create love relationships beyond their wildest dreams! The Diamond Self work is based on research that shows there is no such thing as a fixed structure in the brain that represents the self! The "I" or personal identity you think is permanent is actually a process in your neural network that is always in flux. Noted author Dr. Joe Dispenza describes the process:

> *You are a work in progress. The organization of brain cells that makes up who you are is constantly in flux. Forget the notion that the brain is static, rigid, and fixed. Instead, brain cells are continually remolded and reorganized by our thoughts and experiences...nerve cells can be seen as dancing patterns of delicate electric fibers in an animated web, connecting and disconnecting all the time. This is much closer to the truth of who you are.*

There is a constant play within brain structures that represents your identity. Your brain and its neural networks are that malleable. What this means is that you can train and thereby change your brain's image of self, including its physical representation of you, which is your body image. You can do this by deliberately adding a picture of a new you, your loving, empowered, beloved Diamond Self, into the constantly changing energy flow of identity. Which, of course, over time, changes your whole outlook on love and the reality of your dating life. And this is true no matter how old you are!

Read each section of the Diamond Self Exercise below and then close your eyes, taking your time to do each step of the exercise.

1. Remember a time when you felt good about yourself—alive, real, attractive, passionate, talented, connected, loving—lovable. Put yourself in the picture so that you are looking through your own eyes. If you can't remember a time like this, imagine a scene where you would feel lovable and loving. Feel that completely.

2. Imagine yourself better, even better. Imagine yourself five times better.

3. Now take that image and bring it closer to you. Make it brighter, more colorful, clearer. Give it a sound track, a great sound track, magnify all those good feelings—make them stronger. This is your Diamond Self. Give it a name, a grand name. Here are some examples to get you going:

   • Amazing Grace
   • Vivacious Vixen
   • Deserving Radiant Goddess of Light
   • Saucy Minx
   • Adorable Angel of Joy
   • Beloved Mighty Isis
   • Happy and Fearless Goddess of Unconditional Love
   • Joyful Chosen Magnificent Jewel
   • Sparkling Confident Queen of Love
   • Playful Precious Mesmerizing Lioness
   • Sparkalicious Loving One

   Play with any names that come to you for a minute or two. Then say your Diamond Self name to yourself. (Note—You can always work on or expand it later.)

4. Shrink the Diamond Self, make it tiny, as small as a real diamond. Then put that image aside.

5. Get an image of yourself at a time when you felt rejected, abandoned, betrayed or unlovable, when you were overrun with negative self-talk, like *It's hopeless for me*, or *I'm too fat, too invisible*, or *I'm a loser*. We'll call this your Disappointing Self.

6. Take the image of your Diamond Self, make it the size of a hand grenade, and imagine throwing it right into the center of your Disappointing Self. Imagine it exploding and completely destroying the Disappointing Self.

7. Now, instant replay. Imagine your Disappointing Self and throw the Diamond Self grenade into the center, blowing up the Disappointing Self again.

8. Speed the whole thing up and repeat several more times.

Do this exercise until you cannot get a clear image of the Disappointing Self. Do a quick version of this process whenever you go to an important social event or any time you need a lift!

Here's how to know if a Diamond Self name is "right" for you: When you think or say it, you will feel excited, happy, even thrilled—but also, perhaps a little scared, embarrassed, ashamed, or silly. This is because you are stretching yourself. Bottom line: a true transformative Diamond Self nickname will call to you. In spite of some uncomfortable reactions, it feels good. And when you think or say it, your new nickname has a fun, joyful quality. Your Diamond Self name is so critical to the speed and success of your love journey.

Now that you have your Diamond Self name it is time to go shopping and dress "Lovely Irresistible Dancer," or whoever has emerged as your unique new you. Pull a new look together by thinking about your sensual, beautiful, and lovable name. Buy lingerie and clothes that are in alignment with your new self and show off the parts of your body that you love. Get a haircut that frames and showcases the beauty in that face you see in the mirror. Find jewelry that symbolizes her radiant, lively, sensual, and loving nature. As Jess Scott says, *"The human body is the best work of art."*

Here is an e-mail I received from "Beloved Radiant Goddess Jana," who was rediscovering her own beauty.

I am a stunner. I just had to tell you that Jon and I went shopping today and bought a gorgeous silk dress for tomorrow night. I really should keep taking pictures of myself because I am so hot!

Like Jane, you want to be able to look in the mirror and see your lovely Diamond Self beaming back at you!

4. FACE YOUR FEAR

Act in ways that your Diamond Self yearns to act. Be gorgeous, real, and flirtatious with both the hotties and not-so-hotties. Make a grand entrance as Foxy Locks Laurie, or Passionate Playful Beloved One if you feel like it. Dance yourself out even if no one else at the party is dancing. Feel with your intuition; get a gut sense of what interests you, what you need to say, or which action calls to you. And if fear is there like a demon blocking you, do it anyway. Fear lights the way to mastery.

In some situations, anxiety or fear is a helpful red light that is good to heed. After all, fear signals are hard-wired into our DNA as instincts. Looking both ways, avoiding dark alleyways, and protecting children in public spaces are just a few examples of our innate vigilance. But when fear stops us from meeting new men or trying for a dream job, it is best to see it as a green light showing us what we *must jump into as soon as possible*. And once we dive into these new waters, that fear turns into excitement because at their core, anxiety and excitement are one and the same sensation. It's all in the interpretation. As Joseph Campbell wrote in *The Power of Myth*, "The Demon that you can swallow gives you its power."

Obviously, we first have to ensure safety. But then the task is how to approach the fearful situation and conquer it, whether that involves leaving the house to go to a party alone, texting or calling a new guy on the phone, or going up and introducing yourself to a hottie. In order to do any of these activities, practice relaxation techniques such as deep or belly breathing. Simply put your attention on your in and out breaths, gradually slowing them down. Anchor your attention there and you will relax.

Soothing or inspiring music on your iPod can help you relax, slow your breathing, and quiet your anxiety. Make a play list of calming music and whenever you think about a scary action or event in your future, listen to it. You will train your mind to relax in the face of any frightening situation.

Another way to handle anxiety is by paying careful attention and studying your immediate surroundings. This is a simple yet profound choice that takes your attention off the negative self-talk that is making you nervous. For example, you may be at a party where you don't know anyone, thinking shyness-generating thoughts, like *These people would never be interested in me*, or *I have nothing to say*. If you start really looking around the room, you notice how the food is arranged. As you study the vibrant colors of fruits, the silver platter in the center of the table, the patterns in the tablecloth, you begin to feel more relaxed. When the hostess comes over to you, you now have something to chat about, but you also stay relaxed and observant. As you notice the dress she is wearing and the interesting way she did her eye makeup, you find yourself relaxing more and more. This is because your attention is drawn away from worrying about yourself.

The deliberate practice of relaxing in the face of fear is how we swallow the Demon and gain its power. Study after study has shown that confrontation is the single best approach to overcoming your fears.

As a child, I was afraid to speak up even within my own family. This led to a horrible phobia of public speaking. But the little tomboy in the dress had things to say. I took myself by the scruff of my shirt and forced myself to speak, to just say anything. I didn't always feel good about it— I would judge my statements with a mean and critical eye. Sometimes I would be mortified at what came out of my mouth. But I kept taking small steps. First, I made myself talk to one person here and there; then with a few students at college and graduate school. Once I received my doctorate, I volunteered to teach a small class at a local community college. Over time, I appeared on local TV (and almost fainted in the green room!) but kept going and finally went live nationally.

So what was the reward for following the gauntlet of my fear? Now I can talk to any group, any time. Because I know the journey from being self-hidden to self-expressed, I have been able to understand and help many people when otherwise I could not have. Facing my fear gave me my Diamond Self. Facing yours will do the same.

In sum, your empowered, lovable Diamond Self comes from rediscovering your authentic self, practicing gratitude daily, giving yourself a Diamond Self name that captures the exciting new identity that delights you, and facing your fears that stand in the way of expressing the radiance of the new you. At the end of the chapter you will practice Inner Work exercises that will help you successfully implement each of the four steps. Now that you have confidence, let's get that Diamond Self of yours out there! Here is how one formerly shy student in our Program described networking with her new sense of self:

> I went to a business party with many people I didn't know. I was living into my new name, Wonder Woman of Love. It was very refreshing because I didn't feel petrified to walk up and say hi. I spoke up for who I was and what I did, and I had a meeting of the minds with one guy I met. Then he said he was going out to a date, but I didn't care. I felt a nice click and it was great because he listened to me.

How to Network Like a Pro

Everything in your life can be enhanced by creating relationships and making friends—real friends, the right friends. Successful networking opens new possibilities. If you master the art of getting out, going to activities, and meeting new people, you will discover that there are eligible guys, good friends in the making, and possible mentors out there. Many can help you directly or set you up with others. Show everyone respect, appreciation, and interest; even the most boring or unappealing person can turn out to have a marvelous connection, insight, or lesson for you to learn. As Anais Nin writes, "Each friend represents a world in us, a world possibly not born until they arrive, and it is only by this meeting that a new world is born."

Give yourself a posse of interesting people whom you admire and respect. Hopefully you have increased your networking since your assignments in Chapter 1. Think about new classes, activities, clubs, and meet-ups that sound like fun. Go to different bookstores and coffee shops (both are great because you have coffee or book "props" to comment on), professional or business meetings where you'll have lots in common with the others, philanthropic events, expos and trade shows, and weddings, funerals, and holiday gatherings. Throw bring-a-friend parties. By now making eye contact and saying hello to three guys is a habit. Make sure you also say hello to women.

Whenever you meet new people, you want to project self-confidence. You do that first by being your Diamond Self, and then by using certain magic networking secrets.

NETWORKING WITH YOUR DIAMOND SELF

It is so important simply to be your Diamond Self rather than hiding your light under a bushel. Unfortunately, many women have difficulties showing their best selves in social gatherings. Instead, they are taught to share problems and misfortunes with each other. You want to break through any fears you have about breaking this unspoken women's "contract." Push through discomfort or embarrassment about your beauty, attractiveness, and power. Understand that simply being your shining self does not put anyone else down. Rather, by being your Diamond Self you can actually serve as a role model. This positive phenomenon of empowerment for others is called "vicariousness." When they identify with your realness, spontaneity, and beauty they are often freed and take the attitude, "If you can do it, I can do it!"

Here is a prayer that I read in my workshops to help liberate the Diamond Self:

PRAYER FOR BEAUTY

Mighty I am Presence and beloved Venus
Make me extremely beautiful,
Beautiful as thou art.
See that all who gaze upon me witness their own beauty
And the beauty of all life everywhere.

—JoAnne Karl, *Original Tribe Handbook of Angels*

Anyone who is not happy about you being your Diamond Self has her own self-worth issues and is not your friend. At least not now.

Five Magic Keys to Networking Success

1. IMAGINE THAT THE PERSON IS YOUR BEST FRIEND

Imagine meeting one of your best friends or a dear relative for dinner. Think about how accepted and warm you feel, how comfortable, how real, and how relaxed you are. Now imagine being that connected to a date or friend who is the latest addition to your network. A great fantasy, right?

You can use the same mental rehearsals when meeting a new guy, a new date, or, for that matter, anyone. Simply program yourself to be an old friend or relative who is entirely comfortable with this person. The truth is we are all related, all brothers and sisters. This is not simply some New Age fantasy. According to 2016 genomic studies almost all of us come from one group in Africa. In the biblical tradition, we all come from Adam and Eve, while in India there is a saying, "Treat everyone as if they were your mother in a past life." You get the idea.

So try a little experiment: before you meet someone, close your eyes and think, *This is a wonderful relative, or an old best friend with whom I feel really comfortable and warm.* You will be more relaxed and this attitude in turn will put the person you're with at ease as well.

2. USE A TEN-SECOND SOUND-BITE INTRO

Research says you have from six to thirty seconds to make an impression on someone. The question you will most frequently be asked is, "What do you do?" The last thing you should say is "I'm an accountant," or "I'm an actress." Generally, no one cares what you do for a living. What you need to convey is how you can help them in ten seconds or less. For that, you need to develop a personal sound bite. You want the person to be so intrigued that he or she *must* get to know you. For example, an accountant or bookkeeper might say, *"I help change people's relationship to money."* An actress could say, *"I take people on vacations of the mind."* A real estate agent could open up intrigue by saying, *"I help people to live their lives in beauty and comfort."*

Your own unique sound bite will lead to a much richer opening conversation. Make it a part of any introduction. Remember, you're not just talking to one person; you're potentially talking to a whole new network of family and friends.

3. BE COMPLETELY FOCUSED ON THE OTHER PERSON

Create a positive memorable impression and a strong connection by completely focusing on the other person. Ask questions and allow yourself to discover the special qualities of the person standing in front of you. Suspend your usual inner chatter or typical commentary. Think of the delighted discovery of a mother seeing her infant for the first time. Study the person's face, eyes, listen to the voice, and notice what you truly like. The Eastern traditions talk about seeing Buddha or the divine spark in each person, a powerful, powerful concept. Look for the divine in the person you're getting to know. Not only does this method create bonding, but it truly helps overcome shyness.

4. BE GENEROUS BEYOND EXPECTATION

This is the one-step technique that creates instant friendship. Be surprisingly and thoughtfully generous. You can do this even with a simple, heartfelt compliment; make it specific and detailed. In return, you'll almost always get back a lot of warmth and a sense of immediate connection. Generosity always comes back many times over. Always. Sometimes not in the way you expect. But it does.

For example, one of the students in our Program was in the receiving line of a very well-known female politician. The woman admired her necklace and my student whipped it off her neck and gave it to her. This simple gesture opened a whole new social circle for her that led to huge business opportunities.

5. CREATE A HOME FOR NETWORKING AND COUPLING

Create a place in which you are not embarrassed by your own clutter or dirt, an environment that is a warm, welcoming reflection of your Diamond Self. Organize your stuff, paint, get a cool lamp, plant, or throw. No matter how big or small, make your home inviting to yourself and a man. Get rid of the bachelorette pad (your secret embarrassment) and create a home as if you were already sharing it with your partner. What would it look like? Would you have more groceries, cook more, would it be cleaner, tidier, would the clothes be folded? How about inspirational paintings of couples in love, pieces like Chagall prints to set the mood?

Sixteen Key Flirting Techniques

*I flirted on Monday with Anton while he was taking photos of me for
my online profile. He was fun, cute, engaging, and willing to play. It
was easy for me, because I was supposed to flirt with the camera, and
I winked and held eye contact. When I would go behind him to look at
the pictures he was taking, I would get a little bit closer than needed and
hold his arm. It was fun and created more of a connection. I felt great
and he did, too.*—Liz, *the twenty-something brunette who was formerly caught
in the Just Buddies Deadly Dating Pattern*

Flirting is phenomenal! It is a playful, fun activity that helps you feel
more attractive and boosts your flirtee's self-esteem. Flirting can be a
complete encounter in and of itself; it doesn't mean you have to go any
farther. It is also important in an existing relationship as a kind of mind
foreplay that keeps you in the great feminine-masculine dance. Flirting
gives your date or partner clear "go" signals that say you find him attractive. Flirting is especially important to practice if you are shy or typically
caught in the Hermit, Fade Away, or Just Buddies Deadly Dating Pattern. And, surprisingly enough, flirting is terribly important if you are
very attractive! The good men are often quite intimidated by a beautiful
woman, and you have to be very clear in signaling your interest.

If flirting doesn't come naturally, try it on men who are not threatening to you. Let loose and have fun. Put yourself in the right mood by
doing the Diamond Self exercise, using the "old best friend" technique,
and thinking affirmations, like: *I feel attractive. I feel sexy. I feel beautiful.*
This may be easier when relating to less-attractive men, but *make sure
you eventually build up to the hotties.*

Here are sixteen flirting moves to try out. *Note:* If you are nervous,
blushing, or shy, let it be. This kind of energy is particularly endearing
and attractive!

1. Make eye contact and smile. If he makes lingering or repeated eye contact back, he is probably interested.
2. Wink.
3. Look at him, look away, look back.
4. While sitting, cross your legs and jiggle your foot in his direction.
5. Touch him lightly on the arm, shoulder, or neck.
6. Touch your lips, neck, or chest.
7. Play with your hair, clothing, or an object.
8. Whisper in his ear.
9. Give him a mini-massage.
10. Laugh at his jokes.
11. Compliment him.
12. Say his name a lot; give him a complimentary nickname.
13. Ask open-ended questions.
14. Ask for help with something.
15. Ask what he likes to eat or what sports, hobbies, or movies he likes. Once you find something in common, ask him if he'd like to do it sometime.
16. When leaving, say you'd like to see him again.

✎ Discovering and Using Your Diamond Self: Exercises_____

Choose from among the following suggestions, according to your own intuition.

You now have all the information on creating and using your Diamond Self. The Inner Work exercises will help you hone these skills.

Total Time for Completing All of Them: 45 Minutes

EXERCISE 1: *REDISCOVERING YOUR AUTHENTIC SELF*

Find a photo of yourself as a toddler or young child where you were unabashedly open, happy, and real. Post it where you can look at it every day. Study the original "you" like a perfectly loving mother or father.

EXERCISE 2: *GRATITUDE LISTS*

- Every day this week make a list of five things, small or large, for which you are grateful.
- Write down what you appreciate and are thankful for in terms of each love relationship you've had in the past. Ignore any negative thoughts that pop up and keep writing.

EXERCISE 3: *SELF-APPRECIATION TO-DO LIST*

Make a list of small to large things that will make you happy and do at least one of them each day. As you give yourself something, make affirmations like: *I deserve this, I am worth it, I offer this modest token at the feet of my Diamond Self.*

EXERCISE 4: *BUILD THE HABIT OF POSITIVE SELF-AFFIRMATIONS*

Continue to notice the five TTLC need and claim affirmations from the last chapter that you have posted around the house. Make sure you have given your Diamond Self a wonderful name. Don't be shy—make it grand. Write that name down and put it where you will see it every day. Give yourself at least three positive comments each day. Continue this for the rest of your life.

EXERCISE 5: *FACING YOUR FEARS*

Research on overcoming fears and phobias has isolated the one secret ingredient for success: Face the fear and you'll eventually be free. This exercise, derived from the work of many behavioral therapists, is one I've used successfully with my fearful clients. Pick out a situation that you fear, let's say going to a party alone. Write down a hierarchy of steps that range from least to most anxiety provoking. Rate how much fear you experience thinking about each step on an intensity scale of 1 to 10.

For example: You feel mildly nervous about considering going to a party alone (fear score = 2); more nervous about getting dressed to go (fear score = 4); even more nervous about walking to the door where the party is happening (fear score = 7); you really worry about standing there and being ignored at the party (fear score = 8); you are terrified about seeing a cute guy in a far corner and flirting or talking with him (fear score = 10).

Practice relaxing by sitting in your favorite chair and meditating, or listening to soothing music or a relaxation tape. Do deep breathing— that is, slow breathing from the belly area—and get deeply relaxed. Fold your hands together in your lap as an anchoring gesture that reminds your brain to relax. Start by picturing the least-feared situation in your hierarchy. Describe it to yourself as vividly as possible while you are relaxed. See the scene, hear the sounds, feel the feelings. The end goal is to work your way through the different situations in your hierarchy until you get to the most fearful one, still feeling relaxed.

If a scene involves another person, envision two happy endings to the encounter: it doesn't work out and *you feel at peace about the outcome and proud about yourself for going for it*; or it does work out, you're seeing the person again, and you feel happy and *at peace about it*. Practice this until your rating of anxiety associated with the scene goes down to 0. If you have trouble with this, go back to a scene just before the whole sequence started (e.g., in our example, taking a shower before you find out about the party). Then start again from that point.

Practice this exercise every day for a week and move up the levels in your hierarchy until you have cleared away the anxiety from each step of the situation. Do not go on until you have cleared the previous level. Over time, you'll find that the most terrifying step that was originally a 10 has fallen to a 0 or 1.

Once you've mastered this exercise and reduced your anxiety, you're ready to take your Diamond Self out to play. Using the facing-fears hierarchy you just constructed, follow through and actually do each step for a real party invite. Practice your deep breathing and relax before you make each move. Pick one of the goals on the list and complete it no matter what.

Congratulate yourself. No matter what step you've accomplished, you have succeeded! You have taken a courageous stance and that is what matters. Over time, work your way through the whole list until you've conversed with the cute guy. This person or that may say no to you, but eventually someone will say yes, because you are saying yes to yourself.

EXERCISE 6: *YOUR TEN-SECOND SOUND-BITE INTRO*

What do you have to offer that helps people? Write down the first thoughts that come to mind. Use descriptive and colorful words.

Let's say you are a consultant to women. Your sound bite could be, "I help women get off the treadmill of their lives." Or if you teach Pilates, it could be, "I help people redesign their bodies." If you have customers or clients who can write a testimonial, ask them to do so, just for your own personal use—they will help you capture what you really do that is helpful.

Memorize your Ten-Second Sound-Bite Intro and have fun using it.

♡♡ Homework

Choose from among the following suggestions, according to your own intuition:

1. Step up networking activities and practice using the Diamond Self exercise when meeting new people. Play full out!

2. Use the Best Friend, Ten-Second Sound-Bite Intro, Complete Focus, and Generosity networking techniques.

3. Use your Diamond Self name with your Love Mentor, Team Love, or a few close family members or friends. Don't be shy about it.

4. Practice two or three flirting moves. Start with less-threatening guys and work your way up.

5. If you need to work on your networking skills, do more speed dating. It's like having a dozen or more dates in one night. Remember, this is just for practice and fun—not to find real dates. Try going to www.Pre-Dating.com, which is the largest speed dating site in the U.S.

6. Work two online dating sites/apps using all the search-engine optimization secrets *for at least one-half hour every day (including weekends)*.

7. Fill out your Love in 90 Days Online Dating Report. Upgrade your photo, tweak your screen name or profile, change sites, or sharpen your focus if needed.

8. Work your Program of Three, go on at least two dates, and remember to have *fun*!

Liz describes how using these techniques led to a personal breakthrough:

I did experience a true miracle tonight. I was at a wedding, dressed in my new red dress, feeling into my new Diamond Self name, The Sensual,

Alive, Irresistible Goddess, and practicing flirting. Maybe it was the champagne, maybe that I was feeling really beautiful in my dress and good about my body and spirit. I met a guy and felt like I had a boyfriend for the night. It was so natural, he was just the right height. He was holding my hand and had his arm around me. He danced me and spun me all over the place, and I loved that. He had this calmness but also this real outgoing side. He was really smitten with me and I played into that.

I woke up the next day completely inspired, inspired by love. By what it's like to really fall for someone, and be excited to see that person. There was a spark there, a chemistry that I can't explain and we could work everything else out. It felt so great to be rejuvenated like that again. It reignited my love intention: I met the man of my dreams who electrifies me and is there for me.

Discovering your Diamond Self and facing your fears will ultimately change your life in ways that surprise and delight you. Have fun, and know that I am with you when you go out there.

We close with the life instructions given to us by Pink Floyd:

Shine on you crazy diamond.

One Simple Secret to Irresistible Self-Confidence and Getting the Love You Deserve

But with one step backward taken
I saved myself from going.
A world torn loose went by me.
Then the rain stopped and the blowing,
And the sun came out...

—Robert Frost

OK, My Love, you may be thinking at this point that it is easy for me to suggest that you find the sunlight of your Diamond Self identity and let it shine, but that is not so easy to do! Especially if you are heartbroken. It is not easy at any time or for any person. Accessing the self-confidence of your Diamond Self is a challenging process for all of us. It certainly was a struggle—a major knock-down-drag-out struggle—for me. But, as I struggled, I learned one simple, incredibly powerful secret to creating the confident "me" I wanted to be and the love-filled life I wanted to live.

I learned how to harness the natural and irresistible growth waves of life to help me shine. And that is the secret I want to share with you in this chapter. It will turbocharge your Love in 90 Days Program, as it boosts you up beyond your wildest dreams. This secret certainly has worked big-time for me! I am sitting here, more in love with my hubby Sam than I've ever been, in my dream condo on the 14th floor, with floor-to-ceiling windows overlooking the azure waters of the ocean, blessed to be on my personal Diamond Self mission of writing this chapter to bring love to you! I never ever would have dreamt that I would be able to have the self-confidence to create the life I am living, given my background as an unwanted nobody's girl. But I did. This secret made it so—and rapidly. As you learn about my core secret, you will understand the process that will make your Diamond Self identity and positive self-affirmations pop and manifest. And in this chapter, I'll give you my most powerful tools to harness this secret, in your love journey (and in any other areas of your life!). I use these tools constantly.

If you're like me, I bet you have struggled with making affirmations that don't seem to work for you. I know I did for many years. You proclaim to the universe that you are a catch and then go on a date, get all nervous and clam up. You say you deserve love and you instantly feel undeserving. You proclaim that you will meet amazing guys and all you meet are ghost-types, narcissists or alcoholics. You get demoralized. Your self-confidence wanes.

You start again. You write down all your affirmations. You make a vision board with photos of your ideal career, diet, a great dating life, and dream relationship. One or two affirmations in the areas of your life that are less complicated come true. But the key ones in the love department do not. You struggle some more and your self-confidence dwindles even further. You think, *Louise Hay, thanks for all your gifts, but when it comes to love, the Law of Attraction just does not work for me!*

The Aha I got about making love affirmations is that you are acting ONLY in one direction.

But as Newton's third law puts it, for every action there is an opposite reaction.

Which means that the act of making an affirmation automatically surfaces all the doubts, fears and other reactions that stand in the way of it materializing. You may be thinking, but, Dr. D, Newton was referring to physical objects. Well, these days with the discoveries of quantum physics, we are finding out that there are many spillovers from the physical to what many physicists consider the ground of the universe, i.e., consciousness. If you think about your own experiences, you will get that this law also holds true in the transformational process.

Often you make an affirmation and immediately experience its opposite in the form of conscious and unconscious negative feelings and beliefs from the Disappointing Self identity. If the arena in which you are making the affirmation carries a fair amount of negative baggage, the affirmation will not manifest in your life. This is because you are not working with the entire transformational process, which includes the negativity and self-doubt. You can't simply stuff these emotions and thoughts down by just asserting an affirmation over and over again. If that's what you are doing, no wonder you are not seeing results. As author Dr. Joe Dispenza puts it, *"By itself, conscious positive thinking cannot overcome subconscious negative feelings."*

How do you overcome those nagging doubts and beliefs? By working with the backward pull that you will experience as you attempt to move forward: a two-steps-forward, one-step-back approach. I call it riding the incoming and outgoing transformational waves to get to the destination of your dreams.

For this you need ways to rapidly access and deal with negative feelings and beliefs that block your forward vision. That is what this chapter is all about. Another way to say this is:

> An arrow can only be shot by pulling it backwards.
> —*Anonymous*

This is the one simple secret that can lead you to irresistible self-confidence and the love you absolutely deserve, as it has for thousands of women in the Love in 90 Days Program. It has worked for women of all ages, all shapes and sizes, who suffered from all different love wounds.

These women have broken out of the prison of self-doubt, social anxiety and shyness. And you can too!

Irresistible Self-Confidence

Before we dig deeper into the forward-backward transformational process that can make it all happen for you, let's look carefully at the goal for this chapter—real life, irresistible self-confidence. Yes, yes, yes!!!!! This is the kind of self-confidence that makes you attractive, magnetic, charismatic, the kind of confidence where you can be truly real and authentic, make silly mistakes and elegantly recover your poise, live out your quirks and eccentricities and know that they make you adorable, fun, funny, loving, and lovable. The "it" factor that draws guys to you. Think such self-confidence is impossible for you? Well I want you to hear me right now: I've seen that kind of sparkling self-appreciation emerge over and over in our students' lives, no matter what they have been through!

Confidence: *a feeling of self-assurance arising from one's appreciation of one's own abilities or qualities.*

Yes, I've seen that magic of confidence unfold in students and clients who feel old and over the hill because they are in their 40s, 50s, or 60s; in women who are 50 pounds overweight and feeling that weight in more ways than one, in women who have been cheated on, who feel rejected, crushed or humiliated; in those who have been abandoned, who feel unlovable, unwanted; in those who have never had a lasting relationship, who feel less-than, depressed or hopeless. At first, they come to the Program unempowered and believing that they have to be chosen by a guy—and may never be chosen because of their issues. They believe they have to settle or grasp at whatever crumbs they can get because this is the best they can do.

But then they find a new sliver of hope, use the forward-backward secret and the magic happens. They transform into being more and more grounded, assured, deserving, feeling desirable, into having charisma and mojo. And when they develop that kind of irresistible self-confidence they know that they can do the choosing from among the matches that come to them. And the guys do come to them. Because with this kind of confidence, they are interesting, fun to be with, uplifting and loving toward the men. Which is very attractive. Men choose to be committed to women because they have this way of being. Men who were asked in research studies why they married their wives generally say, "Because I feel good around her!"

Now, let's look at the nuts and bolts of how the experience of self-confidence is created. At its core, confidence is an experience, a sense of self-assurance based on a set of affirming beliefs about yourself. These beliefs are grounded in appreciation of your own personality, beauty (everyone has beautiful aspects!), spirit, sensuality, humor, brains, and unique overall attractiveness. Your self-confidence beliefs are anchored by and part and parcel of your Diamond Self name. So please revisit your Diamond Self name. You may get inspiration in this chapter to add confidence-boosting adjectives to your name and that will, in and of itself, be a super addition to your journey of self-appreciation. Please note, if you don't have a Diamond Self name yet, please go back and give yourself one by doing Step 3 in Chapter 7.

Positive Self-Talk

Using a Diamond Self name and other affirming beliefs lead to positive self-talk, which is very powerful. Positive self-talk has been used to: change behavior in underachieving students, increase nurses' and doctors' well-being and lower their stress levels, reduce breast cancer patients' cortisol levels; and heighten athletic performance. People cope more easily when going into new social situations and are less likely to make downward social comparisons when they practice self-affirmations. Participants in one study who said self-affirmations before a new social encounter reduced their thoughts about being rejected, compared with another group that focused on the event and who would be there.

Let's get started on your journey to positive self-talk and self-confidence. The first step is to find your own unique expression of confidence—one that tickles you, that you find intriguing, or flat out would simply love to have.

Finding Your Affirmations for Irresistible Self-Confidence

How do you develop affirming beliefs that lead to irresistible self-confidence? You start by deliberately making positive statements about yourself in your mind and aloud that are inspiring and nourishing. And you truly allow yourself to play with the process. To be bold and grand, even if you are not feeling it!

Just pretend for a moment you can choose who/how you want to be regardless of any challenging reality or heartbreak you may be facing right now. You got a good start creating your TTLC needs and claim affirmations. Now ramp it up and think of more positive affirmations about yourself that will lead into the kind of confidence you would like to have. Go ahead, play full-out, be creative and push the envelope.

Start jotting down ideas. Get the engine going until you feel freer and freer to write down whatever comes to mind. If a statement feels scary, that is good—you are pushing the edges of your growth. If it feels great to think of a particular affirmation, then it is right on target. Putting your attention on a positive belief about yourself is one of the most powerful creative forces at our disposal. With that in mind, some proven examples of powerful confidence-boosting affirmations are:

> *I am entirely lovable and appealing.*
> *I am fun, funny and irresistible.*
> *I am a beautifully unique child of God.*

I am sparkling and radiantly alive.
I am delightful and adorable.
I radiate and attract love.
I am charismatic and magnetic.
I am charming and captivating.
I am engaging and enchanting.
I am lovely and fascinating in a way that is easy and effortless.
I am entirely deserving of miraculous, surprising, lasting love.

After you jot down a few confidence-building affirmations, use your Diamond Self name in an affirmation. This will allow you to own all the power, deservedness and beauty in your new identity. Feel free to expand your Diamond Self name at this time. You can add any of the adjectives in this section that call to you. Here are a few Diamond Self name affirmations that have been used successfully by the women in our Program.

I am the Magnificent Star—a catch!
I am the Lovable, Sexy, Inuit Sea Princess.
I am the Irresistible Precious Czarina.
I am the Magnetic, Confident Deborah Rose.
I am the Blessed, Radiant Beacon of Love.
I am the Chosen, Beloved Beautiful Belle.
I am the Captivating Bright Light.
I am the Mesmerizing Sparkalicious Susan.

When you make self-affirmations, you build on positive experiences from the past, and, more importantly, you are programming for new fulfillment in the future. Global or glowing affirmations about yourself don't necessarily work in the time frame you would like—usually they take longer. But they do work. Make no mistake about it. The more attention you put on the loving self-declaration, the more quickly it will manifest. But you have to put your attention on it like you would on a mantra—lightly and without attaching to the affirmation too tightly. I call this Mantra Affirmation Activation.

The general rule of Mantra Affirmation Activation is, when doubts or other negatives arise, treat them as if you were sitting in meditation: observe them without judgment. *Notice and acknowledge your self-doubts and do not fight them.* The more you acknowledge the doubts without struggle, the more quickly they will go away. Always return to your affirmation, like you would go back to a mantra after a distracting series of thoughts. In this way you will be flowing with the natural zig-zag pattern of growth.

You can be the prime and sole architect of a deliberate and more positive self-concept or identity using self-affirmations. Over time and with these practices, you will release your negative self-talk and the delimiting inner beliefs of your Disappointing Self identity. The wonderful thing is, you get to decide how you want to experience yourself. You get to decide who you are. Here is how Kiara, a fifty-something hospice social worker, describes her journey into irresistible self-confidence:

> *When I first got divorced I felt like I had to grab whatever attention guys gave me. I was a doormat who put out sexually and in other ways just to hold onto whoever was in my life at the moment. I felt so bad about myself. After I worked on my Diamond Self name and with my coach, everything began to shift. She kept referring to me as the Diamond Goddess of Light. At first it was weird, but then it sent me into peals of laughter. Finally, I began to really feel it!*

Now, let's delve into the exercise that Kiara's coach used—the one that truly harnesses the forward-backward growth process and can catapult you into fabulous self-confidence.

The Five-Minute Manifestation Miracle Exercise

You will be a failure, until you impress the subconscious with the conviction you are a success. This is done by making an affirmation which "clicks."—Florence Scovel Shinn

But what if, despite your best efforts to let go of those pesky self-doubts, they still manage to keep appearing and deflating you? How do you overcome that? By flowing with and exaggerating the backward-pulling thought, feeling, or sensation that keeps reoccurring. And then going right back to the affirmation. What this method does functionally is that it "marries" the affirmation to the neural nets in your brain that relate to the arena you are working on. And as you do the exercise, those neural nets change in the direction of your affirmation! This deliberate stimulation of neural net growth is especially powerful when you do the exercise with affirmations about your Diamond Self identity, because it then comes to supplant your whole shy, fearful, unconfident Disappointing Self identity!

In fact, this exercise is a one-two punch that takes your Disappointing Self identity down. Not only are you injecting your Diamond Self identity into its neural nets, you are also unearthing and exaggerating the objections and negatives, which tends to make them dissipate. It is only when you resist a thought, feeling or sensation that it keeps going and persists. Now you understand why this is true: because of the zig-zag nature of growth, resistance to the underlying self-doubts creates persistence.

But with the Five-Minute Manifestation Miracle you avoid that sticky process, where you try but can't seem to rid yourself of something that is really bothering you. These critical, mean, self-negating thoughts and painful feelings can sometimes come from the unconscious parts of your Disappointing Self identity, where they are buried, but still sabotage your efforts to grow. The Manifestation Miracle exercise can surface and dispel even unconscious issues that stand in your way. Your Disappointing Self identity doesn't stand a chance if you do the work thoroughly!

Here are the steps of the Five-Minute Manifestation Miracle Exercise:

1. Say your **affirmation** out loud.
2. Say a **fear, doubt or other reaction** that comes up, but in an exaggerated way with feeling. *This can include a feeling with no attached thought, i.e., "I am sad!" or a sensation if that is what comes up—i.e., "I have a tightness in my chest, UHH." Deal with only one reaction at a time. Do not explore your reaction; simply voice it ONCE as a single statement while you exaggerate the feeling of it.*
3. Repeat your **affirmation** out loud.
4. Say another (or the same) **fear, doubt or other reaction** that comes up, but in an exaggerated way. *Your reaction may repeat itself, which is fine, or move from negative, i.e. "This is bullshit" to positive, like, "Maybe it could be true." During this process you may also unearth new, liberating positive thoughts.*
5. Repeat your **affirmation** out loud.
6. Continue with the **affirmation/reaction oscillation** until you reach an inner stillness and you feel like the affirmation seems real, believable, even if just for a moment!
7. You will shift into a lighter, more hopeful state!

To make it easy to use this amazing exercise, I have a download of the steps here for you at http://lovein90days.com/manifestation-miracle -exercise/.

Here is an example of how Linda, a very successful lawyer in her 40s worked the Manifestation Miracle exercise using her Diamond Self name. Linda's coach prompted her with the steps by alternately saying, *"Affirmation?"* And then, *"Fears, doubts and other reactions?"* after each repetition of the affirmation. This is another highly effective way to work the exercise.

Using the exercise, Linda was able to discharge negativity about her Disappointing Self identity as well as painful and then liberating thoughts about her ex, Miguel. As Linda worked with her coach, she said the following out loud in response to the prompts:

> *I am the Saucy Sensual Sweetheart of Love.*
> *Ugh, I am just a dried-up work drone.*
> *I am the Saucy Sensual Sweetheart of Love.*
> *I'm a dried-up suit!*
> *I am the Saucy Sensual Sweetheart of Love.*
> *Miguel didn't think so!*
> *I am the Saucy Sensual Sweetheart of Love.*
> *Miguel would never have left me.*
> *I am the Saucy Sensual Sweetheart of Love.*
> *I feel soooo sad!*
> *I am the Saucy Sensual Sweetheart of Love.*
> *Argh, my throat hurts.*
> *I am the Saucy Sensual Sweetheart of Love.*
> *I want Miguel back.*
> *I am the Saucy Sensual Sweetheart of Love.*
> *I REALLY don't want Miguel back.* (This was a surprise revelation and marked a turning point in the exercise!)
> *I am the Saucy Sensual Sweetheart of Love.*
> *Maybe I could find someone better.*
> *I am the Saucy Sensual Sweetheart of Love.*
> *Maybe I really could find someone better!*
> *I am the Saucy Sensual Sweetheart of Love.*
> *Hmm. Maybe I am.*
> *I am the Saucy Sensual Sweetheart of Love.*
> *My new red dress looks pretty hot on me!*
> *I am the Saucy Sensual Sweetheart of Love.*
> *I am the Saucy Sensual Sweetheart of Love!*

When Linda got to this point in the exercise, her affirmation manifested as a belief that seemed real and a big smile broke out on her face. Dr. Joe Dispenza describes how this kind of powerful inner process can alter our brain and cell physiology:

> *The latest research supports the notion that we have a natural ability to change the brain and body by thought alone, so that it looks biologically like some future event has already happened. Because you can make thought more real than anything else, you can change who you are from brain cell to gene, given the right understanding.*

Notice that Dr. Dispenza mentions changing the body by thought alone! This brings us to our next section that is so critical for irresistible self-confidence: Body image.

Irresistible Body Self-Confidence Regardless of Your Age or Dress Size (You Read That Right!)

The sad truth is that when we women relate to our appearance we are almost always in a judgmental, critical, and PICKY mode that is the opposite of confidence. We view our bodies through a distorted lens, so that each pound seems to be ten, each dimple of cellulite is like a sea of orange-peel skin, each wrinkle is like a crevice that draws all the attention. This happens because we unconsciously use a **compare and despair** mode of perception, in which we compare ourselves to impossible-to-achieve size zero, twenty-something ideals of beauty. Ads, TV, movies, and even social media blast out these images of thinness, youth, and perfect airbrushed beauty on a daily basis.

No one has a perfect body. Those photos you see of celebs in magazines are retouched. Those actors in movies and on TV are layered in makeup and have body doubles half the time. Those models you see on the runways are usually struggling with eating disorders that can have them looking like skeletons in real life. The obsession with being thin, young, and perfect-looking is the bane of our culture. If you have ever felt bad about your body—like you have too much cellulite, too many wrinkles, and too many pounds, eyesore pimples, dandruff, a small chest, or fat legs—you are not alone. Every woman in this culture suffers from what I call the body blues at some point in their adolescent and adult lives.

We often compare and despair about never looking good enough. The compare and despair way of thinking and perceiving is vicious in that it operates unconsciously and consciously. It has been wired into our brains' neural networks, which makes it very hard to change. And it affects everything we do in the arena of love.

> A woman who is self-conscious can't relax to let her sensuality come into play. If she is hungry she will be tense. If she is "done up" she will be on the alert for her reflection in his eyes. If she is ashamed of her body, its movement will be stilled. If she does not feel entitled to claim attention, she will not demand that airspace to shine in…(And) he simply will not see her, his real love, standing right before him.—*Naomi Wolf*

Ah, but now we bring out our secret weapon that can free you from the shyness, the anxiety, the self-conscious hiding and discomfort, the invisibility that Naomi is talking about. By using the Miracle Manifestation exercise you'll be able to banish the body blues and LOVE the way you look—dimpled thighs and all! You will reshape your brain's neural networks for how you perceive yourself physically and emotionally, which means you will be confident in many situations that used to be challenging and intimidating. And, drumroll please, with your new body-confidence you will be more at home and open sensually and sexually (which makes you irresistible to your guy). You will be able to have more intimacy, pleasure, and connection when you want it. You will feel, appear, and act very differently inside the bedroom and outside of it. Guys will react more positively to you.

As actress Salma Hayek says,

> People often say that "beauty is in the eye of the beholder," and I say that the most liberating thing about beauty is realizing that you are the beholder.

As Salma realized, our perception of our own beauty lies in recognizing that we own the lens to focus on what we behold. Not anyone else. Simply put, the Manifestation Miracle exercise gives you A NEW PAIR OF GLASSES. That's right: a new pair of glasses that allow you to throw away the old pair that caused you so much suffering.

Here are ideas that you can use to craft your irresistible body self-confidence affirmations:

> My body has luscious, delicious energy.
> I am attractive, sensual and sexy.
> I am irresistibly voluptuous in a unique way.
> I am youthful, vibrant and lovely.
> My body is electrically alive and gorgeous.
> I am curvy and entirely delectable.
> My body is foxy and alluring.
> I exude life-generating juiciness.
> I am uniquely beautiful, warm and inviting.

Here is an example of how Beth, a counselor who was 50 pounds overweight, used the Manifestation Miracle exercise for body self-confidence. Looking at the steps of the exercise, she said her affirmation, alternating with fears, doubts, or other reactions out loud as follows:

> I am irresistibly voluptuous in a unique way.
> I am a blimp!
> I am irresistibly voluptuous in a unique way.

I have to lose weight!
I am irresistibly voluptuous in a unique way.
Maybe the keto diet will work.
I am irresistibly voluptuous in a unique way.
My face is hideous.
I am irresistibly voluptuous in a unique way.
I'm not! Ugh! (She exaggerates a sensation of nausea in her stomach)
I am irresistibly voluptuous in a unique way.
Ugh!
I am irresistibly voluptuous in a unique way.
I'm tired of this stupid exercise.
I am irresistibly voluptuous in a unique way.
Jim did seem to be coming on to me.
I am irresistibly voluptuous in a unique way.
My legs are pretty good. (She begins to shift out of her negativity)
I am irresistibly voluptuous in a unique way.
Well, Jim may think so!
I am irresistibly voluptuous in a unique way.
It could be, in a unique way.
I am irresistibly voluptuous in a unique way.
Well, yeah!
I am irresistibly voluptuous in a unique way!

Beth never did lose any weight. But she did start dressing to showcase the real voluptuous beauty she did have, as her mojo blossomed. I am thrilled to say that after doing a few of these exercises in the context of the whole Love in 90 Days Program, she is happily living with her soulmate Jim.

It is not the body itself that causes suffering and difficulties in relationships; it is the judgmental body image beliefs in your mind that stop you from being present and shining.

Using Your Confidence-Boosting Secret

The Five-Minute Manifestation Miracle exercise is indispensable. It can be used for any of your affirmations, large or small, in any aspect of your life. For example, if you are feeling anxious about a new hottie, you can even run the Manifestation Miracle Exercise before you have a date with him. You might use one of the following affirmations:

> *Sam and I easily and effortlessly have fun on our date.*
> *Steve and I get surprisingly close and loving on our date.*
> *Our next date is a lovely, laughter-filled, joyful experience.*
> *This date tonight goes surprisingly well as we get even closer.*

You get the idea. Craft an affirmation about the date that helps you relax or makes you feel good. Then run the Manifestation Miracle exercise on your affirmation, saying it and then exaggerating each doubt, fear or other reaction as it comes up, and then restating the affirmation. You may encounter objections like, *I won't like him. He won't like me. We will have nothing to say to each other. He just wants to get laid. I don't want to get hurt again this time*, etc. Keep oscillating between the statement of the affirmation and the other reactions one at a time until the affirmation pops as a believable, pleasurable statement. You will have the best time possible on that date!

Remember, you have this handy forward/backward tool in your pocket to use any time you need it! I use it all the time. After you use the exercise, write down the affirmation you used and post it where you can see it every day. It will take on a life of its own as it manifests in your life in surprising and better-than-expected ways.

You Are Deserving and Positively Entitled

If you feel stuck and unable to successfully use the Manifestation Miracle you may be having issues with your sense of deservedness or what I call positive entitlement. This is the self-loving quality that allows you to give yourself magnificent affirmations and then make them come true. So, if you need some work in that arena, deservedness affirmations that increase self-love are great. For example, you can make affirmations like: *I am entitled to miracles. I deserve to have what I need to be happy,* or *Everything I want is here for me and I am entitled to it.*

Run the Manifestation Miracle exercise on your affirmation. Then, to show the Universe you mean business give to yourself every day. Every day; no exceptions. Look for new and special treats you usually deny yourself, experiences you would look forward to.

In our culture, women are taught and expected to be generous to everyone but themselves. For a woman to be giving to herself is often considered selfish. So you must break your conditioning and learn to be self-caretaking especially in areas where you are stingy or withholding. From the smallest acts, like careful listening to your favorite music and giving your life a sound track, getting and wearing cashmere socks, or splurging on a French manicure; to signing up for pole dancing, singing, or Improv; and up to the largest steps, like painting every day and declaring yourself an artist or buying that condo in the building you've been eyeing. Just do it.

Throughout the day, check in with yourself. Take your attention inward and get a sense of how you are feeling. If the feelings are not positive, take a moment to acknowledge them as okay, and then speak kindly to yourself. This is just the usual backward tug of the growth process in action. And then move forward again into kind self-talk. If you are working on a demanding project, promise yourself a wonderful reward. Tell yourself how much you have accomplished and how well you are doing.

Think about what little prize would make work more enjoyable. Heed
the Bard's advice: "Be to yourself as you would to your friend."

And get a move on with activating your wonderful affirmations for
self-confidence in dating and love. You so deserve it!

May you not forget the infinite possibilities what are born of faith in yourself.
May you use those gifts that you have and take in the love that flows to you.
Let a healing presence settle into your bones and allow your soul the freedom
to sing, dance, praise, and love.

—Adapted from St. Teresa of Avila's prayer

9

Field Report on DUDs and STUDs

I think our intentions of being chosen/wanted are coming true. We're choosing ourselves and actually wanting to be in a club that not only accepts us as members but celebrates us. Still no word from Amir. I did speak to Jay, who is chomping at the bit to come to town. I even flirted with the produce guy at Genuardi's. Bought sexy winter boots, putty suede with fur lining, very Nanookie of the north. I sure am crying a lot today, but out of sheer happiness. Something is shifting in me.—*Iris, the redhead caught in Hermit and Crumbs Deadly Dating Patterns in Chapter 2*

Now that your Diamond Self confidence and name are emerging, it's time to put together everything you've learned about Deadly Dating Patterns, the Dating Program of Three, and your TTLC needs. The Field Report on DUDs (Definitely Unworkable Dudes) and STUDs (Seriously Terrific, Utterly Devoted Dudes) will help you do just that. More importantly, it'll help you monitor your progress in the program.

Reviewing and filling in the Field Report each week is like taking a mini Love in 90 Days workshop. This one assignment yields great results. In the Report you will learn to evaluate the pros and cons of each guy, the needs he fulfills, and whether your relationship fits or breaks your Deadly Dating Patterns. As you rid yourself of any DUDs who sneaked into your Program of Three (or whom you let in) and find more fulfilling guys as replacements, you'll simultaneously be breaking your Deadly Dating Patterns and continuously upgrading the men in your pipeline. To help you pinpoint the great men even further, I will give you the latest research on the "marrying kind" of men.

Field Reports on DUDs and STUDs

A copy of page 1 of the Field Report on DUDs and STUDs follows. This worksheet contains three critical questions to ask about any guy who is potentially a Program of Three candidate. Page 196 reviews the steps you can take if you find a great guy but there is no chemistry.

Make copies of the form on the facing page. Once you have had consistent contact with a good candidate, fill in his name after *Is* and check off all the criteria that he fulfills on each of the *Crazy About Me, Willing to Grow,* and *Meeting the Basics* categories. If he makes it as a Program of Three contender in all three areas, put him on your Program of Three list and continue dating him. If he doesn't, quickly terminate the relationship and consider yourself one step closer to finding love. The more DUDs you wade through, the better your Program will be. This is a numbers game. I can't emphasize that enough. Go quickly through lots and lots of DUDs to get to your STUD.

Note: You will notice that I did not mention age range in the *Meeting the Basics* category. This is because I want you to extend yours! These are the expansive days where it can work out gloriously well with a younger man who is mature. And, of course, there are older guys who are settled, have less to prove, and want to focus on a younger woman and often even fulfill her "pregger" needs. So stretch yourself.

The only time I suggest you be delimiting on this criterion is if you do get a huge number of responses online and have to sort through many candidates. If this happens, you can use age plus how well he rates on

Meeting the Basics criteria to sort your catch into A, B, and F categories, where the A types are the ones you check out first, then you work through the Bs. Fs are discarded.

🖐 FIELD REPORT ON DUDs AND STUDs 🗒

PAGE 1

Is _____

I. *Crazy About Me?*
- Eager to see me
- Reluctant to leave me
- Interested in me and my life
- Wants to be helpful
- Is verbally and physically affectionate
- Wants to be sexual with me
- Acts like I am very special; doesn't really want to date others
- Willing to hang in there as I work the Program of Three

Program of Three Contender = Yes on at least 4 of the above

II. *Willing to Grow?*
- Takes suggestions or advice
- Is self-reflective
- Is willing to go to therapy or life coaching
- Takes growth courses
- Meditates or prays
- Is in a 12-step program or men's group

Program of Three Contender = Yes on at least 2 of the above

III. *Meeting the Basics?*
- Is a good guy—reliable, tells the truth, cares about others
- Wants a real, committed relationship
- Willing to have children if I want them
- Is successful—has a good income
- Is a member of my religious faith
- Is not in a relationship with anyone else
- Comes from a stable family of origin
- Is geographically desirable

Program of Three Contender = Yes on at least 4 of the above

No Chemistry Yet?

Use the OPEN Techniques: Think of him as a present wrapped in nested boxes. As you interact with him, you are unwrapping the present and finding out more and more about him that may be wonderful, and opening a delicious chemistry and connection! Use one or two of the following affirmations before each date: *I have fun with this man. I see the hidden possibilities in* (name). *He is a present for my enjoyment. More will be revealed. I uncover and enjoy the wonderful aspects of this man. I find chemistry with* (name). (Name) *is a hottie!* (Name) *turns me on!*

Go on dates that are exciting, novel, and get the adrenaline pumping.

Plan a date where he is in his element and at his best. Wear sexy lingerie, flirt with him, and maybe kiss him.

To give you an idea of the kind of high-level guys you—*yes, you*—can wind up with, here are the actual report write-ups by two advanced students in our coaching program:

Pat, a thirty-nine-year-old schoolteacher, describes a guy she met online who passes all of the Program of Three criteria with flying colors:

<u>Crazy About Me:</u> *I spent four months looking online before I met Roy. He's shorter and older than me. But I gave him a chance and when he came to a family gathering, Roy put on a spontaneous magic show for my toddler nieces and told the funniest stories. We all had the best time. I fell in love with him right then and there. He calls me "Dutchie," which is short for "the Dutchess." And he says I should call him "the Lucky Duke" because of meeting me. It's so easy with him—we spend a lot of time just lying down together, gazing at each other. Roy gets me. He says he treasures my kindness and gifts of the heart.*

<u>Willing to Grow:</u> *Roy and I joined a Joel Osteen meetup group. We are going to hear Joel preach live next month.*

<u>Meeting the Basics:</u> *Roy's a green thumb gardener who values being close to the earth and being of service. That's what I love about him. He wants a best friend companion for life.*

Pat eventually married Roy and they are extremely happy together.

Shelly, the forty-two-year-old accountant we met earlier, describes Harry, a restaurateur whom she is well on the way to marrying:

<u>Crazy About Me:</u> *Harry says he's committed to me and exploring this and isn't seeing anyone else. He came in a car, picked me up at 7 and said he loved my dress. We had drinks and appetizers at the W Hotel and then we went to the theatre and the car waited. After the show he asked, "Where would you like to go next?" I suggested the Rooftop Bar. We went there and talked about the connection we both feel. We talked about last week and my inability to speak out of shyness and he said the most important thing is for me to feel comfortable. But he did see a freckle and he said he wanted to kiss it and it was the most adorable thing. I really felt it in my heart. We were there until 1:30. Then the car took me home. He called when he got home to say goodnight.*

<u>Willing to Grow:</u> *Even though Harry is so successful in business, he has a coach. He said he learned a lot from past relationships and that he*

needs to really listen to a woman. He is interested in taking a personal growth course.

<u>Meeting the Basics:</u> *He is the sweetest, gentlest, smartest person. A real man. He is close to his 20 year old daughter. He is financially successful.*

As you read the examples, realize that these guys have warts and pimples. The first guy was no Brad Pitt, was much older, and initially Pat felt no chemistry. The second guy, Harry, was recently divorced, still very involved with his wife and daughter, and traveled a lot on business. There are no perfect men. But it is critical to focus on the good qualities that are present and to look quickly and cleverly for a good guy who thinks even your "freckles" are adorable.

Now on to page 2 of the Field Report, which you will find on the next page. Make copies and fill out a page for each guy who made it through your checklists on page 1. List his ranking as 1, 2, or 3 in terms of his potential to be your Beloved; under "Positives" journal about how he fulfills the Three Question criteria (*Crazy About Me, Willing to Grow, Meeting the Basics*) plus the TTLC needs he potentially fills (a review list is on page 3 of the Field Report). Then list the guy's "Negative" qualities. Finally, write about how he fits or breaks your Deadly Dating Patterns (a review list is on page 4 of the Field Report).

Make several copies of all the pages in the Field Report. Every week you are actively working the Program complete a Report on the guys in your orbit. Don't be lazy about this task. Remember, you've committed to making love your highest priority. If you are on the 90 Day Program and have been slacking off, now would be a very good time to recommit to fulfilling your goals. We are halfway through and there's still plenty of time to meet the right guys. The more consistently you are doing the weekly assignments and evaluations, the more you will progress toward your ultimate goal. It's that simple.

For every possible Program of Three candidate, rank order him 1, 2, or 3 in terms of potential to be the One and fill in the following:

Number:

Name:

- *Positives (Crazy About Me; Willing to Grow; Meeting the Basics):*

- *TTLC Needs He May Fulfill (see Field Report page 3):*

- *Negatives:*

- *Fits/Breaks My Deadly Dating Patterns (see Field Report page 4):*

I Deserve

- Being chosen and wanted as the special One
- Being helped to feel safe
- Being loved unconditionally
- Commitment
- Hugs and physical affection
- Being understood
- Being prized
- Being told I'm attractive
- Being treated as if I'm desirable
- Being encouraged to live my dreams
- Getting constructive and helpful critiques
- Being helped to explore the world and my place in it
- Getting recognition for my accomplishments
- Being told to "suck it up" when I have to do something difficult or scary
- Getting teaching, advice, or guidance
- Belief in my unique potential and talent
- A "swift kick in the butt" to help me get motivated
- Being praised and rewarded for accomplishments
- Being supported when failing or feeling vulnerable
- Being treated with respect
- Getting constructive limits on my behavior
- Being encouraged to be real
- Being encouraged to play, to find my bliss
- Being forgiven
- Being treated fairly
- Being given to
- Being confronted when I'm out of line
- Being treated as if my wants and needs are very important

👍 FIELD REPORT ON DUDs AND STUDs
DEADLY DATING PATTERNS 🗲

- The Flame-Out

- The Fantasy Relationship

- Crumbs

- The Hermit

- I'll Make You Love Me

- Abuse Recycle

- The Safety Net

- Not Perfect—I'll Pass

- Chase Me

- Fade Away

- Jealousy Trap

- Just Buddies

- The Grass Is Greener

The Field Report mini-course gives a weekly snapshot of which men are offering what you need in the best way possible. Checking the "I Deserve TTLC list" on page 3 will keep you mindful of what you are looking for. Filling out the section on Deadly Dating Patterns will force you to confront whether you are dragging bad dating habits into your future or beginning to break them. If you continue to be stuck in a particular pattern, the next chapter is perfect for you. It will help free you from your dead-end habits once and for all.

Here is how Trish, a beginner in the Program, filled out the page 2 tear-outs on Phil and James, the first two guys she had dated in six years:

Number: *1*
Name: *Phil*

Positives [Crazy About Me; Willing to Grow; Meeting the Basics]: *Gave me The Secret DVD. Interested in my work. Helped me on and off with my coat. Emails me a lot. He's spiritual, thoughtful and we had good conversation. Talks about wanting kids.*

TTLC Needs He May Fulfill: *Feeling safe, being treated with respect, being encouraged to be real, being given to.*

Negatives: *Not sure I'm attracted to him. Almost no chemistry.*

Fits/Breaks My Deadly Dating Patterns: *Breaks me out of being a Hermit or Abuse Recycle.*

Number: *2*
Name: *James*

Positives [Crazy About Me; Willing to Grow; Meeting the Basics]: *Very complimentary. Took me out to dinner at L'Auberge. A psychologist who was in therapy.*

TTLC Needs He May Fulfill: *Getting teaching, advice or guidance. Told me about how to get more hits on my Web site.*

Negatives: *Balding, paunchy. Not sure I'm attracted to him. A little preachy. Divorced with 2 teens—not sure about the ex and him??*

Fits/Breaks My Deadly Dating Patterns: *Breaks me out of being a Hermit. May fit in with my Abuse Recycle pattern!!!*

James stopped calling Trish and fell away, but she continued dating Phil and decided to put her Program of Three on hold. The relationship proved to be a very good entry back into the dating world for her. Phil was very sweet to Trish and she got used to being treated well, taken out to fancy vegan restaurants, and having long philosophical discussions. Trish continued to have a chemistry problem with Phil and in the end broke off the relationship after a few months. She then simply went back on the Program of Three. There is no failure on the road to love if you keep moving on; it's all up to you. You do have the option of packing up your heart, closing the shutters, and quitting. But if you just keep going, you will succeed.

Now let's look at how another student in our Program, Iris, filled out her Field Reports:

Number: *1*

Name: *Rich*

Positives [Crazy About Me; Willing to Grow; Meeting the Basics]: *When I was in Costa Rica he emailed every day and signed his notes with besos and abrazos. He was happy when I was doing fun things. He told me to call when I got back, no matter how late. He let me know he was free for a date Friday or Saturday and for me to choose the day that worked better. He came up with the Rembrandt exhibit in town. Called Saturday morning to say he was going to be a little late and admitted to having a fashion crisis. Too cute. He came to my house, picked me up, said how great I looked. We smooched here and there, he bought a membership so we could go back. We went for dinner and somehow got on the subject of what to call him; he always signs his emails "Richard," but his daughter calls him "Rich." He smiled and said, "Richard" is fine for now, but when the time is right—and you'll know when that is—I'd enjoy hearing you call me "Rich." The next day he sent me a link to an article on the exhibit with a note saying how delightfully distracted he had been with me.*

TTLC Needs He May Fulfill: *Being chosen and wanted as the special one. Being encouraged to find my bliss. Being told I'm attractive, adorable, sexy. Being respected and sought out.*

Negatives: *He's not sure what he wants relationship-wise, since it's still new. He was married for 20 years, divorced two years ago and still trying to figure things out. He brought up his ex a lot. He has practically grown kids, which is great, but will he want to do it again? He seems a bit bitter. He's not a big tipper.*

Fits/Breaks My Deadly Dating Patterns: *He makes me feel sought after, taken care of. He's local, available. He's got money, works hard, plays well with others. He takes good care of himself. He can write a witty email and tells me in writing how much he can't wait to hear from me or see me. He tells me to have fun, enjoy life. Is this a Fantasy Relationship?*

Number: 2

Name: *Dan*

Positives [Crazy About Me; Willing to Grow; Meeting the Basics]: *He writes a great email, hysterical, erudite, very quick. He's been very sweet and consistent. He's called when he said he would and I really enjoyed the conversations. When I said I was coming into the city Saturday he asked if we could meet up. He really wanted to see me. We settled on brunch at Apple. He's traveled the world, wants kids. He emailed me today to wish me good luck on my interview. He's cute and tall.*

TTLC Needs He May Fulfill: *Tells me how attractive I am, makes me feel chosen, wanted, listened to. He thinks I'm smart, cool.*

Negatives: *His mother seems to have a lot of drama in her life. Not sure I want to get involved in all of it. He was married and it didn't end well I don't think. Hope he can just relax with me. We'll see. Seems he has to be "on."*

Fits/Breaks My Deadly Dating Patterns: *Even though he's divorced, he seems like he wants marriage and a child with the right person. He lets me know he's interested. It's early—I don't want to fantasize and make him out to be perfect. He's made some jokes about drinking to excess. I will watch that and see if/how that manifests.*

Number: *3—practically gone from the list, to be replaced with sundry other men whom I'm about to call or who are about to call me.*

Name: *Ben*

Positives [Crazy About Me; Willing to Grow; Meeting the Basics]: *Fun guy to chat with. Marriage-minded, funny. Was calling me every couple of days just for the pleasure of my voice, now it's less so. Loves his son. Understands why his marriage failed. Is into crystals and adventure. Open-minded. Has said some great stuff like "I just want someone who I can laugh in bed with," or "I just want to wake up and think to myself how lucky I am."*

TTLC Needs He May Fulfill: *Feeling that I'm interesting and special. Being encouraged to follow my bliss, as he's following his.*

Negatives: *Geographically undesirable. Lives in Chicago. Has not come here yet to visit me, which is a big bone of contention. Money and his son have been the two factors so far.*

Fits/Breaks My Deadly Dating Patterns: *This is definitely a Fantasy Relationship until I meet him in person.*

As it turned out, Ben *was* a Fantasy Relationship, but because Iris had been diligently monitoring herself weekly, she caught it quickly. Iris replaced Ben, her number three, with Jan, who quickly took over the number one spot. Here's her description of Jan's "Positives":

Jan is amazing, all that and a bag of chips. I could really see myself with this guy and HE can't wait to see me too. He wants to get together again before he leaves for Amsterdam for his dad's birthday. What a lovely first date—only two hours, but what an amazing, lovely soul. His new book on the Amish comes out in November. I checked out his Web site and Googled him, he's legit. I hope his interest is as real as I want it to be. I haven't met someone I could see myself with in a long time and he definitely is one of them. He reminds me of when you talked about "when a man is really ready," and I think he is. He asked if I was open to a child with the right person.

We talked about all sorts of stuff from the trivial to the deep; we even talked alchemy and anthroposophy (he brought them up!). He held my hand for most of our time together. He has very warm lovely hands, said I am very sexy (he was sure others have told me so) with incredible eyes. He even told me how amazing and delightful I was! Dare I say he's cute, but not Hollywood handsome, interesting handsome.

You can see how Iris is progressing to men who are more fulfilling for her. She has left her old Deadly Dating Patterns, which included Hermit, Crumbs, and Fantasy, and has moved on to dating caring guys.

Bel, a thirty-five-year-old boutique owner who was struggling in her business, describes her advanced Dating Program of Three:

Number: *1*
Name: *Andrew*

Positives [Crazy About Me; Willing to Grow; Meeting the Basics]: *I wouldn't have been able to appreciate him six months ago; I think I would have passed on him because he is balding and older. But I can talk to Andrew and have all the deep conversations I love to have. He likes personal growth and he meditates. I wasn't in the mood to meet him on our first date, but I found myself actually really attracted to him without trying. He seems completely smitten when he looks at me. Absolutely loves to take care of me; he loaned me his BMW and offered to pay off all my debts!!! I love that he has that much money. Or maybe it is his self-assurance, a lack of neediness. Andrew's so sweet underneath all that drive. He is proactive, a guy who knows what he wants and how to get it. He wanted to meet me. He came straight over to my table at the wedding and asked to dance with me when I first met him.*

TTLC Needs He May Fulfill: *Being chosen and wanted as the special one. Being helped to feel safe. Being loved unconditionally. Commitment—he is saying that he doesn't want to see other women. Being understood. Being prized. Being told I'm attractive. Being encouraged to be real. Being treated with respect.*

Negatives: *This is the biggest negative: he has an unstable daughter from a previous marriage who is a handful.*

Fits/Breaks My Deadly Dating Patterns: *I have a tendency to do the Not Perfect—I'll Pass, and I can see those thoughts happening already. His weight is OK, but he is not in good shape physically.*

Number: *2*

Name: *Steve*

Positives [Crazy About Me; Willing to Grow; Meeting the Basics]: *He cares about the world, travels and is open to learning. He's financially set and takes me to fascinating lectures at the Met. He's extremely knowledgeable and smart and we have great conversations about all kinds of things. Likes to stay in shape, runs marathons. Seems crazy about me, e.g., asked me to go to Ireland with him.*

TTLC Needs He May Fulfill: *Being chosen and wanted. Swift kick in the butt to get me motivated (gets me to jog). Being taught (world events, art).*

Negatives: *He likes to hear himself talk. I suggested that he take the Landmark Forum [a growth course] and he refused outright. More and more, it appears he is not open or willing to grow. Last night when we went out we argued more than usual. I think he is falling down my list. He is awkward when he kisses me.*

Fits/Breaks My Deadly Dating Patterns: *I know I'm being picky about his not jumping into the course and that fits my Not Perfect—I'll*

Pass pattern, but I think he may have some deep-seated fears about being close. I can only imagine what sex would be like with him. . . .

Number: *3*
Name: *Stephen*
Positives [Crazy About Me; Willing to Grow; Meeting the Basics]:
We've only communicated via text and phone, but I really like hearing his voice. He has a great energy about him. He appears to be stable and is a successful trader. His photo is hot! Seems playful. We are supposed to meet next Saturday for dinner. I don't want to get into a Fantasy pattern. We will have to see!

Bel continued on the Program of Three for two months, at which point it was clear that Andrew was the One. Their relationship continued to flourish and the couple brought Andrew's daughter in for some family therapy sessions, which proved very helpful. Bel married Andrew in a sunset wedding on the grounds of his alma mater, Yale University.

Reading these Field Reports gives you a good sense of what it is like to be on the Dating Program of Three. Typically, as you work the Program, not having any dates will be a thing of the past. You will be able to compare and contrast men and catch yourself when you fall prey to your Deadly Dating Patterns. Though it can take some time at first, filtering out the DUDs and finding the STUDs gets easier and easier the more you do it.

The Marrying Kind: What the Research Shows

Here's another tool to use to help you sort men more effectively. Over the past few years, researchers have looked closely at the types of men who are more likely to be interested in a long-term relationship or marriage and those who are likely to be commitment-phobes or players. And guess what? There are telltale signs that you can use to guide you to the STUDs.

Rutgers University and the National Marriage Project conducted a national study that showed that married men were more likely than single men to have grown up with both biological parents. Almost half of the married men reported going to religious services several times a month, while less than one-quarter of the unmarried men did. When the researchers sorted out the "marrying kind" of single men, they found similarities: Those who came from traditional backgrounds in intact families and those who attended religious services regularly each month were more likely to agree with the following statement: "You'd be ready to marry tomorrow if the right person came along." Also, a Gallup poll showed that the vast majority of these men are seeking a "soulmate" who will fulfill their emotional, sexual, and spiritual desires and will also share breadwinning responsibilities.

The study went on to cite significant differences between the "marrying kind" and the non-marrying kind. Marriage avoiders were more likely to:

- distrust women to tell the truth about prior relationships
- worry more about the risks of divorce
- say they did not want children
- believe that singles have better sex lives than marrieds
- agree with the statement that "there are so many bad marriages today it makes one question the value of marriage"
- say that at this stage of life they just want to have fun
- express the concern that "if you marry, your biggest concern would be losing your personal freedom"

Ladies, there are some important clues here.

Obviously, there are wonderful, available guys who don't fit the complete profile of the "marrying kind." Nevertheless, the research is convincing that good parental role models and a spiritual or religious background help in molding guys who are more serious about commit-ment. If marriage is your goal, you may want to watch early on for info and clues about a guy's upbringing, eagerness for marriage, spiritual or religious activities, general distrust of women, and his fears about losing personal freedom. Don't waste your time on the "non-marrying kind"; they will only break your heart.

Be discerning and find out what any serious partner is offering you. Here's how poet Adelaide Anne Procter confronted her love:

> *Does there within thy dimmest dreams*
> *A possible future shine,*
> *Wherein thy life could henceforth breathe,*
> *Untouched, unshared by mine?*

You will want to question your guy, too. You deserve the loving com-mitment you want.

✎ Field Report on DUDs and STUDs: Exercises ____

Choose from among the following suggestions, according to your own intuition.

Total Time for Completing All of Them: 30 Minutes

EXERCISE 1: *CLOSURE*

Go through all your old boyfriends plus anyone who has potential and put them in the following categories:

1. Old boyfriends who have closure (nothing left unsaid; clear how and why it ended)

2. Old boyfriends who need closure (things left unsaid; not clear on how and why it ended)
3. Guys from the past who have twinkles of possibility
4. Guys who know I'm not interested but are still around

EXERCISE 2: *LETTERS OF CLOSURE*

Write letters of closure to each guy from Category 2 in Exercise 1. In the letters, explore the way the relationship played out, plus his role and your role in ending it. Ask him about anything you feel you need to know. Say whatever is left unsaid to him. End the letter thanking him for lessons learned. For now, just keep the letters in your journal—for your own personal closure.

EXERCISE 3: *FILLING IN YOUR FIELD REPORT ON DUDs AND STUDs*

Make copies of and fill in your Field Report. Do this weekly while you are actively working the Program. Use page 2 as an opportunity to elaborate and really journal about the guys you are seeing. If you don't have three, consider adding an interested-but-rebuffed guy from Category 4 in Exercise 1. Go ahead and let him know you are now interested.

EXERCISE 4: *THE DESERT ISLAND*

Make a list of any five people, living or dead, with whom you would choose to be stranded on a desert island. *Think about not only the need for companionship, but the need to be clever, get things done, and survive.* Write a list of reasons why you chose each person. What does this exercise teach you about an ideal mate?

EXERCISE 5: *IF YOU ARE NOT DATING YET, JOURNAL ABOUT IT*

Write down reasons why you are not dating right now. Maybe you feel stuck, scared, depressed, bored with it all, tired of dating, tired of men, tired of your own dating complaints, just plain tired. Okay, let's pretend or imagine that you are simply in a Hermit Deadly Dating Pattern. End this sentence with whatever comes to mind: *I really can't date right now because*_____. End it again, over and over until you get insight or your mood shifts. If you do this long enough you will go deeper and discover what is holding you in this pattern. It may be a deep-seated attachment to an old flame or bitter, angry feelings, or just a fear that you are truly unlovable. Write it all out.

Now, write down three action items that will pop you out of this time-wasting morass. These can include connecting with a master Love Mentor and asking for help in getting out there, going shopping for your Diamond Self look, jumping in online, or going to a party and networking. Take one of these actions.

 Homework

Choose from among the following suggestions, according to your own intuition:

1. Discuss your Field Reports on DUDs and STUDs with your master Love Mentor and Team Love.
2. Contact any guys from the past with twinkles of possibility from your Exercise 1 list. If it feels right, arrange for a date with them. *Note:* If a guy showed abusive tendencies or you are at risk for getting re-involved in a sticky, unfulfilling pattern with him, do not contact him. If you have any doubt, discuss this with your master Love Mentor and/or Team Love.
3. Contact or send your letter to any ex who needs closure, based on Exercises 1 and 2. Ask him for real feedback about what you did

wrong in the relationship. Tell him to be honest and not to worry about hurting your feelings. This can be invaluable.

> Complete the interaction so that you feel like you are done with this person.
> Do not do this if (1) he was abusive to you; or (2) the connection with him will reactivate a Deadly Dating Pattern!

4. Get more Beauty, Advice, or Matchmaker Mentors as needed.
5. Step up the networking and practice using the Diamond Self, Best Friend, Ten-Second Sound-Bite, Complete Focus, Generosity, and/ or Flirting Techniques.
6. Work two online dating sites/apps using all the search-engine optimization secrets *for at least one-half hour every day (including weekends).*
7. Fill out your Love in 90 Days Online Dating Report. Upgrade your photo, tweak your screen name and profile, change sites, or sharpen your focus if needed.
8. Have at least two dates. Work the Program of Three and make it a point to really appreciate the positive qualities in each guy.

And one last recommendation from a happily married graduate: "Stop shopping for apples at the lemon store!"

Congrats on making it through Chapter 9!

The best journaling advice I can give you is to follow through on filling in your Field Reports on DUDs and STUDs. This is one of your biggest take-aways from the Love in 90 Days course. Filling out these reports weekly will move you along more quickly through the mysterious twists and turns on the road toward love.

As Lao Tzu wrote:

Without words, without even understanding, lovers find each other....
The moment of finding is always a surprise, like meeting an old friend
never before known.

―❦―

Ditching Deadly Dating Patterns Forever

I seek the Prince, he's ready to grow
He's crazy about me and it will show
I will feel his love and support
The Frog will have a selfish retort
I won't get involved too fast
Until a Prince proves he's built to last
And let him go if I get crumbs
Because I am just too good for bums!
I allow the cream of the crop
To prove to me they are the top
To step up for courtship growth
And create a future with dreams for both
I see us at our big fun wedding
So happy in our marriage bedding
—Shelly, a forty-two-year-old graduate

Before Shelly found her prince, she went through some really tough times. Growing up, she was extremely shy and reserved and often could not speak her truth. For a long time she clung to one guy after another who gave her crumbs. Then, after she followed the Love in 90 Days principles, she met a STUD who was a good man and generous beyond her wildest dreams. Much as you try to get out of them, Deadly

Dating Patterns can stick to you like super Velcro. If you are still struggling with a particular pattern, this chapter will help to "unstick" you and propel you forward.

Deadly Dating Patterns always seem to resurface when you experience some type of dating mishap, "rejection" (your interpretation), or real "failure" with a guy you like. Your natural reaction is to start the negative thought machine, the self-pity, the "f*ck-its." Those feelings, in turn, can pull you back into your Fantasy, Crumbs, or Abuse Recycle relationship. Or they can put you right back in your Hermit hut, watching mindless TV, cleaning the bathroom, or even reading your junk e-mail. Rather than saying hello to the cute guy on the train, you get tongue-tied and run the other way. When it comes to finding a new photo for your profile, you see nothing but pimples, warts, and just how big your nose really is.

Or you obsessively write and rewrite e-mails to prospective partners, trying to be more clever, more real, more funny, or more of whatever that mysterious quality is that attracts a cool partner. And when you're on a date with a good-looking (make that threateningly good-looking) partner, you get tongue-tied or start babbling. Or you project these not-liking-me thoughts onto your partners, ruining any chance you have of simply being yourself or of having a good time. Underlying all these Deadly Dating Patterns are the deeper fears: of being rejected, of being unlovable, of being disappointed, hurt, and discarded.

But there are ways to climb out and move beyond these "holes of the spirit." First let's take a look at Portia Nelson's recipe:

AUTOBIOGRAPHY IN FIVE SHORT CHAPTERS

CHAPTER ONE
I walk down the street.
There is a deep hole in the sidewalk.
I fall in.

I am lost...I am helpless.
It is not my fault.
It takes forever to find my way out.

CHAPTER TWO
I walk down the same street.
There is a deep hole in the sidewalk.
I pretend I don't see it.
I fall in.
I can't believe I am in the same place.
But it isn't my fault.
It still takes a long time to get out.

CHAPTER THREE
I walk down the same street.
There is a deep hole in the sidewalk.
I see it there.
I still fall in...It's a habit.
But my eyes are open.
I know where I am.
It is my fault.
I get out immediately.

CHAPTER FOUR
I walk down the same street.
There is a deep hole in the sidewalk.
I walk around it.

CHAPTER FIVE
I walk down another street.

In this chapter you learn how to "walk down another street" once and for all via the Deadly Dating Patterns Fix-It Kit. Read through all the different remedies simply for ideas and inspiration. Then focus on the Fix-It tools specifically designed to break through your unique recurring patterns.

The Deadly Dating Patterns Fix-It Kit

1. THE FLAME-OUT FIX

You need to slow things down! Remember the mantra: *Jump in too fast and it's over fast*. It is critically important for you, of all people, to do a Dating Program of Three. Even though you meet this guy who is totally on your wavelength, who gets you like never before, who brings you yellow peach roses and writes poems about you, who assures you he's never felt like this before *in his whole life*. Even though you are absolutely sure that this is a totally different soulmate experience and can't stop looking at the roses or reliving every move he made in bed that ecstatic night! *Remember, this is your addictive brain chemistry in action. See two other guys. Be smart.*

Listen to your Love Mentor. Make yourself busy so that you are less available for those lost-in-Nirvana five-hour dates. When it starts getting out of hand, limit the amount of time you spend together. Three hours is plenty. Remember, leave him hungry and wanting more. Control your fantasy life. Stop thinking about him so much. Put your attention on other things and other guys. Take on that exciting assignment at work. Go shopping—and not just for what to wear on a date with him. Avoid going to your place or his—because you know what will happen there!

Write up a list of his negative traits to keep your mind more realistic. And ground your mind with meditation, tai chi, chi gong, or other mind/body practices that will diminish the speedy rush into the tunnel of love.

Discuss your Flame-Out tendencies and this hot relationship with

your master Love Mentor. Ask her or him for help in slowing down and
creating a more mature coming together. Get your master Love Mentor's okay before you jump in and have sex. Remember that I've recommended at least eight weeks of consistently improving contact between
you before you open the oxytocin floodgates.

Here's how Dawn courageously ended a highly charged Flame-Out
relationship that set the stage for meeting the man who became her
husband:

> *I have stuck with my commitment of not initiating contact with Billy.
> This has proved to be very difficult today. Especially tonight... Lots of
> stuff started coming up. I got a text and at first I thought, "Oh great,
> I'm doing my work and Billy contacts me." Then it turns out it is a dear
> friend of mine—gay.*
>
> *I got home and I just cried. I felt so sad. I started thinking, "Well, he
> texted me last, so technically, it's my turn... blah blah blah." Yes, it is the
> land of making up stories to justify my behavior and feeling guilty that I
> haven't created a lasting romantic relationship. Yet, there is a win in all
> of this. I didn't overeat; I took off my makeup and flossed—yes, flossed.
> So even though I feel TERRIBLE and I WANT BILLY TO CONTACT
> ME TONIGHT, I am not hurting myself or making myself feel worse by
> not taking care of myself. And that is a MILESTONE.*
>
> *I hate the feeling I am having. I feel like a hurt little girl, yet I know I
> am a grown woman. I feel powerless and stupid. But I don't hate myself.
> In fact, I am thinking that here I am—I look great, I'm successful—
> WHAT IS WRONG WITH HIM?*
>
> *Yet, I do know that I am creating it all. Why am I continuing to
> attract unavailable men and when will I stop?*
>
> *Thank God I'm in class. Thank God for your support. This is some-
> thing that I must change in my life because it is really not working for
> me to be single when what I want is a loving partnership. So, with this
> email, I recommit to NOT INITIATING CONTACT WITH BILLY
> TONIGHT. One day at a time.*

Later that night, Dawn e-mailed me again:

> *I registered with eHarmony with the intent of creating something new. I*
> *haven't heard from Billy. It's about 11:00. I am going to take a bath and*
> *most likely turn off my phone at 11:30. I am so tired of waiting for him*
> *to text night after night. It has been a creation of longing and yearning.*
> *I feel very happy to have had the courage to take a stand for myself*
> *tonight. I am not a chicken. I know good things are coming into my life.*

2. THE FANTASY RELATIONSHIP FIX

You go cold turkey. Nix all thoughts of him. Switch your attention away
from the phantom whenever he enters your mind. Avoid seeing him.
This is dealing with an addiction and you are going into recovery.

In 12-step programs they tell you to avoid "people, places, and things"
that lead to the addictive substance. You do the same. Avoid places
you are likely to see him, anything that reminds you of him, songs you
associate with him, neighborhoods, hang-out joints, and especially his
friends who are likely to fill your head with his goings-on.

Work a Dating Program of Three and put your attention on real men.

If you had a relationship with him in the past, save any mean, angry,
or horrid texts, e-mails, or letters he sent you and keep them where you
can review them. Send copies to your master Love Mentor to use as
ammunition for times when you are drifting back to obsessing or actually seeing him. Stay in close touch with your master Love Mentor as an
emotional anchor until the longing for the fix wanes away.

Jillian, who lived in a Fantasy Relationship with a co-worker, describes
how she finally went cold turkey:

> *I had the hardest time not calling Alan this morning as I drove home on*
> *Christmas from Rhode Island. But I didn't. I kept thinking about how I*
> *wanted to share the holidays with him, how great he would fit in with my*
> *family, how much he would enjoy this day. I was doing all this despite the*

fact that he had never once asked me out on a real honest-to-goodness date. My brain went back and forth until I slammed the steering wheel and said, "You stupid girl! He's never going to be yours. And besides you want a good Christian!" I know I don't want to be doing this when I'm 50. I will not contact Alan. My affirmation is, "I need and I claim love beyond expectation!"

3. THE CRUMBS FIX

Give up the crumbs and take a seat at the banquet table. First, break up with the guys who are only giving you crumbs. Then make a rule: *I only date men who are (a) available and (b) crazy about me (for real).* Try this on for size, even if it means spending time with guys who "aren't good enough" but who treat you like royalty. By the way, if you do this, the crumb-giver may come around. If he starts courting you, give him a chance. But don't jump right back in. Slowly let him prove to you that he is changing. Encourage him to go into therapy or work on himself to see if he can be more giving and the two of you can come together in a way that is fulfilling for both of you.

You need to learn about what it really means to be loved. A master Love Mentor who is very generous can help you with this issue. Be sure to do your Diamond Self work and use that glorious name with your master Love Mentor and Team Love. Make an affirmation to the effect of, "I deserve it all." Post it where you can read it every day. Treat yourself as royally as you can. Practice asking for what you want, no matter how expensive or "inappropriate" or "bothersome" it is. Also, practice receiving and saying yes when those things come to you. Because they will.

Kathie talks about her insights after a Crumbs boyfriend broke up with her:

He couldn't even kiss me the way I wanted to be kissed and even used to put less food on my plate whenever he cooked, which was rarely. And I found out he is taking another girlfriend to his birthday bash;

he planned that while he was still seeing me! What I realize is that I
don't speak up enough about what I need or how I want things to go, so
I shouldn't be surprised when I don't get them. My pattern is to not say
anything and stuff myself with binge eating. I think the eating is out of
that hunger, that need that never gets fulfilled—certainly not with the
a'holes I choose. It is time to work the Program instead of the ice cream!

4. THE HERMIT FIX

There are two kinds of Hermits: those who are "jaded" and those who
are plain scared. If you have been married, divorced, and/or dated
around a lot with no success, you may be "taking a break" for a variety
of reasons, most of which have to do with the fact that you are sick and
tired of meeting DUDs. On the other hand, you may be newly divorced
and feeling fearful about taking the plunge back into the dating pool or
just a shy person who never really got into dating at any age.

No matter which kind of Hermit you are, there's no getting around
it: *Take action.* If you are jaded, bear in mind that working this Program
will open up new worlds of men to choose from. If you are scared, understand that putting yourself out there will become easier and easier.

Shyness is just an inverted need for attention. Once you start getting
it, believe me, you will lap it up. And that is great. A shining, fully
expressed you will free others. Master the keys to networking magic:
the Diamond Self, Best Friend, Ten-Second Sound-Bite Intro, Complete
Focus, Generosity, and Flirting that you learned in Chapter 7. Using
just one of them can set you free!

You just have to start. Baby steps count. If you go to a lecture and
smile at one person as a first step, that's good. Make eye contact and
meet and greet any people around you. In any social situation, remember this rule: Instead of being quiet, *say anything.* It doesn't have to be
profound, make sense, be interesting, or show how clever or cool you
are. Most social conversation is either illogical or boring. People don't
really listen or pay that much attention to each other. Just join in. Try a

little flirtatious eye contact and review the other Flirting Techniques in Chapter 7.

Whether you are a jaded or scared Hermit, take a quick dive into the online dating pool. Do some speed dating with no expectations. Get a tough master Love Mentor who helps get you out and about—one who will come with you is optimal! At the very least, get a good friend to drag you out of the house.

Here's how one client who hadn't dated for over ten years described her first dating adventures:

> For someone who used to wear makeup maybe twice a year, dressing to impress with makeup is a whole new gig. Scary. But I forced myself to do the online thing and I had two first dates this weekend! One date went from just a drink and conversation to walking around town, going to an art opening and dinner. He wants to come kayaking in the harbor. It's my favorite place to go. I haven't heard from him as to when. The second guy I am not so sure about. Felt awkward, or maybe he's awkward. He's a little mysterious. I did Google his name and he is a well-known history prof who writes and lectures. He is coming next week for a swim. Yikes, I need a full body wetsuit pronto!!

5. THE I'LL MAKE YOU LOVE ME FIX

Your one-sided over-giving is just a way to hold on to the guy. It masks your own fear of rejection. Understand that *you can never make anyone love you.* It's either there or it's not. You are addicted to giving and have to go into recovery. It's just like in Al-Anon: You have to realize that you are powerless over another person and whether or not he is attached to you. Your giving just creates the illusion of control.

Force yourself to stop giving so much. Slow way down—do the Program of Three with no sex so that you can get to know a guy.

The giving has to go both ways. Find a man who is very generous to you. Your instinctual reaction will probably be not to like this type, since he wants so badly to be in a club that will have you as a member. But stick with a giver for a while. It will be very uncomfortable at first but then you will get used to it. You need to learn how to take. Also, get yourself a master Love Mentor who enjoys giving to you. Hard as it is, grit your teeth and take it like a woman!

Here is how a student in our Program who was just emerging from this Deadly Dating Pattern describes the dynamics in the I'll Make You Love Me Fix:

> *When you pursue them they get scared. Common male problem. Because when you pursue them they feel, "Uh-oh, do I want to get involved or am I just in it for the chase?" I think you have to avoid the intimate things until they are crazy mad about you. If they get sex before they fall in love with you, they stop thinking about how to please you and start thinking about their dinky. Not being so available allows them to make a clear choice. Not pursuing feels crazy but it works. Some people enjoy making it a fun game and acquire a skill at it. Think JFK Jr. and Carolyn; she was merciless on him and would walk off with other guys if he stopped paying attention to her.*

6. THE ABUSE RECYCLE FIX

Empower yourself and take the driver's seat by doing the Dating Program of Three. When you meet a guy, look carefully for signs of a judgmental nature, blurred boundaries, or uncontrolled anger. Ask him about his history of failed relationships. Listen to how he talks about his ex. Is he high handed and judgmental? Do you feel bad or insecure after you have been with the guy? If you experience *any* of these signs, run the other way.

You must take action to address the self-hate that brings you into abusive relationships. Meditation, therapy, 12-step programs, growth courses, or setting up a Team Love would be possible steps to take. Some folks who have had a very troubling childhood *always* need to be in some type of growth activity. I know I do. I meditate and regularly take yoga and other spiritual or personal growth courses. If I don't, I can spiral into negative self-talk.

Find a master Love Mentor or use a Love Mentor® coach who will call you on your choice of abusers and help you get away from them. And, finally, write out a projection of what you will be like in ten years if you keep on accepting abuse. Here is one student's projection of her lonely future:

The year is 2028—10 years from 2018.

Barbara is now 50 and no longer sexy, and no longer remembers what it's like to feel like a princess. What has made her that way? Hanging on to a fantasy of fixing things that never materialized. She tries every once in a while to pull herself together and dress up, but all she sees in the mirror is the surface, because she let the inner part of her die. She has no light shining and runs from anything that seems to shine. Yes, she has dates occasionally with over the hill, tired playboys, who also pulled it together for one night. They only remind her of herself. Always seeking the fantasy, never accepting a person who is real into her life. Who were the real possibilities? There must have been other guys interested, but she never looked twice, dismissing the nice ones, for the narcissistic fantasy of having a guy that would make her look good even if he treated her like dirt.

She had a chance ten years ago to step forward, deal with her fears... but was too scared and searched for every reason to stay. She could change him; she couldn't accept her participation in this failed relationship. It hurt too much on many levels. So she became passive and just waited, and clung.

Now she's living in a dead fantasy world, replayed like an old cassette tape, rewind, play, rewind, play.

Barbara, I am happy to say, has moved on and is currently dating good guys with real potential.

7. THE SAFETY NET FIX

Either leave or help this guy grow into someone you could fall for! This person is a projection screen for all that you truly believe is wrong with *you*. If you see him as passive, unsuccessful, or unattractive, examine where you find the same qualities in yourself. You need to work on yourself, much like a woman who runs the Abuse Recycle. Develop a master Love Mentor relationship with someone you really admire and look up to. A person you feel you don't really deserve. This will give you practice taking in love from someone you respect.

Another path is available if the guy is willing to grow. Sometimes Safety Net DUDs can turn into wonderful STUDs. Loni was a client who wound up starting a hot relationship with Gil, a guy who seemed at first to be a definite DUD. She met eight-years-younger Gil while he was in graduate school and she was a nurse. Gil was a smart *schlemiel* who was smitten with Loni. He wore nerdy clothes and awful glasses, and had no idea about romance or flirting. Loni decided to help him out and he cooperated. She got him tight jeans, contacts, plus a haircut at one of the trendiest salons in NYC. After the haircut, Loni saw other women flirting with Gil and actually felt turned on to him. A few months later, they made love. She discovered to her surprise that he had a slow hand in bed. And once he got over the initial awkwardness, he became a great lover!

8. THE NOT PERFECT—I'LL PASS FIX

Listen to the voice in your head that is hypercritical of *you*. Then you won't be projecting so much. If you start feeling turned off when he spills his coffee, as you help him find some napkins to clean up the mess, say to yourself, *I'm being picky and critical in some way of myself, just like my mother (or father)*. Even though this feels strange, it will change the way you look at men. This pattern is a manifestation of you being critical of you and is surely a reflection of some harsh, picky parenting you had along the way. Find a master Love Mentor who is unconditionally prizing of you—who thinks you are perfect!

While usually you are the one who does most of the rejecting, some guys sense when you are in this one-up, judgmental pattern and will abandon you before you reject them. Rachel wrote this description about a guy who dumped her in a Not Perfect—I'll Pass pattern:

> *Mitchell is very insecure and needs someone to make him feel secure and special. He knew he was going to have to step up with a girl like me and he wasn't up for the challenge. He even realized that I was too good for him and that he couldn't put things over on me. Also, that I wasn't going to buy into his dramas. He knew he had met a match above his head and so he had to walk.*
>
> *I just had some realizations as I write this: I think I frequently make up a defensive story about how the guy is no good in my head. It is my way of avoiding that idea that I was rejected and the guy just wasn't that into me. Ouch. Maybe I need to just accept that I was rejected, feel it and move on.*
>
> *I think that I could actually be a little softer and more forgiving. I can be too critical and expect a lot. That is why I need persistent pushy guys. They need to prove themselves to me and then I will let my guard down and move mountains for them. I need to be forgiving early on. The wall I put up is my own protective measure.*

9. THE CHASE ME FIX

Unless he's a real jerk, no testiness or running off! Instead, take a chance—hang in there and be real with him. You need to slow things down! Remember this mantra: *Jump in too fast and you'll scare yourself right out.* Let the relationship unfold so that you can become secure in his attachment to you.

Learn meditation, yoga, or any spiritual discipline that helps you settle down and be less anxious and impulsive. Get a master Love Mentor who will stop you from copping out and running away. And you must screw up your courage. Sometimes the very hardest challenge is to allow someone to love you. It hurts. It brings up all the wounds and pains of the past. But a good guy will hang in there while you process that pain. In the early days when I would hit a rough patch, Sam used to draw me a bath and sit with me while I cried, processing old father wounds.

Meagen, a ponytailed brunette given to running away, describes the Chase Me Deadly Dating Pattern:

> *I need to recognize that I'm not honest in a relationship in order to protect the guy's feelings. Yet if I am not honest, I am not truly showing up and I set him up to fail with me. My pattern is to not say anything, use those unexpressed feelings to plan my escape route, and then tell the guy (like a bomb) when I am walking out the door. The emotional bomb kills off both of us—I am devastated and he feels like crap, but he doesn't really have a clue about what happened. I am going to speak to my Love Mentor every day to help me get over this assured-mutual-destruction insanity.*

10. THE FADE AWAY FIX

Be sure to use your Diamond Self exercise before each date. Dress the part. Be in love with yourself before you walk out that door! Imagine many guys competing for you, as if you were an adorable prize. Remember, you are not ordinary! There are no ordinary people. Use the networking secrets, including the Ten-Second Sound-Bite Intro, Complete Focus, Generosity, and Flirting. Make it a point to review the Flirting Techniques in Chapter 7. Use at least two with any date who has even a hint of possibility. You have to be giving guys clear "go" signals.

Remember to close your eyes and imagine that the person you're about to meet is a dear old friend you haven't seen in years. Greet the guy and start the evening with that friendly vibe. Ask him open-ended questions about himself. Have fun. If you like him, make sure to send a brief text or e-mail that is appreciative of the date.

Here is how Maria, an overworked copywriter, described her Fade Away issues:

> *It seems like guys might be interested, but I am not so interested. I am try-*
> *ing to be open to the present (i.e. unwrapping the present), but because*
> *I don't really care either way, I am a bit distant and willing to push off*
> *seeing them. They kind of get a subtle message and it fizzles. I need to*
> *understand this issue of "not caring." I think I just never expect it to go*
> *anywhere and I don't want to get my hopes up. I have to stop that. And*
> *stop letting days go by before I respond to a guy's message because I am*
> *"too busy."*

11. THE JEALOUSY TRAP FIX

Work your Program of Three so you feel like the one who is choosing. Write down an affirmation like *I am the special one*, and set it up where you will see it every day. Envision your man looking over at another woman and then back at you and clearly choosing you, with all the satisfying feelings that scene brings up. Practice positive self-talk and make sure to work on all the self-love exercises in the Program. And work on personal growth outside the Program. You have to be totally in love with yourself!

Here's how Alisha successfully dealt with her Jealousy Trap thinking and avoided creating a fight based on that paranoia:

> *Paul and I were supposed to get together this past weekend. He said he'd*
> *call me Monday late-morning. I didn't hear from him. Immediately, the*
> *old records started playing, e.g., "He's with someone else who he's more*
> *interested in etc." I took a deep breath and thought, "positive self-talk!"*
> *I sent him a text and said, "Is everything OK? I thought we were on for*
> *today." He sent me a text back within five minutes: "I'm really sorry. I*
> *got called into work early"—He'd told me that he would be on-call, but*
> *I had forgotten—"and haven't had a chance to come up for air. It's been*

one of those days." When he got home that night we exchanged several
sweet text messages and he said, "Let's do something soon. I'll call you."
Now I feel like he just needs more shaping. I think he's crazy about me
because he sent me an email when he returned from a week in San Fran-
cisco and when I didn't respond within a day he called me.

12. THE JUST BUDDIES FIX

Stop dressing and acting like one of the guys. Start wearing clothes that
highlight your best feminine assets, complete with heels, makeup, and
jewelry. Review the Flirting Techniques in Chapter 7 and practice flirting wherever you go.

By all means, whenever you're around guys, use the magic question:
"Would you help me, please?" Men are wired to solve problems and take
care of women. They love it. Let them. Being buddies rarely gets you
to the goal. You have enough friends already! Don't dispense advice to
a guy about another woman unless he's willing to introduce you to his
brother, best friend, etc. Don't waste any extra time hanging out with
someone who does not respond romantically. You need a lot of Beauty,
Advice, and Matchmaker Mentors as well as a good master Love Mentor. Find a master Love Mentor who sees the great feminine Diamond
Self in you.

Liz came out of her plain shell by getting a number of mentors to help
her emerge as a rather glam hipster in four-inch heels. She had this to
say about her transformation:

> *So . . . my skirts are working! I am meeting some more men. Sometimes we*
> *exchange numbers, sometimes they take my number or I take their number*
> *and sometimes we talk about getting dinner. I completely agree that I*
> *want them to make an effort to try to get in touch with me and spend time*
> *with me and help me (I'm very needy, but I'm petrified of being seen as*
> *high maintenance and whiny. So I act tough and laid back). This is my*
> *next challenge, to let them pay for dinner or help me pick out a computer.*

13. THE GRASS IS GREENER FIX

The great mathematician Frederick Mosteller has shown that you will maximize your odds of finding the best possible spouse if you date about 37 percent of the available candidates in your life, and then choose to stay with the next one who is better than all the rest. Any other strategy, whether choosing earlier *or* later, will significantly decrease your chances of success.

For example: Suppose you expect to meet 100 potential partners in your lifetime. If you marry the first one, your chances of having found the best one are 1/100. If you wait to the last one, your chances are again 1/100. By sampling the first 37 percent of the total pool of candidates, not only will you learn about the various types of men and your responses to them, you will have entered the sweet spot of the probability curve where your chances are at their best.

Now review all the men you've dated at least once since high school. Write them down in your journal and start counting. Pick the number of men you realistically expect to date over the next twenty to thirty years. Now do the math. If you're under the 37 percent you still have some dating to do, but keep in mind you are looking for the guy who is better than all the rest. If you're over the magic number, start thinking about your most recent guys in terms of the DUDs and STUDs Report and find the one with the most potential. If an old boyfriend turns out to be the best, contact him and see if he is still available. In any case, the next few guys you meet are likely to be suitable candidates. Remember, you are looking to maximize your chances of picking the best guy from among those you've already met or are likely to meet. Stop your magical thinking about princes riding in on white horses.

You don't think any of the guys you dated were suitable for you? Practice imagining the guy as if he were with another girl! This will change your ability to appreciate all the things that are right with him. In fact, making a list of all your old boyfriends and what was absolutely right with them is a very helpful exercise. It brings you face-to-face with your own fears.

Lina went through her exes:

> *Eddy is patient. Brett is a really nice person....Elliot is strong, brilliant....George is a little crazy, but he is giving, a powerhouse, an inspiration! I realize that these men gave me all they had to give. But I could never be sure. I just could never settle. As I've dug deeper into myself I sense an internal block that has kept me from choosing a man. I think it has to do with being afraid that I am inept, cannot make a good decision, and sadly, that I cannot trust myself. But, when it all comes down to it, I think the block is all about my own self-esteem issues, and not wanting to be with a guy who would choose the not-so-lovable me.*

Happily, Lina ended up with George, the giving powerhouse. She couldn't be happier with her choice.

Taking a Stand for Love

The Deadly Dating Pattern Fix-It Kit involves brutally honest self-reflection, self-discipline, and courage to take right action. Many Fixes involve cutting off contact with an abusive, unavailable, or withholding man in order to move out of a situation that is not working and make room for one that does.

Facing loss and the possibility of being alone is one of the hardest human challenges. But if you do not take a stand for yourself, who will? This is where a Love Mentor Coach and/or Team Love comes in (http://www.Lovein90Days.com/dating-coach). A support team makes it so much easier for you to make the big moves. Hold on to the vision of love that you have created for yourself. And be ready to risk losing the DUDs you cling to in order to help real love blossom.

✎ Ditching Deadly Dating Patterns Forever: Exercises _____

Choose from among the following suggestions, according to your own intuition.

Total Time for Completing All of Them: 30 Minutes

EXERCISE 1: *STEPPING OUT OF YOUR DEADLY DATING PATTERNS*

Based on what you've read in this chapter, what are your next steps to breaking out of your Deadly Dating Patterns? What could you do that would take you even further?

   If you are struggling and have to pull away from a DUD to end one of your Deadly Dating Patterns:

- Write another ten-year projection like Barbara did in the Abuse Recycle section, describing what you will be like in ten years if you continue on with this unfulfilling relationship.
- What small steps could you take that would make you feel more empowered? Could you speak up and ask your partner more clearly for what you need? Could you slowly spend less and less time with him? Who could give you emotional support while you shift away?

EXERCISE 2: *LETTER FROM A PERFECTLY LOVING PARTNER*

Once again it is important to put your attention on what you want, rather than on what you do not want. Write yourself a letter from a perfectly loving partner.

EXERCISE 3: *MIRACLE DAY*

If you were to experience a true miracle tonight, and as you slept all your love fears and self-sabotaging patterns disappeared, what would you be like tomorrow? Write a description of the newly transformed person you've become. *For the next day act as if that miracle has occurred.* Buy yourself a present that symbolizes the new you and keep it near you.

EXERCISE 4: *ENVISIONING GOALS*

We are now two months into the course. Based on your newly acquired understanding of your fears, resistances, and the realities of the men you are dealing with, it is time to reexamine your goals. Some may have been achieved already, which means that it's time to set higher ones. Or your original goals may have been unrealistic and based in fantasy. In order to be successful, you should be stretching but setting realistic goals.

Revisit the program goals on page 234.

Write down any new goal and a timeline for achieving it. Envision each step between where you are now and achieving that goal. Experience each step as a scene by feeling, seeing, and hearing the details. Then write out the scenes.

Here's how one student in our Program re-envisioned a scene from her new goal:

The Proposal

He knows that even though I'm not into traditional gender roles, the bended knee thing is something I would not object to. He is professing his undying love, how he thinks the moon and sun rise and set on me, on his world with me. He's chosen a gorgeous square diamond, very unusual setting. It is so touching, so incredible, so magical when he asks, I feel like we're in a bubble of some sort, I have no reservations. Yes, I say, yes.

EXERCISE 5: *ANCHORING GOALS: YOUR LOVE SONG*

Listen to a love song that speaks to your heart. As you do, imagine how great it will feel when you meet your goals. Listen to this song often.

The Ten Love in 90 Days Goals

1. Create an exciting love intention or affirmation.

2. Create greater self-esteem, deservedness, and self-love.

3. Break out of Deadly Dating Patterns and create a successful Dating Program of Three.

4. Move up the ladder to better men.

5. Meet someone who has tremendous potential for a love relationship with you and graduate from the Program of Three.

6. Declare love for each other.

7. Talk seriously with your Beloved about what each of you needs and wants in a fulfilling love relationship.

8. Create a loving win-win contract that gives each of you roots (stability and dedication) and wings (fulfilling your dreams).

9. Commit to moving in together or getting engaged to your Beloved.

10. Marry or make a lifetime commitment to live out your dreams together.

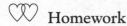 **Homework**

Choose from among the following suggestions, according to your own intuition:

1. Fill out your Field Reports on DUDs and STUDs with an attitude of total thankfulness and gratitude. Journal about what a difference your attitude makes!

2. Discuss your Field Reports on DUDs and STUDs with your master Love Mentor and Team Love.

3. If possible, contact some of your ex's friends and ask them for honest feedback about what you did wrong in the relationship with him. I know this is hard. But students in our Love Mentor® coaching program would tell you that this act of courage was invaluable in giving them insights into their Deadly Dating Patterns and helped them change.

4. Get more Beauty, Advice, or Matchmaker Mentors as needed.

5. Keep up the networking and practice using the Diamond Self, Best Friend, Ten-Second Sound-Bite, Complete Focus, Generosity, and Flirting Techniques. Have the new people you meet set you up with guys.

6. Work two online dating sites/apps using all the search-engine optimization secrets *for at least one-half hour every day (including weekends).*

7. Fill out your Love in 90 Days Online Dating Report. Upgrade your photo, tweak your screen name and profile, change sites, or sharpen your focus if needed.

8. Have at least two dates this week. Work your Program of Three!

As you complete your second month, remember that love, whether it is in the form of love of self or love with a partner, can and will break through the most unmovable glaciers of the heart. As the *I Ching* says:

> *When two people are at one in their inmost hearts,*
> *they shatter even the strength of iron or bronze.*

PART III

The Third Month

First Aid for Heartache

For even as love crowns you so shall he crucify you.
Even as he is for your growth, so is he for your pruning.
Even as he ascends to your height
And caresses your tenderest branches that quiver in the sun,
So shall he descend to your roots and shake them in their clinging to the earth.

—*Khalil Gibran*

It takes staggering courage to open yourself to love. After the crowning, the walking on air, and the sheer bliss of new love's caress, often comes the fall, a loss made that much greater because of the heights you reached. Emotionally, it can feel like you've been thrown down into a very black hole or nailed to a cross and then abandoned. You desperately want to stuff yourself until you're sick, or you can't eat at all. You have crying jags where you feel empty, worthless, and sick. Your gut aches, your heart hurts, you're ruminating about what happened, and you can't sleep or concentrate. Crazy things come to mind, like showing up at the place where your Beloved works. Nothing matters, not even the biggest win at work.

During the third month of the program, you may hit a wall while running the marathon of love. You may be dealing with major heartbreak, or you may be slowly sliding into hopelessness. For getting this far, I admire you! We should all get medals for answering love's call, for living through its harsh torment several times, and yet rising up like phoenix goddesses, ready to face the pain again, if necessary, to find that one truly healing, empowering man.

In this chapter, I'm going to give you all the first aid tools you need to soothe that anguish, recharge your batteries, and allow you to rebound as quickly as possible. I'll share research about the real physical and psychological nature of heartbreak and what these findings suggest in terms of healing. We will look at how the process of growth always includes setbacks—all of us take two steps forward and one step backward over and over again. Understanding this fundamental human pattern will help you uncover and rid yourself of deeper negative beliefs that fuel your heartbreak. We'll cover revenge and why it is not a good reaction to betrayal or an attack made by your ex. And we will take a look at why spiritual or religious practices can help heal your heart. Use any or all of these lessons whenever you are suffering after a loss or if you are tempted to drop out of the program or fall back into old dating habits.

Note: Even if you are not dealing with the challenge of heartache right now, I want you to continue reading this chapter's material and do the exercises and some of the homework anyway. The greatest love can and will disappoint us at one point or another; every single relationship has discouraging times, times of betrayal, or the sting of loss. Understanding this is simply a matter of having realistic expectations about relationships. I am certainly not suggesting that you be cynical or negative about love! Quite the contrary. But expecting these downturns and working through them is what allows us to grow. C. S. Lewis describes what happens if we do not take this heroic path:

> *Love anything, and your heart will certainly be wrung and possibly be broken. If you want to make sure of keeping it intact, you must give your heart to no one, not even to an animal. Wrap it carefully round with hobbies and little luxuries; avoid all entanglements; lock it up safe in the casket or coffin of your selfishness. But in that casket—safe, dark,*

motionless, airless—it will change. It will not be broken; it will become
unbreakable, impenetrable, irredeemable.

Let's look at the downside of the brave decision to love and learn how
to process the pain quickly and generate new and better love experiences.

The Chemistry of Breaking Up

When the Love in 90 Days course brings you from dreams and possibility into new dating, you are excited, curious, and hopeful. Wonderful
breakthroughs occur. But you still need to be prepared for both outer
and inner obstacles. When "the One" turns out to be a jerk, when you
are sitting there alone in your apartment feeling frustrated, rejected, or
abandoned, your love sickness can set in. Why? Your brain is in a state
of love-drug withdrawal. Your dopamine is surging because of your
loss and you are just like a coke addict writhing on a bed, craving. Not
sleeping or eating right messes up your brain chemistry even further.
This explains why you may feel driven to try to get your Beloved back,
sending him sixteen text messages, phoning his new girlfriend, or almost
turning stalkerish.

But as your dopamine levels settle back down, symptoms of depression and despair can take over. You are sitting in emotional traffic, held
back by old fears, sadness, and other feelings based on limiting beliefs
and negative self-talk that no longer serve you. This inner programming
can be floating just under the surface of your mind like secrets you keep
from yourself. For example, one love student wrote after her hottie
melted into the air:

I never realized it, but deep down I believe that I am a truly damaged
unlovable person. In some secret compartment of my heart I feel love is
impossible for me.

At this point your natural instinct is to run back to known territory, even if it is to stay in your ratty bathrobe eating Ben & Jerry's, bury yourself in work, or to go back to an empty, painful relationship. It's perfectly okay to feel that emotional pull and to even take a little time to hole out and regroup. (But it is definitely not okay to go back to a bad-deal relationship!)

This setback will pass. It always does. But meanwhile, I know, it hurts. Let's take a look at why and all the different ways you can bounce back so that you are even stronger than before.

Breaking Up Hurts—For Real

In studies of life's most stressful events, being divorced is the number two top life stressor, following right behind number one, being widowed. Both can plunge you into severe depression and health problems. If you fall into either of these categories, you absolutely need to take care of yourself and do all the activities we discuss.

Women who hadn't gotten over a relationship by sixteen weeks after the breakup had decreased activity in brain regions associated with emotion, motivation, and attention. This is a physical change in the brain. That's why it is so hard to concentrate on anything—so hard to get up and go. *Do not let yourself go for several months' time without taking steps to get over your loss.*

Researchers at UCLA have pinpointed the part of the brain that registers the pain of a breakup. Being rejected activates one of the same areas of the brain as physical pain! In the study, the more ignored the people felt, the more activity they had in the anterior cingulate, which also registers physical distress. Your pain is physiological.

Other researchers at the Johns Hopkins University School of Medicine have found that a breakup can create physical heart pain and shortness of breath. They call it broken heart syndrome (BHS) and, of course, it affects more women than men. Emotional stress or rage can actually precipitate a heart attack, so if you experience the symptoms of

BHS—physical heart pain and shortness of breath—you need to get it checked out by a medical professional.

Getting Over the Heartbreak

Here is the good news: There are definite, clinically proven methods to beat the blues!

SHARING

Talking about your negative feelings has been shown to lessen the activity in the pain-feeling part of the brain, and being with close friends causes the brain to release natural opioids, which are like the painkillers found in opium. So make a beeline for your master Love Mentor and Team Love members and talk it out!

MEDITATION AND RELAXATION

Johns Hopkins researchers recommend practicing relaxation techniques to get rid of heartache. These include meditation, deep breathing, or journaling out your feelings. Later on in the chapter we will explore more spiritually based meditative approaches.

SLEEP

Sleep is very important in helping to elevate mood. When you're depressed, however, sleep may be hard to come by. This is another reason to consider starting a regular relaxation or meditation program—these have been shown to help people sleep better. You can also try a warm bath with lavender oil and/or cutting off stimulating activities like texting, Facebooking, checking e-mail, watching TV, or surfing the Web a few hours before bedtime.

EXERCISE

Exercise releases opioids, those all-natural painkillers. Hitting the gym regularly can help you feel good about yourself. To start, just try ten minutes of walking, stretching, or any kind of physical exercise and see what happens. Those ten minutes can carry you forward in every way!

IMAGINARY CONVERSATIONS WITH YOUR EX

People who have imaginary conversations with their partners that help them to say good-bye have more relief from grief than those who don't. Later you will have an exercise designed to help you complete a healing imaginary conversation.

Here is one that Julia, the diminutive dentist, had with her very narcissistic ex:

> *You are so classically narcissistic! You only think of yourself. You sucked me in at first with all this generosity, but once you had me, you only took, took, took. And you were the one who abandoned the relationship, even though I bent over backward for you, you jerk! You withdrew slowly from me to the point where there was nothing left. You stonewalling jerk!! Even though you were the one withdrawing, you provoked me into ending it by actually going on Match and chatting online in the same room as me— how humiliating! And now I hear you are happy. It makes me so upset! You never deserved me and I hope in your next relationships you'll get exactly what you dealt out—a lot of b.s. in a charming voice. You wasted my time and my life these past 2 years. I fell for it, I didn't self-protect, I was too anxious to be in a relationship and I ignored the signs. I wanted someone else to do the hard work for me. Well, I have learned that I have to do it. I will watch out for myself. I will speak up for myself!*

Airing these pent-up issues and feelings helped Julia let go and move forward. Similarly, allowing yourself to process your own thoughts and feelings, no matter how painful they are, will allow you to move far beyond them and the guy who triggered it all. It's part of the grand pattern that governs all change: *the dance of two steps forward, one step back.*

Two Steps Forward, One Step Back

As we discussed in Chapter 8, we are wired genetically to zigzag up and down on the path of growth. This process occurs not only in our minds, but also in the trajectory of interpersonal healing. Think of a young toddler at a windy beach. She dashes into the dancing waves, only to get frightened and run back crying to her mom. The mom reassures her and walks her back, showing her how to play in the water. This is how we safely learn about the world. Throughout our lifetimes we continue growing through this dynamic, moving forward and then turning to others for mentoring and the anchoring of safety and love.

Just as in other areas of life, there are no straight lines when we are climbing the mountain of finding love. As we press upward, our heavy old baggage of fear sometimes pulls us back down. Upset, we don't really know the best way to proceed. So we touch base with a "hiking guide"— a master Love Mentor—who teaches us and encourages us to climb higher.

You take two steps forward when you move out of a relationship that is not working and begin to date with a clear intention to find the One. The inevitable forward-backward growth pattern means that these courageous steps will lead to fears, self-doubt, and other feelings based on negative beliefs and, most profoundly, identities that don't serve the new experience. This is your one step back. Your old identities act as inner saboteurs and bring up the garbage stored in the basement of your mind, giving rise to self-talk like: *I am a damaged, unlovable person. I am an invisible woman. I'm a whale.*

When you suffer through a breakup, these beliefs about yourself may threaten to take you over. You might want to reestablish an old destructive relationship or hide out as a Hermit, if only to silence the inner saboteurs. But the paradox is that in order to be free of these old identities, you have to welcome them. Expect the garbage. Accept and sit with painful ideas and uncomfortable feelings so that you can then let them go.

The best way to do this is to turn to one or more loving maternal figures to soothe and guide you—your master Love Mentor or Team Love group. In these safe havens you can let out your pain, sadness, grief, anger, and fear. You can listen to your own thought process as you talk out loud and find the hopelessness and other garbage thinking that needs to surface. As loving others listen, you can identify and reflect on your negative beliefs and painful identities. And the bonus is, after you let it all out, you also feel much better. The research I mentioned earlier supports this suggestion; turning to your Love Mentors will release opioids that reduce your pain and help deactivate the pain center of your brain.

Now you'll be able to take in encouragement, prizing, and coaching from your loving mentors. This fuel helps you think differently about yourself and act in new ways that lead to success. Loving words help co-create a healthier identity that is in line with your Diamond Self. A new, stronger you is at the end of this whole bloody process.

Breakups and setbacks are par for the course. So welcome them, and make a beeline for your Love Mentors. Open up with them, unearth your secret saboteur thinking, and you will be able to step away from it to create what you want and be more of your Diamond Self. You can then do the Five-Minute Manifestation Miracle exercise from Chapter 8 and create a vision of the brand new future you are living into.

Here is an example of the forward-backward dance in action. Carol, a musician who was quite shy offstage, took her two steps forward by getting herself a master Love Mentor, Susan, a neighbor in her building who was an amateur matchmaker. Carol took Susan out to lunch and spent a lot of time with her. But when Susan actually introduced Carol to a dream guy, a gorgeous Italian writer, Carol got the jitters and clammed up on the first date. Afterward she consoled herself by saying "two steps forward, one step back" over and over like a mantra. She called Susan the next day and spent an hour on the phone, talking about what a "f*-up she felt like." Susan laughed about it, which helped Carol to calm down. Susan told her to call the guy and invite him to her next concert so that he could see Sexy Divine Love Diva, her Diamond Self. Carol followed through, Mr. Dreamy Writer came, and later she was able to go out to coffee and focus her attention outwardly on him instead of nervously on herself. After this she was able to date the guy comfortably.

During the Love in 90 Days course the students write themselves letters of encouragement to be read when they are feeling bad and stranded in one-step-back land. They also share them with their coaches or Team Love group. Here is one:

> Dear Prevailing Angel of the Light Iris,
> I know you feel like crap right now but not to worry my dear, it will pass AND it means things are shaking up which means you are no longer stuck. CONGRATULATIONS! That's huge. Please know you are not alone on this leg of the journey. When you need help, ask and it will be there for you, take the chance, believe it. You have surrounded yourself with loving, capable souls like yourself.
>
> Be a good friend to you. You would never let someone else down. Be as trustworthy and kind to yourself. It'll all be worth it, I guarantee that statement. You at 75 thanks you. You at 50 thanks you. You at 45 can't thank you enough. Your grandchildren thank you. You have freed yourself and infinite possibilities await and abound. Feeling bad is good. It's temporary, it means you can still feel. I'll be here for you cheering you on, kicking you in the butt lovingly so you know someone is watching and someone cares enough to watch closely. You rock. You go girl. You're my hero.

Iris read this letter aloud to her coach, who leaped up and applauded her. If you don't have a master Love Mentor/professional coach or Team

Love, get one or both. It's not too late. Now that you are down you may find that your need fuels you to find strong loving support. Giving yourself the gift of loving mentorship would be another huge step forward in your life. If you can't find a great person or a team of friends to work with informally, I have a team of awesome fairy-godmother Love Mentor® coaches handpicked and trained by me. You can go to www .Lovein90Days.com/dating-coach/ and have a complimentary session.

Revenge Not Taken

It is a natural reaction to want to hurt the person who hurts you. This tendency comes from the cerebellum, the primitive part of the brain, which is wired for fight or flight. Love and hate are two sides of the same coin. A few of the most passionately in-love couples I've treated have actually come close to killing each other.

There is a myth in this culture that revenge gives you relief from your upset, that it will make you feel better and help you get over the relationship. But this unforgiving knee-jerk reaction can really backfire on you. A lack of forgiveness leads to:

- more stress
- health problems, including heart disease and cancer
- negative changes in blood pressure, muscle tension, and immune response

Why does revenge backfire? Because focusing over and over again on your ex and obsessing about your wounds can only lead to more obsessing and more raging.

You get more of whatever you put your attention on.

A vengeful lack of forgiveness leads to less personal awareness and growth for you. It always takes two to fox trot; if you focus only on what the other person did wrong, you won't ever learn what you did wrong—and that means you are likely to do it again. Lack of awareness is the deadly infrastructure of the Deadly Dating Patterns.

If you are deeply hurt and raging, don't injure yourself and squander your energy by seeking revenge. Give yourself peace and a new beginning by working on forgiveness.

- *Analyze your own bottom-line thinking about how he hurt or damaged you.* You may think, *He ruined my life. I can never trust again.* Ask yourself, Is this really true? Another person can act horrifically, but you are the one who has control over your own thoughts and reactions.

Julia, who had the imaginary conversation earlier, realized that after her breakup she believed that her ex had taken away any opportunity for her to bear children. When she asked herself, Is this really true? she realized that she had been the one who had stalled the conversation when he asked her about having a baby.

- *Ask yourself how you contributed to the problems.* How did you set up the situation in ways you acted or did not act? You will feel like less of a victim if you see your own hand in what happened. Coldness or subtle rejection can be just as cutting as overt verbal attacks.

Bree had a relationship with a cold and distant guy. Nonetheless, she wrote the following about her part in the breakup:

> *I brought expectations to the relationship to fulfill everything I hadn't received up to this point from my family and life, and placed those expectations on you, actually wanting and expecting you to fulfill them all. How would anyone be capable of such a Herculean task? I am very sorry for putting you on that impossible pedestal and then asking to be served by you. I also take responsibility for not loving you for who you really are. Is there anything more horrible than this? I kept looking to the*

*ideal instead of seeing and appreciating the real you. I am sorry for that.
I wanted to see the knight in shining armor, instead of Brian. I wanted
to wipe away anything I considered to be a flaw. I grew up criticizing
and judging myself, always wanting to be the ideal me right now. I was
supposed to be the perfect student, perfect daughter and do good for
others. Always looking at the ideal you, I couldn't then love the real you,
because I couldn't love the real me. All this doesn't excuse my behavior
and now I am sorry.*

- *Use the loss or crisis to become a better person.* If you are feeling angry,
channel it into working on yourself. Get a facial or work on a new
wardrobe. Exercise to youthify and tone your body. Initially thinking about how sorry he will be when he sees how fantastic you have
become can be fuel for your rebirth! Get yourself a dynamite master Love Mentor, learn to meditate, go to a 12-step program, start
counseling, or pray more. Turn the painful relationship into a gift of
transformation for yourself. Julia describes how much better she felt
when she turned to God instead of pursuing an act of revenge on
her ex:

*I asked God to bless me and I started to cry. I decided right then as a
Christian, I am using my faith to help lead my actions and moving closer
to the fellowship in my church. And then life came out in 3D for me.*

Spirituality: The Ultimate First Aid for Heartbreak

Just as Julia's quote shows, turning to God, a spiritual practice, or a
Higher Power can be the ultimate first aid for heartache. Spiritual practices can provide stress relief, peacefulness, and a sense of connectedness and love. They help soothe the speed-like craving that the love
chemical dopamine creates. When you connect to a Higher Power, no
matter how you understand it, you don't have to go the distance alone

and make healing happen by sheer will. Which is next to impossible. Instead, relief is available to you when you turn to Something Greater than yourself. Simply being **willing** to try such an approach gives you a clearinghouse for your resentments, pain, and upset; a balm for your spirit; and a renewed faith in life and love. Over time you develop a sense that the universe is benevolent and will provide what you really need.

Usually our attention is so focused on getting our to-do lists done, on acquiring and taking care of our possessions, and on our achievements or lack of them that most of us, if we stopped for a few moments, would feel empty and at a loss. Heartbreak makes us stop and truly feel the emptiness that comes from disconnection and separateness from the present moment. The profound aloneness. But the excruciating pain can bring about an opening to the spiritual dimension and the kind of awakening that has alleviated suffering for thousands of years.

Maybe the idea of "God" turns you off. You may think of yourself as an agnostic, atheist, or rationalist. If so, the only thing I want you to consider is that there seems to be much more going on here than what our rational minds can comprehend. Maybe you have heard certain music that sent you to another dimension of bliss. Or you have magical experiences with wildlife, the ocean, the mountains, or other places in nature that bring you soaring spiritual feelings. Or you have noticed synchronicities: you get a gut feeling that a particular event, like bumping into an old best friend, is going to happen, and there she is right in the middle of the street in a bustling city. These experiences suggest that there are many things happening that are beyond our awareness and understanding. And just maybe a power or force underlies all there is.

There are tons of benefits from spiritual practice designed to connect us to a Higher Power. Studies show that prayer and meditation can and do heal. Even when prayer takes place at a distance from a sick person, and those who are praying do not know those they are helping. Yet, research shows that there is a positive and healing physical effect. Thousands of other studies reveal that meditation strengthens the immune system and helps prevent PMS, heart disease and chronic pain.

Meditation also lowers stress, anxiety, fear, and blood pressure while increasing feelings of being in the present and in a state of connection, compassion, and serenity.

On a physical level, a spiritual practice like meditation activates the parasympathetic nervous system (PNS), which controls life-giving things like breathing, digestion, and your cardiovascular and immune systems. When you stimulate the PNS, you spread calm through your brain and your body. Brain researchers have found that meditation:

- Increases gray matter in certain areas of the brain.
- Reduces the brain shrinking effect of aging in the prefrontal lobe.
- Increases activation of the left frontal lobes, which reduces depression and lifts your mood.

"At the end of the day, I can end up just totally wacky, because I've made mountains out of molehills. With meditation, I can keep them as molehills."—*Ringo Starr*

Whether through meditation, prayer, music, or nature, please be willing to open yourself to a Higher Power or Something Greater than yourself. It could be life, the universe, spirit, light, angels, power animals, or love itself. It also could be the 12 steps of your recovery program. When you connect to Something Greater, no matter how you understand it, you don't have to be alone, struggling with your heartbreak with all its painful and deflating images, flashbacks, thoughts and feelings. Over time you will develop a sense that the universe has your back and trust that it will provide support for you, even when things seem to be shockingly negative or your life is falling apart.

This is the ultimate healing path that allows you to be PRESENT and able to experience what is really happening without negative or fearful stories about the past in your head. Chances are you are not even interacting with the one who broke your heart for many hours, days or months. **Which means the painful interactions are not happening**

now. So be here now. Don't get stuck in the Disappointing Self's swamp of negativity and suffering.

FREEING YOURSELF FROM SUFFERING

Often our attention is so focused on being right in the conflicts with our ex, on "knowing" what is best for ourselves and him and "knowing" whether some event or situation is good or bad. Whether we admit it or not we often pretend to ourselves that we run the universe—our own little universe of ourselves and loved ones. Or we pretend that we know how it SHOULD be run. Especially when it comes to men, i.e., thinking, *He should have worked it out with me. He should have not disappeared on me, etc. etc.*

I call this Playing God. And when you play God, you create suffering for yourself. Because you have no trust that the falling apart of one relationship may be the springboard of a larger plan for good, a plan that is beyond your comprehension right now.

Why not stop your struggling and float on downstream? Why not surrender to Something Greater? Why not imagine it all in the hands of a benevolent Force or God(dess)? Instead of your own hands. Or your ex's. Just for this hour. Just for today.

Invite your HP to infuse you and your life with divine love, healing, and inspiration. This invitation may involve prayer, reading for spiritual inspiration, studying Kabbalah, the Bible or other scriptures, practicing meditation, or watching YouTube videos with spiritual masters, like Mooji, Eckhart Tolle, or Byron Katie, yoga, tai chi, chi gong or yogic breathing. Try renewing a religious practice you learned in childhood. Or you can seek out a new church, synagogue, or fellowship that feels soothing. Make sure you use a living spiritual practice instead of rote prayer. For those with drinking, codependency, drugging, or food issues I also recommend twelve-step programs such as Alcoholics Anonymous, Al-Anon, Overeaters Anonymous, and the like. The meetings are oases of love and spiritual connection and set you up for support and ultimately serenity no matter what you've experienced or are still going through.

The "Divine Has Your Back" Exercise for Healing Heartbreak

- Take a minute and imagine that there is a loving and good Higher Power or Divine Consciousness that is working seen and unseen throughout your life. Even if you do not believe it. And if you do believe in God, try to get a sense of Him or Her that is fresh, new, and in the moment. Go on, close your eyes now. Get a feeling of Divine Presence. Get a Divine Image. Hear a Voice or a sound or some music in your imagination.

- Now imagine that this loving Divine Force has orchestrated all your misfortunes as lessons for you, as events that you can gain wisdom and growth from.

- And finally imagine that the Divine Force has led you to a new happiness and a love relationship with someone who has all the good qualities of your ex, but so much more going for him. I will call this new guy your Better STUD! Whereas your ex was narcissistic, your Better STUD is attentive and compassionate. Whereas your ex was cheating, your Better STUD is extremely loyal and devoted. Yes, keep going with this. Get a picture in your mind of the new higher reality your Higher Power is plotting and planning to help you create!

- Imagine a scene with the two of you in a marvelous connection, in a staggeringly beautiful location, with all the lovely sights, sounds and feelings of the bliss of that moment.

OK, great job!

Here's what's going to happen: Anchored in your new Spiritual connection you will become able to receive intuitive hunches or messages that help you and, in turn, the whole situation you are in. Usually these new inspired solutions offer both you and everyone concerned a way to get your needs met that did not seem possible before. This is the Spiritual path. It connects you to your own Higher Power and takes you out of the role of being separate and alone in the world. It saves you from all the responsibility and stress of figuring out what is good or bad, and what you and everyone else should do to make it all work according to your own self-limiting plan. Opening to the Spiritual path takes you to present-time connection and acceptance, to serenity, peace and happiness. Which, in turn, takes you to true love that is surprisingly wonderful in ways you never even expected or planned.

So use your heartbreak as fuel to invite the Divine to connect to you right now—and you need to do it every day hereafter.

When you feel that bond on a regular basis—preferably always—you will experience yourself as a "fragment of the divine" and will be buffered from the pains of lost love.

Next, I offer you the gift of a simple portal to healing peace and presence through nature called the Being in the Moment Meditation. I would like you to read the instructions, then put down this book, go out and do the exercise until you feel shifted into a lighter place.

The Being in the Moment Meditation

The being-in-the-moment exercise is one practice that will lead you in this soothing direction. It is an outwardly focused meditation where you put your awareness on an object in the present moment, truly seeing it as it is, in all its glory. Being-in-the-moment is an amazing salve for emotional pain. The practice is easiest to do somewhere in nature: a park, an undeveloped field or forest near your home, a lake or beach area. If you are in the city, use trees, plants, flowers, birds, squirrels, water flowing in a fountain, or clouds-and-sky. For fifteen minutes each day, take a being-in-the-moment walk. It's best to create a time slot for the exercise outside of your daily routine. But you can also do it whenever you are outside, going to work or walking home. Beauty is everywhere.

Use your full attention. Initially put your attention on something you don't usually notice, like blades of grass or a squirrel. Study the object. Take it in with your senses. If thoughts or feelings come, accept them and then bring your mind gently back to the object before you. Appreciate and find the beauty in the object, even if it is just a patch of grass. As it says in an ancient Sanskrit manuscript, "Look lovingly on some object. Do not go on to another object. Here in the middle of this object lies the blessing."

Once you get a feeling of oneness with the object, walk on slowly and choose another. Gradually, you will emerge from the auto-hypnotic trance that most of us are in all the time that focuses on the past or worries about the future. Breaking that trance means you can come into the present. You can then reconnect with God, stillness, or All-that-is. When that happens, you'll realize that you're never alone. As Sri Daya Mata says in *Enter the Quiet Heart,*

> Realize that we are not alone,
> That we never have been
> And never will be alone.

Miracles small and large can happen to you when you are in the present. This is especially true when you are in the great balm of nature, where, as Emerson puts it, "a wild delight runs through the [wo]man in spite of real sorrows." Allowing yourself to be present with an arching oak tree, the caressing wind, or a shiny tiny hummingbird can help you release your sadness and anger so that it passes through your heart easily and effortlessly. After your feelings pass, you may feel more detached from negative thoughts about your pain, ex, or breakup. You can pass through the dark nightmare of pain into a new light of peace and even gratitude.

Taking Action

Okay, so you've processed your hurt feelings, done some spiritual exercises or prayer, and worked on forgiveness. All good Inner Work. Next comes the Outer Work.

First, if you are in an active state of love sickness and withdrawal from your ex, you need to take action immediately. Avoid any people, places, or things that remind you of him. Do not text, e-mail, phone, or contact him in any way. If he contacts you, do not respond. If you have even the slightest contact with anything to do with him, it will fire up the love-addiction process and make you want him more, and that will make you hurt more. Ask your girlfriends and Love Mentors to help you avoid slipping into dangerous waters by reminding you of all the trouble and pain this guy brings with him. Also, any 12-step recovery group can help provide the steps and slogans that can be adapted to help you stay away from your "drug": contact with your ex. A number of my students have successfully used the 12-step daily meetings, groups, and philosophy to help them detox and successfully withdraw from addiction to a man.

The most powerful way to hasten this healing process and take the two steps forward is to get out there and work your Dating Program of Three. This will take your attention off your ex and the past much more quickly. Even if it is soon after your loss, jump in. You don't need to worry about getting entangled in a rebound relationship that is likely to fail, because you will be dating three guys. New research shows that people who actually marry on the rebound are no more likely to fail than those who wait. So go for it.

Take other actions that will offset the messed-up brain chemistry of love withdrawal. Distract yourself from thoughts of him by taking on new challenges at work or going on a trip. Take that Improv or tai chi class you have been dying to enroll in. Exercise while listening to your favorite music (not love songs!).

Finally, if none of this works and you are not sleeping or eating properly, are constantly obsessing about him and what happened, are anxious, raging, in despair, and unable to pick yourself up and get going, consider going into therapy or taking an antidepressant, especially if you have thoughts of suicide or hurting someone. Both psychotherapy and antidepressant drugs can help you out of that dark place. Ask your master Love Mentor, Team Love, friends, family members, minister, or doctor for referrals to a talented psychiatrist or therapist in your area. In the United States you can also go to the American Psychological Association online at http://locator.apa.org or call them at 1-800-964-2000 to find a psychologist. Once you get three names, have a consultation visit with at least two of them before you choose one. In this way you will get help from a talented mental health professional who is a good fit for you. As your depression lifts you will gain deeper insight into your dynamics and a clearer vision of what you want to create in your life.

In sum, you can use this whole heartbreaking experience as a vehicle to make things better—much better. You can connect with God, find new peace, gain insight into yourself, and find new closeness with your love support team. And, you will move on to better men.

✎ First Aid for Heartache: Exercises _____

Choose from among the following suggestions, according to your own intuition.

Total Time for Completing All of Them: 35 Minutes

EXERCISE 1: *IMAGINARY CONVERSATION WITH AN EX*

Have an imaginary conversation with an ex who still carries a negative emotional charge. Set up a pillow as "him" in one chair while you sit in another and talk to him. Express fully whatever you are feeling. Talk about your anger, feelings of betrayal, how he let you down or disappointed you, and what you wished he would have done. Talk about any insights about yourself that come to mind or what you wished you would have done.

Add anything else that comes to mind. End by saying good-bye.
If this is too difficult, do the whole process as a journaling exercise.

EXERCISE 2: WORK YOUR ONE STEP BACK—DISCOVER SECRET NEGATIVE BELIEFS ABOUT YOURSELF

Make two columns in your journal. At the top of the left one, write *What Happened*. At the top of the right one, write *This means that I am*. In the first column describe negative events that happened. Just write the facts, not any judgments about the facts: e.g., *Joe slept with Rosie*. For each event, write in the right-hand column what you think the event means about you. For instance, you might put down: *I cannot trust my judgment. I always pick players.*

Continue doing this until there are no more facts or conclusions left. Take each conclusion and ask yourself, Is this really true about me? Remember that nothing is always true!

EXERCISE 3: WRITE AN ENCOURAGEMENT LETTER TO YOURSELF

Write a letter to yourself that is meant to be read when you are experiencing the one step back and are feeling hopeless or low. Encourage yourself to feel the painful, angry, sad, or scary feelings and to make the right moves anyway. Give yourself the big zigzag picture of growth.

EXERCISE 4: WORK ON FORGIVENESS

For any ex you are angry with, take a courageous look at what you did to create the situation. Imagine that all the complaints this person might have about you are really true. Try them on for size. They probably have at least a sliver of truth in them. What did you do or not do to set up the relationship to fail? Were you not clear in asking for what you needed or wanted? Were you subtly rejecting? Negative and judgmental? Journal about all this. What did you learn from the person? What did you gain? Your freedom? Your ability to see what you really want? An understanding of the importance of speaking up for yourself? What positives did you notice in yourself in handling the relationship? What was the hidden gift for you in the whole experience?

EXERCISE 5: *SPIRITUAL PRACTICE*

Whether you are experiencing heartbreak or not, I would like you to commit to a daily spiritual practice at least until the end of the Love in 90 Days Program. This means praying, meditating, or perhaps doing the being-in-the-moment exercise for as little as ten minutes a day. The goal is to make a connection with all that is around you, whether you call that God, Nature, or your Higher Power as you experience her, him, or it. This will help you navigate the social jungle as a solid person who radiates connection and selfhood, not arrogance, iciness, fear, or disconnection. A spiritual connection is the perfect setting for your Diamond Self.

Write down what your daily spiritual program will be for the next few weeks. If you miss a day, do a double session the next time. In two weeks the world will look brighter—and so will you.

EXERCISE 6: *HEART AFFIRMATION*

When the emptiness, sadness, and fear are very strong, you can play the role of the healing Love Mentor with yourself. Use the following two-step technique:

1. Make two loose fists and with your fists gently tap the areas above and below your heart for about a minute. Imagine your pain as black shapes in the heart that are falling down and out of you as you tap.

2. Put your hand over your heart and say this sentence over and over again: *Even though I feel* [whatever you are feeling: *bad, sad, angry, devastated, depressed*] *about* [what happened with your Beloved, e.g., *John cheating on me*], *I deeply accept and love myself.* Do this second part until your feelings shift into a more neutral or positive state. *Note:* This is a useful exercise to do even when you are in an ongoing relationship.

Here's an e-mail I received from a married Love in 90 Days graduate:

Oh, what a wonderful exercise this is. I just did it again now, and it feels good!! I love it and I think that it truly gives hope to the soul, especially when we are on the journey of creating what we want and experience set backs....As I celebrate my 2 month wedding anniversary today, I can tell you that you have helped me to change my life and the trajectory of where I can be since love is leading the way.

 Homework

Choose from among the following suggestions, according to your own intuition:

1. If you are dealing with heartbreak, use the two-steps-forward-one-step-back process:
   a. Connect to a loving, powerful master Love Mentor and use her love and her presence to fill and soothe you. If necessary, call her every day. Ask her to be close to you in whatever way you need and to be the safe haven until you can create the next level of love. Let her envision and dream for you and help push you forward.
   b. Avoid people, places, and things that remind you of your ex. Instead, get yourself out there on a Program of Three. Go online

right now and work it. You have no idea who is waiting to come to you right there in your computer!

2. Fill out your Field Reports on DUDs and STUDs.

3. Discuss your Field Reports on DUDs and STUDs with your master Love Mentor and Team Love.

4. Take yourself out on an extra special date—leave work early and go see that art exhibit you've been missing; go hiking in the park you enjoyed as a child.

5. Get more Beauty, Advice, or Matchmaker Mentors as needed. If the feeling strikes you, splurge and get yourself a very special treat.

6. Keep up the networking and practice using the Diamond Self, Best Friend, Ten-Second Sound-Bite, Complete Focus, Generosity, and Flirting Techniques. But this week make sure to attend some events that will make you laugh. Have the new people you meet set you up with guys.

7. Work two online dating sites/apps using all the search-engine optimization secrets *for at least one-half hour every day (including weekends)*. (Yes, even though you may feel like crap!)

8. Fill out your Love in 90 Days Online Dating Report. Upgrade your photo, tweak your screen name and profile, change sites, or sharpen your focus if needed.

9. Have at least two dates this week. Work your Program of Three! I know it's hard, but you need to suck it up.

Okay, courageous one, as we end this chapter I want to share the restorative and uplifting words of Joseph Campbell:

> *It is by going down into the abyss that we recover the treasures of life. Where you stumble, there lies your treasure.*

Beware of Frenemies

HOW FAMILY AND FRIENDS CAN BE
ROADBLOCKS TO LOVE

It is difficult to say who do you the most mischief: enemies
with the worst intentions or friends with the best.—*Edward
Bulwer-Lytton*

Finding love is a challenge. Unfortunately, relating to family
members and friends can sometimes make it even tougher.
When people in your inner circle become negative, pessimistic,
competitive, jealous, or don't show you appreciation and/or encouragement, it inflames your own doubts and fears. If you are in a new love
relationship, these reactions can come on suddenly, or they may be
familiar and ingrained parts of lifetime relationships that are so subtle
you may not even be fully aware of them. In either case, unsupportive
reactions can pull you back into being hopeless about yourself or about
love and undermine all the work you've been doing. They can stop
you from getting out there and dating, or, in extreme cases, they can
sabotage a budding relationship with a guy who could have been the
One!

Some people call these members of your posse Frenemies. Ask yourself whether any of these descriptions sound familiar:

- A "best friend" who takes an instant dislike to a guy you really like
- A sister or brother who reminds you of your past failures or the DUDs you've fallen for
- A dad who criticizes any guy you bring around
- A mom who clucks about how men would find you more attractive if you only lost those ten pounds
- Your two closest friends who are no-shows at the first dinner party you are hosting with your number one guy

In this chapter I'll show you how to distinguish between friends and Frenemies and give you four steps that will reshape your support system into one that validates your love intention. The exercises and homework at the end of this chapter are designed to help create an inner circle of people who support your Diamond Self and the stand you are taking for love.

Note: Even if you don't have any challenges in this department right now, read over the material and do the exercises. Sometimes you cannot foresee problems that may come up. A number of the most successful students in our Program have been shocked when a trusted member of their innermost circle suddenly reacted like a Frenemy.

Step 1: Uncovering Your Frenemies

I have no trouble with my enemies. But my g*dam friends...they are the ones that keep me walking the floor nights.—*President Warren G. Harding*

FRENEMY TYPE A

We often find ourselves hanging out with close friends and family covering the same old ground, with the same kinds of conversations, over and over again. What's happening here? Basically, we all carry out habitual patterns that we don't really question or examine. Sometimes after spending time with these people, we feel deflated, down, hopeless, or resentful. These reactions are especially common after being with our women friends.

Women tend to seek consensus, and they often calibrate moods and thoughts with one another using something called "sharing troubles" talk: your friend or family member airs a complaint or problem and you feel like you should share a similar one. Guess what? Whatever the level of frustration or lack of fulfillment your friend has in her life, she will tend to bring you down to it. You begin to commiserate about how you are sick and tired of dating, how horrible it is out there in dating land, how the men in (fill in your city's name) won't commit or aren't good enough, and how the good ones are all taken and the rest are jerks and losers. So what? you ask. Repetitive and habitual deflating experiences with Frenemies foster and reinforce your own pessimistic and self-defeating beliefs about love. And whatever you believe you will tend to re-create and reexperience over and over again as a self-fulfilling prophecy.

FRENEMY TYPE B

Needy or narcissistic people who always seem to be in a jam and demand your time, attention, and help are attention vampires. You may feel like a good person, spending hours texting and on the phone with them as they process their latest betrayal, but if you pay careful attention, you'll discover that your needs are really not important to them. This type of relationship runs counter to what you are trying to do right now. You need to fulfill yourself, love yourself, and give yourself what you need. If pulling back and concentrating on yourself sounds too selfish, you need to work on feeling more deserving. Post new copies of your "I need and claim" TTLC affirmations from Chapter 6 somewhere in your closet and read them every day.

FRENEMY TYPE C

Some women cannot tolerate your success in love. Notice who gets picky and puts down every guy you date, sulks or starts fights when you find a STUD and spend less time with her, or expresses serious doubts about a great guy who could be your prince. She may simply say that she does not want to hang out with the three of you because he gets on her nerves. This type of Frenemy can often turn out to be your very best friend.

FRENEMY TYPE D

"Cynics" believe that a good marriage is impossible and let you know it at every turn or even in their blogs. *Philadelphia* magazine writer Jessica Pressler found that her friends included many Cynics, who reacted very coolly to her engagement. Her best friend, Maria, for example, asked if she had seen a *Time* magazine article on couples therapy in which all the couples hated each other. Then Maria posted the conversation she had with Pressler on her blog, ending with "Is the secret to a happy marriage utter and comprehensive denial about how bad it can be?"

Another Pressler Frenemy said, "Oh, I can't hang out with you—you're a boring old married lady."

UNDERSTANDING YOUR FRENEMIES

How can we better understand the underlying motivation of these four types of friends or family members? My work over many years, including significant numbers of interviews with Frenemies, indicates that their behavior is influenced by a potent combination of three factors: negative programming, jealousy, and envy. Negative programming can be overt or subtle. Cynics openly express their own hopelessness and pessimism about love-that-works or a happy marriage, while other Frenemies subtly express their wish for you to remain as the old you, the "you" they are comfortable around. In other words, the "you" with all your bad habits, gloomy beliefs, and rampant self-doubts! With jealousy, your Frenemy wants to possess you and have you to herself for many reasons, including escaping her own loneliness. And, finally, there is envy: she wants what you have—a loving man. All three characteristics are found in your most toxic Frenemies, but one or two of them are common to all. Watch for the presence of these red flags and you'll be on your way to weeding out friends from foes.

FAMILY FRENEMIES

When a parent or family member is negative, uncaring, demanding your attention, living an unfulfilled love life, or sharing pessimistic beliefs about love, the impact on you can be even more powerful. Family members and their relationships are your earliest and most profound role models and teachers.

Let's briefly review some fundamentals of psychodynamic psychotherapy. For over fifty years, clinical research on how we form love attachments, the origin of our deepest fears, and the impact of our parents on our well-being and outlook has pointed to the crucial role of our childhood experiences. John Bowlby, who spent his life studying young children, concluded that parents directly give the first experience of what love is through what he called their "attachment behavior"—and it is that behavior that forms our basic template for how to attach to someone else in an intimate relationship.

Let's focus here on three types of early attachments that have been shown to leave an indelible mark on later relationships.

Parental attachments that are cold and distant create one type of template that we see in certain Deadly Dating Patterns such as the Hermit or Crumbs. If your parents were not consistently nurturing or emotionally available as you were growing up, you can be left with chronic fears of abandonment. The deeply held belief that results is: *No one will ever choose or love me.* The unconscious childish fear is: I will waste away and die. You know you have this pattern when the deepest need you have is to be claimed and to have unconditional love, yet your pattern is to hide out, accept relationships that give you very little, or push caring people away.

A second basic type of attachment results from a parent who is narcissistic, intrusive, or smothering. The resulting inner love model is riddled with fears of engulfment. How does this play out in an adult relationship? We firmly believe that the only way to get love is to disappear as a person in the couple and just respond to the other's needs and wants. In the end, our identity is lost. The I'll Make You Love Me Deadly Dating Pattern illustrates this perfectly. On the other hand, we may be so frightened of engulfment that we shy away from commitment and play out the Grass Is Greener pattern.

Parental attachments that are anxiety ridden or even violent may leave you with deep scars around trust. If a parent was often angry or raging, you may fear being hurt or even killed in an intimate relationship. Bowlby called this annihilation fear. Because of your own anger, you may unconsciously fear hurting a loved one yourself. In relationships, you pick fights or drive people away, or you simply avoid relationships altogether. The Deadly Dating Patterns that result from anxiety-ridden or violent parental attachments include Abuse Recycle or Chase Me.

In cases of sexual and physical abuse, all of these basic fears may play out with severe and long-standing consequences. In these instances, long-term therapy or counseling is a must; research convincingly shows that therapy for survivors can be very effective in improving their love relationships.

Remnants of these family patterns usually continue when you are an adult. We are biologically wired to take in the beliefs of our parents and to model ourselves directly or indirectly on their behavior. No matter what your parents have taught you—perhaps that you can't trust anyone and to go it alone, or that you are too needy, unworthy, unimportant, or slutty—you have internalized their messages. These messages shape how you form and behave in your romantic relationships. You will either follow them or you will rebel against them, proving yourself to be the opposite of what they've said, attempting to form an identity that is not needy or slutty or fill-in-the-blank. Unfortunately, these acts of rebellion all too often leave you back where you started: in a Deadly Dating Pattern that is unfulfilling at best and self-destructive at worst. Either way, negative family programming tends to lock you up in rigid ways of behaving that are contrary to your natural, spontaneous Diamond Self.

Also, your parents' marriage—whether healthy or dysfunctional—or their lack of relationship forms an additional model for you to follow. If you grew up in a family where your parents divorced, argued, were distant, or acted crazy or violent with each other, these experiences shaped your early road maps for intimacy.

Step 2: Journaling About Your Reactions to Friends and Frenemies

Begin to examine the quality of your relationships with your closest friends and family. Journal about their reactions to you after you've shared your excitement about a date, a particular guy, or the experiences you're having on the Love in 90 Days Program. Have their attitudes toward you changed? Are they less encouraging or supportive than before? Are they picky or hostile about the guys you see? Journal about your feelings, reactions, and moods after interacting with each of them. Keep careful notes after each interaction, especially observing whether your best friend, sister, etc., left you feeling inspired or deflated. Be honest with yourself and take responsibility if you were negative, defensive, or hostile to begin with. But if you notice there is a problematic pattern developing or a long-standing habitual way they undermine you, you're going to have to deal with them directly. We'll cover that in Step 3. For now, please continue to observe and journal.

One technique we've taught our clients that has helped them clarify their feelings about difficult family members is writing letters in their journals *that are not sent.* This method will help you identify any ongoing negative programming, including abandonment, abuse, or intrusiveness. It may be present in family members' relationships, in their attitude and treatment of you, or in how they react to your being in a relationship. Here is a Frenemy letter that twenty-nine-year-old Brooke wrote in her journal:

> *Mummy, I have memories where you were so unbelievably hyper-critical about relating to boys and you really affected me. I felt shameful and used if I even kissed someone and that really sucks. I'm thinking about one time in particular when you screamed at me for having a hickey and for falling asleep in the basement. As a result I felt I couldn't talk to you about anything at all. I feel like I had to get severely depressed in order to talk to you about what was going on inside without you judging me. This really affects me. It makes me want to spend weeks without talking to you. What I need from you is for you to not judge me and to look at who I am as good enough.*

Here is a letter written by a forty-something student to her dad that helped her realize how his marriage affected her beliefs about love. This simple but powerful exercise helped to free her from her parent's problematic role modeling.

> *Dear Dad,*
> *I'm still mad at you. You could have loved mom in a dear and true way. Why did you cling to your earlier sweetheart? Why did we as kids know you had loved this past girlfriend? Who cares? Who was she to us? You live with mom and made us with her, but somehow you locked your heart away in the past.*
> *   Did you ever love mom? Were you just being a narcissist and picking mom because she was beautiful, innocent and from a good family? Mom, 15 years younger than you, was ready to love you,*

but you never showed her how to love you. How you liked to be challenged and participate in building things together and being praised. If you'd shown her how to love you, she could have done so.

Would it truly have been such a stretch for you? It couldn't be that hard. You would've needed to let go a little bit each day of the other love, but filled it with something present, new, mom's love. And we could have grown up seeing the love between you two. As it was, we only knew you both loved us children, but we never witnessed the display or words of affection between you two. Dutiful love, that's what we experienced. And it felt empty somehow, like a forgotten room in a house.

Dad, was it worth it? To stay all shut up inside your emotional self? To have us watch your loneliness erupt in weird ways? Dad, didn't you see how it was hurting us? Did you ever see beyond your own needs to show love for mom for us? Did you know it was going to be detrimental to me? That it would fuel my fears about re-creating a dutiful but loveless marriage? An OK state of affairs; good enough to pass your days as companions but little more.

The next step after distinguishing Frenemies from your true friends and journaling your observations is to work on changing the way you relate to them.

Step 3: Turning Frenemies into Friends

As Gandhi put it, you need to "be the change you want to see in the world." In order to turn Frenemies into friends, you need to relate more positively to them and shape their behavior so that it is more validating. If you are unsuccessful in your efforts, you may want to build a boundary around them (more in Step 4).

BREAKING NEGATIVE PATTERNS

First of all, are you yourself constantly complaining and whining about your dating life, so that you are shaping your friends to feed back your stinking thinking? The first order of business is to stop your own repetitive complaining. Break these obnoxious patterns when you are with them and you'll alter the interaction. You may have more wonderfully positive moments together.

Next, when your Frenemies do make pessimistic, negative statements to you, politely ask them to stop. Catch them when they are saying that dating is hopeless, that all men are losers, or that you are going to wind up together sitting on rocking chairs in assisted living. Stop them even when they are making jokes about how bleak your situations are. When they tell you to lighten up, simply say something like, "Our gallows humor about love is getting old. I've decided to try a new tack and to be more positive about my future. I really hope you can support me in that intention." Follow through whenever your friend slips.

A more toxic situation arises when a close friend starts acting jealous or envious when you meet with success in dating. She's the friend who repeatedly puts down a guy who is possibly the One, or who keeps saying, "He's not taking you out on Saturday night—I bet he's with another woman!" She may complain that since you've been on the Love in 90 Days Program she never ever sees you. Or she may intrude on your relationship, tagging along on dates and possibly even coming on to your boyfriend.

Every time one of your friends or family members behaves or talks in an unsupportive way, say, "Please stop." Repeat the speech about your love intention and how you hope they can support it.

Remember the three components of negative programming, jealousy, and envy we described? Be on the lookout for these signs and spring into action calmly and deliberately. Your friends will almost certainly be surprised by your new attitude. They may accuse you of being touchy or defensive. Take a deep breath and, with your Diamond Self in full display, tell them you care about them and hope they will honor your wishes to change your attitudes and actions so that you can have love in your life.

SHAPING PEOPLE TO COME THROUGH FOR YOU

Next, begin shaping your Frenemies' behavior so that they become more optimistic, attentive, supportive, and uplifting. You will feel better—and, after they get the hang of it, they will, too! To accomplish this goal, you will use what I call Positive Shaping Talk: clearly and lovingly ask for exactly what you want and need.

Positive Shaping Talk works best when it comes from what I call Positive Paranoia. Here's what I mean: You know that the people in your posse love you and mean well but don't always know how to show it. Often we do not focus on the love that is truly there for us but are distracted instead by surface interactions. We dwell on what a family member or friend is doing and saying in the moment, which can be quite dim-witted, unloving, or even unconsciously cruel. This puts us in a state of paranoia, where we suspect that the person may not care for us all that much. *Focus instead on how much the person at their core really does love you*, and you will get more of their caring. Refocusing on the love that might not be evident in the moment is Positive Paranoia.

Look on your Frenemies from a place of Positive Paranoia and practice Positive Shaping Talk with them. You will come right out and ask for attention, validation, nurturance, or encouragement for your vision. You can be talking to your distant father and say things like, "*I would love for you to pay attention and show me how much you appreciate* (my singing, my gifts, my creativity, my success)." "*Give me a kiss.*" "*I'm ready for applause for my* (performance, etc.)." One sentence that really works is, "*I'd really love it if you would say (or do)* _____."

Here is Alisha's description of her Positive Shaping Talk experiences:

When I was in Omaha for the holidays a musical incident came up. I played some Christmas songs with my mom. She played piano, I played guitar and the family sang. I was hurt because my family only acknowledged my mom's piano playing, not my guitar playing. So, before I left, I asked a few of my family members to listen to a couple of my latest songs. I said, "It's important to me that you hear what I've been writing and playing. Please listen." Afterward, they were really complimentary.

My brother was in DC visiting me. In the past he's had a tendency to rely on others to pay for things. This time I told him, "I want you to pay for a couple of nice dinners for me. I think that would be a kind, loving gesture on your part. You're in DC for only a few days. I want you to think, 'I'm gonna show my sister how thankful I am for the opportunity to stay with her and explore DC together.'" It worked out really well! We had a wonderful time together. Also, my brother has had a tendency to forward many, many emails to me. Most of them are junk. So, I also told him, "I want you to be more discerning about the emails that you forward to me. Choose one email a week that you think is worth forwarding to me...not 10." He appreciated that I was so straightforward without being bitchy. I've gotten two from him in the past two weeks and they both made me laugh!

Alisha felt more empowered and appreciated after she transformed her family interactions, and this success enabled her to relate more authentically to men. She went from being in the Crumbs Deadly Dating Pattern to asking her dates for what she wanted—and getting much more of it.

Okay, I hear you—now you're saying, "That's all well and good, but that's not my gang. They are a lot tougher; I can do all the Positive Shaping Talk in the world and nothing will change."

First of all, remember that Step 1 is to become the change you want to see in others. Look at the previous letters; these women altered their behavior first and then began shaping others'. Then make a determined and consistent effort at using Positive Paranoia to shape your Frenemies before you decide that your family or close friends won't respond. While you are practicing these skills, try building a bridge to or reconnecting with family members who are distant. If necessary, limit your contact with those who are negative, intrusive, or abusive. Tell your close friends what you really need from them. If you try all these techniques repeatedly over a period of at least a month and your Frenemies continually fail you, it is best to distance yourself from them.

Step 4: Building a Boundary Around Toxic People

When close friends or family members fail to come through for you even though you have acted more upbeat and used Positive Paranoia and Positive Shaping Talk, it is time to put some distance between you. Move to a more cordial relationship where you do not discuss personal matters. If they are too negative or abusive you may temporarily need to break off the relationship so that your energy is freely devoted to creating love.

Note: This is quite different from dropping all your girlfriends whenever you get into a relationship with a guy. It is very important to keep your good friends around you when you are entering the addictive realm of love. They will help keep you sane and support you. You are going to distance yourself only from Frenemies who are stuck in dark, unsupportive places. This can be a temporary thing—maybe just for a few months.

Here is a letter that Patricia, a forty-four-year-old nurse, sent to her best friend, who was ill and being an attention vampire:

> *When you say, "This is killing me," that is an example of manipulation. When I feel manipulated by what you are saying, I feel angry. When you criticize me for what I am doing or how I am handling something, it is not constructive criticism. It is destructive criticism and it tears me down. This feels abusive to me. When you keep pushing and pushing and pushing for an answer and you don't hear me say stop, I feel abused. All of these behaviors have been a destructive dysfunctional dynamic in*

our relationship and they are no longer acceptable to me. This is why I am not talking to you on the phone. I do not want to engage you and these behaviors which trigger me into a rage because I feel attacked and abused. I have had enough. I am not manipulating you, criticizing you, pushing you or threatening you. I am just trying to take care of myself the best way I know how, in a way that feels safe to me.

After Patricia disengaged from this Frenemy she had a lot more energy to devote to herself and her own path of love.

Detaching from Frenemies is especially critical when you are in the beginning of an important relationship with a guy who could be the One. Your Frenemy can easily fan the sparks of your own doubts and fears and help to destroy the budding romance. One clear sign of problems at this juncture is if you suddenly feel like you have to choose between your hottie and your friend.

Tyra, a Love in 90 Days student who was in her thirties, found a great new STUD and faced that situation with Eva, a "best friend" Frenemy and colleague who worked many long hours with her every day. She chose the STUD and simply stopped sharing the details of her love affair with Eva. Things were going great guns for the couple until he decided to have sex with his ex in order to "see if it was over." Even though Tyra was tempted to call her Frenemy and dish about the crisis, she did not. Instead she handled it maturely and used Positive Shaping Talk to deepen her relationship with her new boyfriend. Here is the e-mail she sent me:

Thank you for helping me to create boundaries with Eva. If I had called her for her opinion after he was with his ex, I would have handled it in the wrong way, creating drama with too much emotion, rather than focusing on confronting him with the truth and asking him to make it up to me—to show me a clear choice that he wants a future with me. The conversation turned to creating connection and moving the relationship with him up a notch...I said, "I need to hear you say you love me." And he just got this big smile and came over and hugged me and said "I love you" and tears were streaming down his face. Big tears. And I said "I love you too." I said, "Say it again." And he did.

Gossip is a tear-down thing. I can't tell you how happy and relieved I feel that I haven't ruined the situation and publicized my business by calling any girlfriends to dish and dramatize. I could have created more pain for myself. Healing the situation is much better than drama. What a good lesson!!! The whole experience actually turned out to be a real gift.

So, as hard as it may be, it is best to clear your posse of any Frenemies who do not respond to your Positive Shaping Talk. Putting a boundary around your Frenemies will free up your time and attention and help you build skills that are invaluable in dealing with the men in your love life. You will absolutely need to be skilled in using Positive Paranoia and Positive Shaping Talk when you are in your love relationship! We will return to this topic in Chapter 14.

✎ Beware of Frenemies: Exercises _____

Choose from among the following suggestions, according to your own intuition.

Total Time for Completing All of Them: 30 Minutes

EXERCISE 1: *UNCOVERING FRENEMIES*

With whom do you spend the most time socially? For each person journal about the following:

1. Are they single? Are they in a relationship? If so, do they generally describe it as loving or not?

2. Do you feel good hanging around them? How do you feel right after being with them?
3. Are they supportive of your self-esteem and attractiveness, your Diamond Self?
4. What are their attitudes toward love, men, or relationships in general?
5. What is their outlook on your ability to find real love?
6. How do they react when you are in a relationship?

EXERCISE 2: *LETTERS TO FAMILY FRENEMIES*

In your journal, write letters to any family members with whom you have unfinished business. Write about whatever comes to mind. Feel whatever feelings come up as you write. These letters are not meant for you to send—they serve to uncover some of the experiences, beliefs, and negative programming that you have as an ongoing legacy of your relationship with that person.

EXERCISE 3: *STOP YOUR WHINING*

For three days, take a notebook and make a note of every time you complain to anyone. For the next three days complain to no one. Journal about your experiences as a non-whiner.

EXERCISE 4: *MAKE A LIST OF WHAT YOU NEED FROM FRENEMIES*

For each Frenemy, make a list of what you need from the person. For example, one student wrote:

- *What I need from my dad is some really long hugs, and a lot of attention no matter what I do.*
- *What I need from my dad is encouragement, for him to say I ask very good questions, no matter what my question is.*

- *What I need from my parents is acknowledgment for going down the path of growth by myself without them and for really taking charge of my own life and psyche.*
- *What I need from my parents is not to worry so much about wasting money—not coming from scarcity.*
- *What I need from my friends is that they help me not take things too seriously.*
- *What I need from my boss is for him to reward me with a higher salary.*

♡♡ Homework

Choose from among the following suggestions, according to your own intuition:

1. Practice "being the change you want to see" so that you are more hopeful and upbeat with your Frenemies.
2. Practice using Positive Paranoia and Positive Shaping Talk with family or friends so that they give you more of what you need: attention, validation, nurturance, or encouragement for your vision. Remember, you can say things like, *"Please listen to me." "I would love for you to pay attention and show me how much you appreciate* (my singing, my gifts, my creativity, my success)." *"I could use a hug and a kiss." "I'm ready for applause for my* (performance, etc.)." *"I'd really love it if you would say* (or *do*) _____."
3. Distance yourself from the problematic Frenemies you identified in Exercise 1.
4. Fill out your Field Reports on DUDs and STUDs with an attitude of total appreciation and gratitude.
5. Discuss your Field Reports on DUDs and STUDs with your master Love Mentor and Team Love.
6. Get more Beauty, Advice, or Matchmaker Mentors as needed.
7. Keep up the networking and practice using the Diamond Self, Best Friend, Ten-Second Sound-Bite, Complete Focus, Generosity, and

Flirting Techniques. Have the new people you meet set you up with guys.

8. Work two online dating sites/apps using all the search-engine optimization secrets *for at least one-half hour every day (including weekends)*.

9. Fill out your Love in 90 Days Online Dating Report and make any needed adjustments.

10. Have at least two dates this week. Work your Program of Three!

11. If you are thinking about choosing the One and graduating from the Program of Three, review "Choose the One Only After Months on the Program" and "Follow the Guidelines for Graduating from the Program of Three," which are sections 10 and 11 in Chapter 4. If you feel that your current number one guy is your own true love, ignore the last three assignments, follow the guidelines, and complete your graduation. Big congratulations!

12. Once you have graduated from the Dating Program of Three, continue to focus on developing yourself—do some of the networking and personal growth exercises and homework over the remaining few weeks of the course. Also, focus on shaping your love relationship so that it becomes a deeply satisfying, win-win partnership. Chapter 14 provides a road map for making this precious love last and get better over time. Refer to it often. Use Positive Paranoia and Positive Shaping Talk to help your Beloved fulfill your needs. Come through for your Beloved and fill his deepest desires so that love takes root and grows. Most importantly: Don't forget to have lots of fun together!

Here is Iris's description of positive shaping with her family and the results:

My folks were preparing to go on a cruise for the first time. I asked my sisters if we could have a get together bon voyage and then approached my parents, who did their usual "we don't want to put anyone out" thing.

I was very clear with them: this is supposed to be nice, a party in your honor. We all want to do this. They said they'd love to and we had a lovely time. Instead of being like them, I've started learning about what I truly want and then asking people to give me those things.

We are in the final chapters now. With your loving posse solidly behind you, keep on trucking and practice Proust's advice:

Let us be grateful to people who make us happy;
they are the charming gardeners who make our souls blossom.

13

Love Secrets Just for You

AFRICAN-AMERICANS, SINGLE MOTHERS, COLLEGE-EDUCATED OR SUCCESSFUL WOMEN, OR WOMEN FORTY-FIVE AND OVER

Every situation, properly perceived, becomes an opportunity.
—*Helen Schucman*

Most of you fall into at least one of these categories: You are African-American, a single parent, a college graduate, financially successful, or over forty-five. Each of these categories carries its own realities and concerns and can create unique barriers to forming a love relationship. In this chapter we will focus on one group at a time, looking at how these special issues shape a woman's love path. In each case we will examine your specific challenges and share the secrets by which they can be turned into opportunities. Even if you do not fall into a particular group, read each section anyway. We are all more similar than different and you may be enlightened or inspired by material on the different types of obstacles. As Paul de Rapin said, "Our strength often increases in proportion to the obstacles imposed upon it."

African-American Women

By the time black women reach their child-bearing years, they find that there are fewer *available* African-American men than women. The media has extensively covered the reasons why, including the rate of incarceration for young black men, which increased throughout the 1990s and has continued to climb, and an underground practice called the "down low," where black men who are married or seemingly straight secretly engage in unprotected sex with men, increasing the number of HIV/AIDS cases. Research has also shown that after they leave prison, black men often find it more difficult than white men to find employment, affordable housing, or health care. African-American men have poorer health and live on average 7.1 years less than any other American racial group.

In contrast, African-American women are better educated and more successful than the men. They have higher college and graduate school completion rates and higher incomes. In fact, college-educated black women are now as successful as their white peers. As a result of the differences between black women and men, the media has coined a new term, the "marriage squeeze," to dramatize the challenges of African-American women.

In addition, several research articles from OkCupid and the Facebook app *Are You Interested* show that black women get fewer digital dating responses. We know from experience in our Program that this lack of interest has put a damper on the moods of African-American women looking for love. Recognize, however, that there are still many tens of thousands of great guys looking for great black women right now! And this book will show you how to improve your odds and connect to them.

Because of the pessimism in the press and culture, black women often struggle with a defensive attitude when it comes to dating. Keisha, a very successful African-American artist and student in our Love Mentor® coaching program, says:

*You meet a black guy and you think he probably (a) has been in jail; (b)
needs help financially because he has no job; (c) is struggling with a drug
and alcohol problem; (d) is a player; or, (e) is on the down low. A lot of
African-American men are intimidated by what a woman has accomplished. If you have an opinion, they think you are headstrong and just
want you for a booty call. They all seem to want white women and their
egos are tied to how many white women they've slept with. I just don't see
examples of black love around me.*

Keisha used the techniques in this book that allowed her to date
smarter and put her ahead of the curve. She no longer feels the same
way about the lack of successful black men or happy African-American
marriages because she has learned that there is much more to the story,
as we will see in a moment.

But first, I want to share with you Maya Angelou's stirring and inspiring words:

*You may encounter many defeats, but you must not be defeated. In fact,
it may be necessary to encounter the defeats, so you can know who you
are, what you can rise from, how you can still come out of it.*

And there are such great victories (even though they don't often get
the same amount of media attention). The pluses that have come from
defeats are many, and it is critical to shift your thinking to the up side.
African-American women have profited from the models in the black
community of women as "doers." The support of extended kin in assist-
ing women with family responsibilities and the pressure on black women
to be economically productive and financially independent have led to
increased self-confidence and greater success. There is now a tradition of
black women being as strong as the tree of life—the backbone of a race,
which many scientists believe is the mother race of mankind! According
to the Out of Africa Model, modern man first evolved in Africa and
eventually migrated and replaced those humans who lived in Asia and

Europe (with a small degree of interbreeding). DNA research has validated this theory and has concluded that for the most part we are all descended from one African woman in particular who has been called Mitochondrial Eve. Take ownership and pride in the knowledge that the mother of all mankind may have been black.

Susan Taylor,* the visionary founder of *Essence* magazine, says, "Black women can provide the healing for African-American men, who have emerged from a 250-year legacy of forced labor building the infrastructure of this country. They can offer healing for all that men have given and lost. And they can offer love. Black women can lead the way."

Indeed, black women have blazed the trail for successful relationships. The truth is that there are many good, solid African-American marriages. And there are successful, loving, responsible black men out there. Will Smith does exist. In *Voices of Successful African-American Men*, Lois Merriweather Moore gives rich and detailed interviews of very accomplished black men. Her work is a refreshing and authentic look at real black males that counters mass media stereotypes. And these accomplished men are everywhere. For example, the 100 Black Men of America, Inc., is a national organization with local chapters around the country dedicated to leadership in each one of their communities.

A 2015 Pew Research study showed that 75 percent of recently married black men were married to black women. The reality is that black men who marry black women are the norm. And the percentage was *even higher* for college educated black men and those who earned more than $100,000 per year, according to Howard University researchers.

Surprised, right? Well here's more good news. In a series of studies, economist Elaina Rose found that the more educated you are, the more likely it is that you'll walk down the aisle by age forty when compared with women who have less formal schooling.

Like other urban legends I've tried to dispel in this book, the ones

---

*The author thanks Ms. Taylor for her thoughtful review of this section. Her comments were invaluable.

surrounding black men have been hyped by uncritical media looking to sell magazines and ad time. In the third section of this chapter, I hope to put to rest one of the greatest and false myths of our time: that successful men prefer to marry down.

INTERRACIAL DATING ON THE RISE

In this digital dating age, more black women are opening their dating options to include other races. After the first dating sites started in 1995, interracial marriage increased. From 2000 to 2010, new interracial marriages climbed from about 10 percent to 15 percent. Then, after Tinder launched, the number jumped to around 17 percent. This is because women are often matched with greater numbers of men based on similar interests, goals, and other preferences and without regard to race. And if you are going to date outside your type, per the Dating Program of Three, there are many options open to you, including racially different guys.

For now, know this: *If you are an educated and successful black woman, you have a world of available opportunities with really great and successful men.*

Are they easy to find? No, and that's why I want you working a Dating Program of Three. Don't let your love life become a statistic in the unwed group. Start by affirming the possibility of meeting a great man. Then get beyond any knee-jerk judgment of a single black guy. One study found that marital satisfaction and dissatisfaction among African-Americans depended on the amount of internalized racism of the spouses; that means that negative judgments about black people that you hold in any secret corners of your mind have to go. Remember all those exercises aimed at promoting self-love? Focus your attention on the power of your race, rich heritage, and cultural contributions to humankind. The more you love yourself as a black woman, the sooner you will attract a guy who is more appropriate for you.

As my friend Susan Batson, the world-renowned African-American acting coach who mentored the likes of Nicole Kidman and Sean Combs, says:

> We must recognize that the men's struggle to survive is sometimes even more complicated than ours. Often we don't know how to share this experience with each other, how to love, how to connect. We don't give ourselves love and therefore do not give love to the men.

So how have my black students given themselves more self-love? Keisha, whom we met earlier, started out all gloomy about her chances at finding love. She had weight issues that made her even more pessimistic. But she changed by using daily affirmations like: *I believe I'm more than a booty call. I accept myself at the weight I am. I am the fabulous partner any man would want. I believe that I'm worthy of a full relationship where the man loves, trusts, and adores me.* The affirmations brought Keisha into a much more peaceful and open frame of mind. Following the Love in 90 Days Program, she started smiling and saying hello to people around her. One day she said hi to a good-looking African-American man on a train. He turned out to be a lovely professional guy who started dating her.

Keisha says:

> I'm continuing to learn about the power of women and what it means to be a woman. Absolutely he should be paying for everything I want. Because what he's gonna get in return, you can't put a price on that— someone who loves him and believes in him, has faith in him and will support him. He'll get someone who will open his world and he will be able to access anything he wants.

When asked about the so-called marriage squeeze, Keisha replied:

> A lot of sisters sacrifice themselves for too many things. They won't date white men. I understand cultural and racial allegiance, but are you going to sacrifice your happiness for that? To me it doesn't matter if he

is black, white, or whatever. The number-one goal is to be happy in your
life and for him to make you happy because that's what he wants. Go out
and just see who you like.

Susan Batson adds this advice:

First we need to look at ourselves and ask ourselves what we truly need.
We get so caught up looking outside of ourselves, trying to survive. When
we are focused on love and not just on making it, then we can be our
honest, authentic selves. That's when we can be in an authentic and
whole relationship. Seeing an African-American relationship between a
powerful man and woman creates the hope, the possibility, that you can
emulate. Find or take a photo of a loving couple and put it where you
can see it.

Susan Taylor, who is happily married to noted author and playwright
Khephra Burns, says: "There are good, beautiful African-American men
out there for you."
And I add, "And many others, if you so choose!"

DR. DIANA'S TIPS FOR AFRICAN-AMERICAN WOMEN

- ♦ Use positive self-talk—about your unique heritage, about yourself,
  and about African-American men.
- ♦ Take risks and open yourself to meeting new people.
- ♦ Quickly screen out the few guys who may be on the down low.
  Telltale signs may include:
  - Nonverbal signals, including eye contact, a touch, or a hug that
    has undertones of an intimate connection between your date
    and another man
  - Secretive behavior or lying
  - Clues that "just happen" to be on his computer (e.g., gay Web
    sites)

- Homophobic remarks or defensiveness about his masculinity
- A history that includes a prison sentence
♦ Do not have unprotected sex until your partner is tested for STDs and you feel confident about his fidelity.
♦ Try dating against type and see what truly makes *you* happy.
♦ Practice receiving from guys.
♦ Make it a point to find and hang around good, loving role models who are living out the kind of relationship you want.

Maya Angelou puts it this way: "Ask for what you want and be prepared to get it."

Okay, so you're going to do the Inner Work. But just where are the single Will Smiths? you ask. Some good places to meet them include Match.com, BlackPeopleMeet.com, EliteSingles.com, or a Meetup.com group for African-American professionals. EliteSingles.com claims that two-thirds of their members hold a bachelor's, masters, or Ph.D. degree and they have a special section for black singles. Also, please do a few rounds of speed dating and practice positive self-talk about you and men. And don't forget to look continuously and ask to meet STUDs in your social, work, and alumni network of family and friends.

Single Mothers

You are not alone! According to the 2017 U.S. Census, there are 12 million single parent households and 80% of them are headed by single mothers. Single parents face the daunting challenges of providing financially and being both mother and father to their brood. Studies show that single mothers were more prone to psychological distress and clinical depression than married moms. Ellie, a single mom, sums it up:

Working and picking the kids up from school and taking care of their needs means it's challenging to find any time for myself. Most single mothers are exhausted because they don't create the time to rejuvenate. And it is difficult to date or maintain relationships because our main focus is the children.

Debra, a seasoned single mother, says, "It's a challenge balancing our own needs while making sure our children's needs are not forgotten or not being met."

In order to address these issues, the first order of business is to feel satisfied that one's children are attended to. The key here is to give the children what they need most: doses of undivided time and attention from you. Then you can proceed to take care of yourself relatively guilt free! What I prescribe for my single mothers is that they give each child Special Time once a week. This is time where the child gets to pick an activity to do all alone with you that is not centered on buying anything. During Special Time, your phone is shut off; there is no texting, e-mail, or phoning—no matter what is going on in your work or love life. You are focused on your child, talking together, playing, hugging, loving, and teaching.

Depending on the child's age, the two of you might be playing with toys or games, watching and discussing a special movie or DVD, going to the park or a beach, vegetable or fruit picking, or going out for ice cream or a meal. My daughter is now grown up and we still have pedicure sessions together for our Special Time (the loving now goes both ways).

Once you have the Special Time going with your kids, create Special Time for yourself. As Ellie says:

> *It is important for women who are single to make a commitment for their own happiness. It will ultimately be great for the kids. I truly feel that sacrificing is not helpful for anybody and sets a bad example.*

So give yourself Special Time in which you work your Love in 90 Days Program. Let's go through the steps. First, identify the negative beliefs about being a single mother that tend to sabotage your love life. Some common attitudes are: *I can't do it all. All I want to do is sleep. I feel guilty about leaving the kids. I am not a good mother. No man wants a woman with kids.* Replace each sentence of negative self-talk with affirmations that counter it.

Look, there are great men out there who absolutely love children and appreciate single moms. A survey titled "Single Moms and Dating: What Do Men Think?" listed several reasons why single men might prefer dating a single mother. These included knowing that a mom is more likely to be: strong, responsible, and independent; appreciative of quality rather than quantity of time; and open to a mature relationship.

One of my single mothers with an adolescent at home recently did the Inner Work, followed a Dating Program of Three, and within a few months met a wonderfully loving guy who is now talking marriage.

Ellie tells us, "Your children need to see a refreshed you who is enjoying life. Your children need to see you role model being in a healthy loving relationship."

Of course it is important to explain your dating life to the children in such a way that they do not feel threatened. Debra comments:

> Communication with our children is very important. We need to help them understand that we are human and that it would be normal for us to want to reconnect with a man at some point. But, also that they—our children—will always come first.

Your initial dates can be short-and-sweet coffee meets. You don't have any time to waste and want to sort through the guys quickly. It is important to choose a mature man who can understand that your children come first. If the children are living with you, he needs to be able to relate well to them.

Keep your dating life away from the kids. Studies show that a single mother's dating behavior affects the sexuality of her adolescent children. Children raised by a single parent engage in sexual activity sooner and more frequently. Also, if the kids become emotionally involved with a guy you are seeing who is a fleeting presence, they can be hurt when he leaves. Debra describes one situation like this:

> One man I dated was wonderfully attentive and caring, but the relationship was not meant to become more serious. When we broke up, my eight-year-old son was feeling sad as he had formed some sort of bond with him.

Once you graduate from the Program of Three and start dating one guy exclusively, you can introduce him to your children, but be sure he enters the family system as a positive, prizing, and giving figure. Bringing a man into your family means a certain loss for your children—a loss of the cushy family unit in which they did not have to share you—so make sure that when your boyfriend is around they have engaging and fun activities to do. You want your kids to associate good things with the new man in your life.

If he truly is the One and you wind up marrying, the best way to divide up parenting duties is to have him be more nurturing and you more of the limit-setter and disciplinarian. If you have kids or teens who act out of control at times, it may be tempting for him to step in, confront them, and break out of the nurturing role. Do not allow this—instead have him be neutral with the kids and function behind the scenes as your supportive secret weapon. He can be a sounding board and adviser on how to deal with your children's problems and issues. Of course he still needs to back up any rules you set. This teaming and division of roles will help your child settle down. In my clinical experience, this type of role division should go on for at least five years because it sets your man up as a facilitator at home and prevents him from becoming the hated disciplinarian and enemy of the child. When the new man becomes the stricter one, inevitably the woman feels torn and forced to choose between her husband and her children. Then everyone suffers.

Similarly, if he has kids, you want to join his family as a sweet, understanding presence and avoid falling into the trap of being the judgmental "wicked stepmother." You will rarely, if ever, become their mother. Aim for being a supportive, nurturing presence and if his kids are older, be their friend or older sister. Don't try to replace anyone or move in as a total role model. Be as loving, generous, and kind as possible with his kids, and it will work out better.

One more piece of guidance: When you are becoming a blended family, it can also be helpful to have a few sessions with a family therapist who is experienced in working with stepfamilies. In the United States the American Association for Marriage and Family Therapy in Washington, DC, provides referrals at www.therapistlocator.net. The American Psychological Association, which is also in DC, will direct you to a family psychologist at http://locator.apa.org.

Here is a success story that Ellie shares:

> *My friend was divorced and has two children. She met her boyfriend at her kids' school. He happened to be divorced with two children also. After dating him for about 4–6 weeks she introduced him to her kids. They have kept their parenting pretty separate with their kids, and that seems to work. They got married and the four teenagers all get along. They started therapy fairly immediately on how to integrate the family and had a strong intention to succeed.*
>
> *They are very happy together.*

So there you have it. Create a strong intention to succeed.

DR. DIANA'S TIPS FOR SINGLE MOTHERS

- ♦ Work with your affirmations.
- ♦ Arrange Special Time weekly for each child.
- ♦ Create Special Time for yourself.

- ♦ Team with your ex around the kids. Forget the fighting! The kids' mental health and well-being depend on it, and so do yours.
- ♦ As you date, sort quickly through the men to find mature ones who can relate to your kids.
- ♦ Let your children know they come first.
- ♦ When you find the One, help him join the family as a nurturing figure to the children.

As a single mother you are in a unique position to bring more love, inspiration, and vision to your children. How? Find a wonderful soulmate who helps you and the children grow to your fullest potential. The kids get all the emotional and tangible goodies and the worlds he has to offer, and they can see you happy, teaming, and in love.

College-Educated, Professional, and/or Successful Women

December 14, 2004, is when it all started. On this date the psyches of successful single women were singed with worry when journalist John Schwartz wrote a *New York Times* article titled "Glass Ceiling at Altar as Well as Bedroom." He claimed that "men would rather marry their sec-retaries than their bosses." The following year, Maureen Dowd followed with another *Times* column (and a book, *Are Men Necessary?*), agreeing with Schwartz. The authors' clear thesis: Men prefer to marry down. Since then both online and offline media have continued with this story.

Many of my college-educated, professional, or financially successful students in our Program worry that they are overqualified for love. Some think it best to hide their success when they meet a guy. Others feel like they have to hold on to the one DUD they've got, even though he is not working out, because their chances out there are not good. This is true even for twenty-somethings like Jo, who works in the financial sector. "It's simple; I feel nervous talking about work on a first date."

It is time to address those anxieties and separate myth from fact.

Both Schwartz and Dowd relied on one study to support their claims. Let's scrutinize this study, which was published in the *Journal of Evolution and Human Behavior*. Researchers tested 120 male undergraduates by asking them to rate their attraction to a photo of a woman who was described as a "supervisor," "co-worker," or "assistant." When it came to dating or marriage, these undergraduates indicated that they were more attracted to the "assistants." That's it. From this study of undergraduates, the authors concluded that men prefer nonthreatening women as life partners.

The research has at least four serious flaws. To begin with, this was a study of students at a university, not men who were at an age where they would normally be choosing a mate. Second, there were only 120 subjects, not an especially large sample from which to draw such sweeping conclusions. Third, the "supervisor" was described as someone who has "responsibility for disciplining absence or poor performance on your part, for rewarding reliable or creative performance." These young men were rejecting a woman who had hypothetical control over their careers! They were not rejecting a woman who was simply described as powerful. Finally, the study's design was all in relation to a photo with no real interaction. In conversation, brighter women might easily have an edge in relating to smart men. By all clinical and research accounts (as you'll soon see), intelligence and intelligent conversation play pretty important roles in mate selection! In short, Schwartz and Dowd's premise is built on a house of cards.

There is one other study that does show evidence for more successful men marrying down. In 1993, a researcher at Stanford published a brief report (one page) concluding that men with MBAs tended to marry down, whereas women with MBAs tended to marry up. Of course, these were people with advanced business degrees, which is a very specialized subgroup. These findings have not been reproduced elsewhere and, as we'll soon see, they've been contradicted.

Is the notion that successful men tend to marry down borne out by other research? The answer is a resounding "No." Many studies of mate selection conducted around the world find that the rule of homogamy applies—that is, spouses tend to show similar educational achievements! They also marry partners who are similar in attitudes, religion, and values. In the last thirty years, as women have become better educated, they have tended to marry educated men. This trend has replaced the historical pattern where, because of a lack of educational opportunities, women were more prone to marry the more educated males—that is, to marry up. Today, because people spend so much time in school, they deliberately look for partners in college or graduate school.

In 2003, researchers Blossfeld and Tim, who have studied homogamy for over a decade, found that educational homogamy rates have *increased* over the last century. For women in their forties in the U.S., over half—that is, 51 percent—married a partner with the same degree; only 27 percent married up and 21 percent married down. Education has changed our society, and women have not been hurt by this. In fact, they are the primary benefactors.

Two recent studies conducted in Europe and Australia show that smart men prefer smart women and are happier for it. First, in a study of educational homogamy in marriage in twenty-two European countries, fourteen countries showed a strong tendency toward homogamy, while in seven, the *men* actually married up! Second, the Australian study on 5,000 subjects revealed that men who married educated women are happier than those who partnered with uneducated ones. Furthermore, the author concluded that a man's happiness level grew by 8 percent for each year of his wife's post-high-school education. So a college graduate brought her man 32 percent more happiness than a high school grad. In other words, solid research on marriage conducted around the world shows that the more educated women have become, the more attractive they are to the opposite sex.

A 2017 study shows that the number of women with advanced degrees is now greater than the number of guys at the same educational level. These researchers looked at U.S. census data which showed that the number of men who marry down is decreasing, while the number of men who marry up is increasing. For men in the 1990s, 38 percent married down and only 25 percent married up. In the latest figures (2009–2011), 28 percent married down, while 35 percent married up. It's clear that men of all types are becoming more and more attracted to successful women. Christine Whelan's *Why Smart Men Marry Smart Women* continued to explore this theme. In a Harris Interactive poll she commissioned, 71 percent of high-earning or graduate-educated men said a woman's career or educational success makes her *more* desirable as a wife, 68 percent report that smart women make better mothers, and 90 percent of high-achieving men say they want to marry—or are already married to—a woman who is *as* or *more* intelligent than they are. The men she interviewed said they were looking for an equal companion who could co-create the kind of future they want.

Another finding that Whelan reports is something we all know but with a twist: Beauty plays a key role in the romantic selections men make. But here's the surprise: smarter women actually tend to take better care of their bodies and therefore may be more appealing visually. Being visually appealing or, as researchers term it, having body symmetry, has long been known to be an important component in mating, not just with humans but in the entire animal kingdom. Whelan concludes that smart women have both beauty and brains and are therefore more appealing. Her bottom line is, "Gentlemen prefer brains."

The news is good, ladies: You do not need to worry about your ambition and power destroying your chances for love.

Now, if you are in a career slump or don't have a college degree, you may feel like you have the opposite issue. Iris puts it this way:

> When I'm in between jobs, if it's been busy, I'm glad for the breather and happy to get out and date. But when the "in between" gets longer and longer, I start to think that it makes me less desirable....I feel like men wouldn't want to take me on as I'd be a drain financially.

Note to those of you who have to play catch-up: If you are in a job situation where you are floundering or unhappy, it is never too late to use the information we reviewed to good effect: No matter what your age, consider heading off to school and studying something you love. Doing so will upgrade the kind of men you are meeting and open new avenues of happiness. So get loans, go part time, do whatever it takes. Slow still gets you there.

DR. DIANA'S TIPS FOR SUCCESSFUL AND EDUCATED WOMEN

+ Counter your negative beliefs with positive affirmations based on solid research.
+ Remember to make love a priority.
+ Get more education if you need it.
+ Explore your receptive and beautiful feminine side with men.
+ Let men be helpful.

A final note on issues of success and having babies: With the advent of increased higher education for women has come a delay in the age at which women marry and bear children. But they can still do both—and not necessarily in that order! As we've shown throughout this section, study after study has concluded that education is becoming less of an impediment to both motherhood and marriage.

So file all these positive realities in your mind.

These days you can have success, marriage, and children if you want them *and* be with a loving guy who is a winner.

Age Forty-Five and Over

Dating can be daunting. And when you're forty-five or older, it may seem next to impossible. You might be coming out of a long-term marriage, or emerging from a period where you were consumed with raising children or caring for elderly parents—or perhaps you still are responsible for kids and/or parents. Have your "dating muscles" atrophied? You may feel like you don't have the slightest idea how to go about flirting and meeting the opposite sex, much less handling issues of sexually transmitted diseases. You might feel like your body is showing the wear and tear of all those miles. Disrobing in front of a romantic partner? Definitely not.

Plus, today's dating world doesn't remotely resemble the one you knew. This brings on worries and negative self-talk. How proactive are women in your age group supposed to be? What about HIV? Is online dating reliable, safe, or even right for a boomer-age woman? In this youth-obsessed culture can you really compete with younger women?

Yes, it is a whole new world out there. But it is a *great* world, filled with possibility. We are living longer, healthier lives; there are demographers who claim we should think of middle age as extending all the way to age eighty-five because of the increasing percentage of men and women who are fully functional at that age! And the giddy swirl of romantic passion can be just as strong for those over forty-five as for those under twenty-five.

Much larger studies of baby boomers have validated that they've changed all the rules on dating and sex. Seventy percent of single baby boomers actively date, and 45 percent of men and 38 percent of women between the ages of 40 and 59 have sex once a week. Boomers have also taken to online dating in increasing numbers. Lavalife.com, a dating site known for its younger clientele, reported a 39 percent increase in boomer use from 2003 to 2006; Match.com indicates that the fifty-plus age group is its fastest-growing segment.

Australian neuroscientists recently studied people ranging in age from adolescence to their late seventies and found that the older adults showed "positive changes in the emotional brain." They had better control of their reactions to other people's anger, fear, and other negative emotions, all of which leads to greater contentment and happiness. The scientists concluded that "becoming mellower" with age is a physiological process that can actually be seen in the brain's electrical activity and fMRI pictures.

The maturity that comes with age opens you to more positive

relationships, even with younger men. The media has helped to open up a whole new role model: "the cougar," an older woman who dates or marries a younger guy by focusing on celebrities like Kris Jenner, the matriarch of the Kardashian clan, who is 62, and her love, Corey Gamble, 37, and actress Priyanka Chopra, 36, who is engaged to singer Nick Jonas, 25. Being older and having kids are not death blows to meeting a STUD.

Many women over forty-five have gone out there and had the adventure and excitement of their teenage years all over again. With the wisdom of their years, they've made their lives even better! Anne, a fifty-seven-year-old, describes how she met her new husband, Jay, a recent widower who was a friend of a friend:

> We were on our way to a concert. Jay drove and I sat up front with him. Within fifteen minutes Jay looked me square in the eyes and said, "Who are you and what are you doing in southern Montana?" His look and the tone of his voice seemed as if he had found his long lost love at last, reuniting with her after spending millenniums apart. I felt a kinship, intrigued by our many similar delights. I quickly put aside any biases I had about lawyers and we discovered our similar taste in music, ethnic food, travel, love of getting out in nature, philosophy, open-minded spiritual exploration, and joy in sharing about our families. This meeting and the synchronicities that brought us together surprised both of us. We have been together ever since.

Many women who are over forty-five have created the kind of deeply fulfilling love that offers true friendship along with the chemistry of lovers. Love, of course, is good for us. As we detailed in Chapter 1, research convincingly shows that married people are healthier both emotionally and physically. An active sex life may lead to a longer life, a better immune system, greater heart health, an improved mood, even the ability to prevent certain cancers and ward off pain. Intercourse typically burns around 200 calories, which is equivalent to running on the treadmill for thirty minutes! Plus, it releases endorphins, which elevate mood and lower pain levels.

Older students in our Love Mentor® coaching program often comment that once they really get into dating, they feel more confident, clearer about what they want, and, therefore, more attractive. They are more empowered and more affluent than ever before. The good news is that often, younger women *cannot* compete with over-forty-fives for an older guy's attention. The thirty-somethings are too active and demanding in terms of nightlife and other activities, whereas a boomer man may prefer the seasoned, wise companionship of a woman who has been there and done that.

In other words, you are in a position to pick and choose whom you want to date, whether it is a younger STUD or an older guy. The Love in 90 Days Program works just as well for you as it does for younger women.

In one of my recent love workshops, I had about sixteen single women, including a stunning willowy blonde model in her early twenties and an unadorned, hardworking fifty-five-year-old artist. Who was the star of that group—the one woman who quickly got a Beauty Mentor, a master Love Mentor, ran a Dating Program of Three, and found the One, Ron, a few months later? Hint: It was not the model.

The fifty-five-year-old, Roz, wrote this e-mail to her Team Love mates four months after the workshop:

> *How are all of you beautiful women? I have two hot ones and a third I am making plans to meet. I am on date seven with Bill and Ron. A little about each:*
>
> *Bill is my age, works in the arts, a former singer, songwriter, musician. . . . He adores me. Just hearing my voice brightens his day. He finds me absolutely amazing and can't believe I winked at him online. We've met for dinner, gone horseback riding together, walked along one of my favorite special beaches collecting seashells, gone to his arts exhibit, had lunch at the beach, been to the movies. He's written a poem for me.*
>
> *Ron is a little older. He's very tall, 6'4". He's had many careers, all high level executive positions. We've been to some great restaurants, gone to a play and a jazz concert. He's brought treats for my Pomeranians and*

been very patient when I have had to attend to one. I emailed him when I saw he was in Montauk (Long Island, NY) and a sailor. I am too.

Ford lives the furthest away. He too is a sailor and has a boat that can get him to Montauk in an hour. He's a little younger, retired. Looking for something he can do that helps the world. He's athletic and active and has three kids, 18, 19 and 20. We are setting up date #1.

All of these guys I either winked at or sent the first email from a big online site. I am having fun dressing up, getting my hair, nails and toes done. I feel comfortable and completely at ease to be myself. What a nice change from dating years ago.

By the way, this is the same Roz you met in Chapter 6 who e-mailed saying she was a "dead mouse" who was not getting any second dates when she first started the program. Roz stayed the course. Two months later she e-mailed her Team Love again:

I have been having a blast getting to know Ron better. We've been exclusive since September and loving every minute together. We talk and email 3 or 4 times a day. We laugh a lot and play a lot. Ron gave me the most incredible gift I have ever received, a gorgeous emerald bracelet from Tiffany's. Just opening that blue box was amazing! He also introduced me to ballroom dancing and we have a great time just dancing away in my living room! I've been going every week for a group lesson. Last Saturday there was a big holiday party and it was my first opportunity to dance outside of a lesson. I surprised Ron by taking a private lesson a few days beforehand to perfect more techniques. When the music came up Saturday night and I said "let's dance" he was thrilled!!! I highly recommend dancing as an activity anyone can enjoy.

So, what are you waiting for? Join the party! Here are four key steps.

First you need to youthify. As you can read between the lines in Roz's e-mail, you must be active and healthy in order to enjoy the hunt, and the fruits of your labor. Exercise is the key. Exercise creates happiness, stamina, a youthful body, and is the perfect tonic for getting over a failed relationship. Meditation and other mind/body practices also help reverse the aging process.

For the outer and inner you, start a regular cardio and weight-lifting program with your doctor's permission. Exercising regularly lays the groundwork for health, which is the foundation for a vital sexual life. A comprehensive study of more than 3,000 adults showed that 73 percent ages 57 to 64 and 53 percent of those ages 65 to 74 were sexually active; even more important was the finding that among those who reported good or excellent health, a whopping 81 percent of the men and 51 percent of the women said they had been sexually active in the past year, versus only 47 percent and 26 percent of men and women who had health issues. Around half of both men and women under seventy-five had engaged in oral sex in the previous twelve months. These findings do not surprise me. In my clinical experience many older women find that they are more in touch with what they want in the bedroom and more comfortable asking for it.

Here's how Roz describes a ten-day love-fest in Costa Rica that she spent with Ron, who is sixty.

> We had the best, best time!! We made love three times a day and used about 50 condoms! I have never been so comfortable sexually and discovered that I am now multi-orgasmic. I must have had about 200 orgasms! I am over the moon! Wow, has my life changed.

The second step to a vital life is to give yourself a makeover and a trendy haircut so that you look great and up-to-date in your own eyes. Go shopping and try out those clothes that your friend wears that give her that special sexy oomph.

Third, it is important to counter any of your negative self-talk about no available men, saggy breasts, wrinkles, and all the other garbage thinking with positive affirmations. Anne, whom we met earlier, describes the inner process that ultimately led to her dating better men:

It became obvious to me that I needed to take a good look in the mirror to see why I had a repeated pattern of attracting less than satisfying partners. I began doing some inner house cleaning, no holds barred. I started to be really honest, to move out of self-deception and pretense. I realized that if I wanted a really great guy, I needed to become a really great woman, and a terrific human being. . . . I appreciated and cultivated my better qualities and accepted the flaws. I focused on what was right and uplifting and gave up caring about the more superficial nit-picky things that had nagged at me and made me feel self-conscious. . . .

One day I realized that I was seeing relationship potentials through some unexamined limiting beliefs. I discovered through Byron Katie's course that I held a belief that I couldn't do the work I loved, travel and have my friends, family and sacred time alone if I had a partner. . . . I started discovering other sabotaging beliefs, about relationships, sacrifices, difficulties, shortage of good men available in this age range, my attractiveness (or lack thereof) as a golden girl, etc. When I had cleaned house, I saw exactly what had been preventing my meeting the right-for-me partner. I deliberately created a new belief that I was with a loving partner who was supportive, healthy, and caring. Two weeks later I met Jay.

Anne is now happily married to Jay.

Fourth, no matter what your age, don't be shy—date off- and online. Put the word out in your network that you are looking. Remember, 66 percent of relationships come from a person's network of friends, co-workers, and family. Definitely do not miss out on online dating. Using the Internet is essential because it gives you a sense of the wide variety of singles who are out there right now. Sixteen million singles have used online dating in the U.S., according to the latest independent research. You can partake of this smorgasbord of possibilities right there at your computer. Spend the time and work two sites. In addition to the sites mentioned earlier that have growing numbers of boomer members, there are more specialized sites like BigChurch.com for Christians and JDate.com if you're Jewish.

All the Program of Three rules still apply. Because there are fewer single men, older women have to be more proactive than younger women. It is best to browse the guys and electronically "wink" at or e-mail ones you are interested in right at the get-go. You can then be a bit more passive and let them work at courting you. This particular pattern will really show you who is interested.

If you are going to be sexually active, make sure you use condoms and dental dams. Boomers are often naïve when it comes to the reality of HIV, which can be transmitted through both intercourse and oral sex. The AARP study cited earlier showed that only 39 percent of those who were having regular sex used protection. And the number of AIDS cases in women age fifty and older is growing, because thinner vaginal walls are more susceptible to tears. Remember, safe sex can still be great sex.

DR. DIANA'S TIPS FOR OVER-FORTY-FIVES

- Counter negative self-talk with affirmations about the advantages of being older.
- Get out there and date even if you're just divorced or widowed. It's okay to derive comfort from compassionate guys. Plus, the sooner you get out there, the sooner you move on.
- Consider younger as well as older guys.
- Youthify—make sure you exercise daily.
- Use anger as fuel for your Love in 90 Days Program. Initially thinking about how sorry your ex will be when he sees how fantastic you have become can fuel your rebirth.
- Be more proactive in flirting with men off- and online.
- Once you graduate to having sex, make sure it is safe until he is HIV tested.

I will close this section with advice from Anne:

Be bold. Be discerning. Be interested. Be honest. Be healthy. Be yourself. See beyond chemistry, biases and appearances. Develop strength in those areas you want your partner to be strong in: communication, respect, romance, financial stability, etc. Don't expect perfection. Accept him as is and see the "coupleship" as an opportunity to encourage each other to grow together as ongoing "works-in-progress."

You now have the knowledge and tools for overcoming obstacles regarding your race, parenthood, success, or age and turning them into opportunities for personal growth and the cultivation of love. *If you have jumped ahead to this chapter, go back and start the whole Love in 90 Days Program from the beginning.*

✎ Love Secrets Just for You: Exercises _____

Choose from among the following suggestions, according to your own intuition.

Please note that if none of the material in this chapter seems to apply to you, simply go back and complete any exercises or homework that you need to finish up from previous chapters. Then do the homework below that does apply to you.

Total Time for Completing All of Them: 20 Minutes

EXERCISE 1: *JOURNALING ABOUT YOUR ISSUES*

Reread any sections in this chapter's lessons that pertain to you, and as you do so, make notes in your journal about any thoughts you have, especially negative beliefs and barriers that come up for you.

EXERCISE 2: *YOUR SPECIALIZED AFFIRMATIONS*

Make a list of affirmations that counter your negative self-talk and any other beliefs that came up in doing Exercise 1.

EXERCISE 3: *YOUR SPECIAL-ISSUES TO-DO LIST*

Review the tips in any lesson that pertains to you. Make a to-do list for yourself.

 Homework

Choose from among the following suggestions, according to your own intuition:

1. Start or complete activities in your Special-Issues To-Do List.
2. Continue practicing Positive Paranoia and Positive Shaping Talk with family, friends, and guys you are dating so that they give you more of what you need.
3. Fill out your Field Reports on DUDs and STUDs with an attitude of total appreciation and gratitude.
4. Discuss your Field Reports on DUDs and STUDs with your master Love Mentor and Team Love.
5. Get more Beauty, Advice, or Matchmaker Mentors as needed.
6. Keep up the networking and practice using the Diamond Self, Best Friend, Ten-Second Sound-Bite, Complete Focus, Generosity, and Flirting Techniques. Have the new people you meet set you up with guys.
7. Work two online dating sites/apps using all the search-engine optimization secrets *for at least one-half hour every day (including weekends)*.
8. Fill out your Love in 90 Days Online Dating Report. Upgrade your photo, tweak your screen name and profile, change sites, or sharpen your focus if needed.

9. Have at least two dates this week. Work your Program of Three!

10. If you are thinking about choosing the One and graduating from the Program of Three, review "Choose the One Only After Months on the Program" and "Follow the Guidelines for Graduating from the Program of Three," which are sections 10 and 11 in Chapter 4. If you feel that your current number one guy is your own true love, ignore the last three assignments, follow the guidelines, and complete your graduation. Big congratulations!

11. Once you have graduated from the Dating Program of Three, continue to focus on developing yourself—do some of the networking and personal growth exercises and homework over the remaining two weeks of the course. Also, focus on shaping your love relationship so that it becomes a deeply satisfying, win-win partnership. Chapter 14 provides a road map for making this precious love last and even get better over time. Refer to it often. Use Positive Paranoia and Positive Shaping Talk to help your Beloved fulfill your needs. Come through for your Beloved and fill his deepest desires so that love takes root and grows. Most importantly: Don't forget to have lots of fun together!

Congratulations for making it this far in the program. I cannot tell you how proud I am of you! Your growth in self-understanding and self-care and your search for love is expanding your universe. As Anais Nin eloquently wrote in her *Diary*,

Life shrinks or expands in proportion to one's courage.

14

How Happy Couples Work

THE EIGHT HABITS OF LIVING LOVE

This day I will marry my friend, the one I laugh with, live for, dream with, love.—*Anonymous*

Your Frenemies can carp all they want about bridezillas and not selling out to the wedding industrial complex and how married people are boring. However, what the research really shows is that married people are healthier, wealthier, and happier. Marital happiness contributes far more to personal happiness than anything else, including work and friendship satisfaction. High-fives to you for putting your time and attention into creating a committed, loving relationship.

Unfortunately, chances are you have had few role models of a win-win relationship, the kind that makes you healthier, happier, and wealthier. It may have been hard to envision this kind of relationship for yourself and challenging to learn the skills and habits that couples routinely use to create this happily-ever-after. Until now.

Here's how Dawn describes the problem:

I didn't have any good data on how a relationship could be fulfilling or beautiful. Growing up, I had always seen my parents' relationship as a place of harsh sacrifice and not as a sanctuary. I learned Dr. Diana's Eight Habits and it changed what I thought was possible in love. I created the intention, "I give myself a loving partner who respects and supports my dreams" on December 18th. On the 19th I met a guy online and we are now married. He loves me in ways that seemed impossible before. What a blessing!

In this chapter we look at the Eight Habits of Living Love and learn how to master them. I gave the Habits this name because *love* is an action verb. A soulmate does not just come to you as a perfectly fitting puzzle piece or twin personality. A soulmate is a person who develops and maintains a state of living love in word and deed with you. The Habits are made of the all-important skills underlying that oscillating back-and-forth current of caring. These are the practices that make love work and make love last.

To some extent, most of the Habits of Living Love can be practiced with everyone, including friends, children, family, and the guys you are dating. Practicing these Habits is a lifelong endeavor that truly will allow you to be the change you want to see in your life. The Habits help you conquer fears and develop self-discipline and allow you to know, appreciate, and love yourself. You will have better relationships all around. Most importantly, you will be happier.

Keeping your loving skills sharp will serve you well in many relationships, but most of all they will allow you to create love that is deep and fulfilling. You will be the brightest light you can be, attracting a light of the same magnitude. The Habits will carry you and your Beloved into the flowering of a beautifully shared future. As the Baal Shem Tov says:

> *From every human being there rises a light that reaches straight to heaven, and when two souls that are designed to be together find each other, their streams of light flow together and a single, brighter light goes forth from their united being.*

The Eight Habits of Living Love form the backbone of the growing and lasting love journey, which we will examine next. They provide a model of a healthy relationship, which is grounded in intimacy, appreciation, devotion, respect, and good collaboration. First we will go over the love journey, then the Habits. After each one is presented, I will show you how to build it into your daily life.

Note: If you are in a committed relationship, examine to what extent the light is shining through in these Habits in the relationship as it is right now. Make sure that you are regularly experiencing and practicing most of these Habits with your chosen STUD. Remember, the beginning of a relationship should be a very fulfilling time. If you are still evaluating whether a guy is the One, observe, for example, if the current contender is truly a devoted giver (Dedication). If you find that the Love Habits are hard for either of you to practice with each other, please contact me at www.Lovein 90Days.com/dating-coach/ and I will assign you an expert relationship coach who will evaluate your specific situation and make suggestions.

The Love Journey

All those dopamine-fueled falling-in-love fireworks, the brain chemicals that fire you up and get you hotly addicted to your Beloved, are designed to fade with time. After about two to three years, the biologically based craving and passion for each other die down and the lovers invariably wind up disappointing and wounding each other.

But there is a flip side to this story: We have selected prototypes of the very people we so dearly wanted to love us—our parents. When our mates break our hearts, they do so in ways that echo our childhood wounds. This means they become even more like our parents. And therefore our mates also have the unique and powerful opportunity to help us heal from our past hurts.

In a healthy relationship, the partners work through the wounding process and healing slowly takes place. Instead of simply reacting to each other like hurt children, they work to transcend their reactivity, be mature, and give each other forgiveness, attention, understanding, and validation.

This creates an intense bond that is totally unique—you get at last exactly the love you desired from a person who represents your mother or father. It is symbolically having the good parent you have always wanted.

My dad was not very interested in me and certainly did not look at me very much. When I first met Sam, he had a hard time making eye contact when we were discussing emotional topics. This would upset me no end; my childhood wounds flared and I was sure it meant that I was not important and that he didn't love me. Luckily, I learned about Positive Shaping Talk and asked him to look at me. And he did. His look, his attention, was profoundly healing for me. Still is.

> Love wing'd my hopes and taught me how to fly.
>
> —*Anonymous*

In a healthy relationship each partner functions as a master Love Mentor to the other. In this powerful coming together, both lovers have their unmet needs filled so they feel secure and understood (roots) as well as supported in pursuing their own dreams (wings). The Tender and Tough Loving Care (TTLC) rhythmically flows both ways based on their deepest needs. It is a spiral of giving and taking that gets better and better over time.

The lovers quarrel. One partner really needs to be grounded, held, and reassured that she or he is lovable. The other comes through. The receiving partner becomes reassured, feels more whole, grateful, and able to give more back when her turn comes. The partners heal each other and become more secure and empowered over time, which means they can help each other more effectively. This cycle of benevolence leads to deepening gratitude, commitment, and dedication. Out of this healing love relationship the partners grow together and each evolves to his or her fullest capacity. Many studies have shown that spouses in long marriages shape each other positively over time.

As this healing spirals on, there is less fear and wounding of each other and room for deeper emotional and physical intimacy. This creates a flow of brain chemicals that generates attachment—more of that feel-good oxytocin for women and vasopressin for men. In order to keep these cuddle, tend-and-befriend hormones going, the members of a couple have to continue to communicate, nurture each other, and team together in a loving win-win way that weathers all the disputes and storms of life.

But what about the sparks, the irresistible yummy passion? Here's a love news flash: Partners who are healing childhood wounds and growing through their relationship are automatically regenerating chemistry! As they evolve, their behavior becomes more novel and spontaneous—and novelty leads to more dopamine. The personal transformation of the partners means they say and do unexpected things; funny, creative, thoughtful, or intimate openings occur and create the opportunity to fall in love all over again.

Healthy couples shepherd this regenerative process along by having an ongoing affair—with each other. They create novel and exciting ways to flirt with, romance, and bed each other. In this way they create an established and committed relationship that gets progressively richer and sexier instead of diminishing with time.

The Eight Habits of Living Love

> *All happy families resemble one another.*
> *Each unhappy family is unique in its grief.*
> —Leo Tolstoy, *Anna Karenina*

Tolstoy's powerful observation was this: There is a commonality among happy families. The ways in which they talk and act with each other are strikingly similar and 180 degrees different from what goes on in unhappy families. Researchers have identified almost all of these healthy patterns, or what I call the Habits of Living Love, by studying tens of thousands of happy couples. My husband, Sam, and I studied the skills of healthy couples at the Institute for Comprehensive Family Therapy and have used them in our own lab, our marriage. The Habits have not only allowed us to weather the family upsets, setbacks, losses, and other assorted slings and arrows, but they have also given us increasing emotional connectedness, happiness, personal empowerment, and moments of rapturous bliss. I've also prescribed these powerful practices to help thousands of other couples create real love that lasts.

The Eight Habits are:

1. Cultivating Intimacy

2. Acting Out of Dedication and Service

3. Acting from Enlightened Selfishness

4. Considering the Cost of Loss

5. Showing Appreciation and Gratitude

6. Practicing Care-Full Communication

7. Following Fight Club Rules

8. Collaborating as Teammates

THE HABIT OF CULTIVATING INTIMACY

It's not just the fabulous hiking adventures, riding the tandem bike across the desert, the deep conversations about delicate issues, relishing exotic meals or surprising each other with the simple gift of a heart-shaped rock. On a deeper level, it's the ineffable intimacy evoked by a glance, an outstretched hand, a smile that matters most.—*Anne, on her two-year-old marriage*

Intimacy is the creation of verbal, emotional, physical, and sexual sharing and closeness. In long-term healthy couples, the partners know each other. They spend time together, talk, share, and listen. The partners are genuinely interested in each other's past, present, and future, their work, and social and daily activities. They spend time discovering each other's deeper needs and wants. The lovers are authentic with each other and speak their truths. They are compassionate and feel for each other.

Loving couples share rituals that bond them and create intimacy. They have little signals and signs that set the stage for sex, dates, and romance. They may routinely have quiet time together after coffee, or say silly endearing things to each other before bed or when they leave for work. They have their ways of cooking and eating a meal together, taking care of each other when one is sick, or ritualized vacations, like "We always go skiing in Colorado after Christmas." Celebrations of each partner's triumphs are very important, even more important than rituals of consolation after a setback. All these rituals create a sense of "we"-ness and lay the foundation for more loving interactions.

One of the key research markers of a happy relationship is spending time alone as a couple. In fact, about 80 percent of people who divorce say that the reason the marriage ended was that they grew apart and lost the feeling of being loved, appreciated, and being close. Thus, spending time together and away from friends, family, and children is crucial.

Loving couples also share physical and sexual intimacy. As we've already discussed, dopamine, oxytocin, and vasopressin are primary contributors to the focused attention and infatuation and, later, attachment and intimacy in couples. Testosterone, the sexual hormone engine for both men and women, also generates connection. Researchers have found that there are three primary ways in which couples interact with each other sexually: sexual trance, partner engagement, and role play.

- *Sexual trance is an inward focus in which very little talking takes place.* Each partner focuses on his or her own pleasure and sensations and creates a fulfilling sexual release.

- *Partner engagement is interactive sex and sex play.* This includes foreplay, kissing, hugging, and eye-gazing. Sex talk revolves around romantic endearments. The Beloved is seen as a separate person whose happiness and satisfaction are as important as one's own. At the highest level of partner engagement there is rapture and bliss, plus a feeling of oneness with each other and humanity.

- *The last type of sexual intimacy comes from role play.* The couple creates a kind of magic theater where sex is a stage for each partner to share and enact fantasies with each other. This helps the partners to explore all the different aspects of self.

Skill-Building

- You can practice the habit of intimacy by having straight talk with trustworthy family members, friends, and men you are dating.
- Practice your listening skills with them as well.
- If you are not used to it, practice giving and receiving hugs, kisses, and affection.
- Whether you are in a couple or not, ultimately you are responsible for knowing your body and creating the conditions for your own

sexual pleasure. You can work on sexual trance by using what the legendary sex researchers Masters and Johnson described as sensate focus. This simple but effective technique requires only that you be in an undisturbed place where you playfully touch parts of your body and learn about what sensations feel good to you. The more you know about your own body the better you and your lover will be able to please you.

- Once you graduate from the Program and are with the One, take your time and slowly open up to the various types of sexual intimacy with a man that you want to explore.

THE HABIT OF ACTING OUT OF DEDICATION AND SERVICE

Stephen did all the research and was the desire for my vision; I am so grateful for his mind's creation, this clear, crisp world that doesn't cloud over, this absence of pain.—Byron Katie, describing how her husband arranged for trailblazing cornea surgery that restored her failing vision

The Habit of Acting Out of Dedication and Service starts with commitment. Both partners completely commit to each other and the relationship for the long-term future. They talk the talk and walk the walk, speaking and acting in ways that show they have made a decision to maintain a love relationship solely with each other. It is dedication and commitment that get a healthy couple through the inevitable wounding, conflict, and hard times so that they can heal and grow together. Commitment is related to better relationship quality, greater happiness, better communication, and less destructive behavior.

Commitment includes the practice of fidelity, which means that the partners do not have affairs with others. Faithfulness is a key to a happy marriage, and ongoing infidelity can be a death knell. However, contrary to urban legend, it is not infidelity that usually kills marriages; many couples have weathered an affair through apologies, reparations, and forgiveness. Paradoxically, working through the affair can strengthen the relationship as the partners discuss what led up to the affair, acknowledge their part in it, confess their unmet needs and wants, and recommit to the Eight Habits.

Dedication and commitment mean that the needs of the couple or the other partner come first before personal needs. The partners consider each other's needs and wants as if they were their own. Each member is willing to sacrifice and invest time and energy for the sake of the relationship. Service to the Beloved is the action of love. Service is love made real.

Emotional affairs are avoided—this is when a parent, family member, or best friend comes between the partners. In triangles such as these, the partner having the emotional affair shows dedication by choosing to satisfy his or her mate's needs as a number one priority—the partner's needs come first over others' needs.

Dedication also involves a willingness to function as a master Love Mentor for your partner. Even after quarreling, feeling wounded, or being in a funk, a healthy partner eventually gets back to being dedicated to healing and giving to his or her Beloved. Bottom line: Both act from healthy selflessness and true generosity of spirit. They work to understand the TTLC (Tender and Tough Loving Care) the other requires and try to fill those needs. When one falls, literally and figuratively, the other holds him or her as needed, providing a safe haven of care, listening, reassurance, and emotional communion. And when it comes time to go back out there, a loving partner gives encouragement, advice, prizing, and, at the moment of success, heartfelt celebration. A loving partner co-creates a vision of success for his Beloved, often seeing real potential unnoticed by the Beloved herself. Then, he encourages his Beloved to dream big and go for it.

In short, healthy partners are dedicated to the development of each other's Diamond Self. This is not pie in the sky. I am describing this from direct experience. I could not be the "me" I am, writing this book for you, without the dedication Sam has shown me for over twenty-five years. Yes, we fight. But we come back together; we suck it up and apologize for the sake of the relationship. Sometimes I'll bring him some yummy quiche even when I'm still mad, because I know food means a lot to him. And he'll give me a tender little kiss on the cheek, which jump-starts the physical connection I need. This is how dedication works. You give more than 100 percent and more than 100 percent comes back to you.

And, as study after study has shown, it works this way in many other couples.

Skill-Building

- You can practice Dedication with your best friend, with your Team Love and family members, and, if you have graduated from the Program of Three, with your new man. It doesn't have to entail everything involved in a fully committed couple. Simply be more thoughtful, giving, and in service to them. This practice is especially important if you tend to be more diva-like and self-centered.
- Work on understanding the TTLC needs that people who are close to you have and be dedicated to helping them grow and manifest their Diamond Selves.

THE HABIT OF ACTING FROM ENLIGHTENED SELFISHNESS

I came to realize how much he needed to stretch, to prove himself in the world in order to please me! Like a knight wearing his lady's colors in battle, he loved winning for and with me. My silence, my fears about asking for too much, my not saying what would make me truly happy, were crippling him and stunting his joy. I decided to give him that chance as my knight. The more I asked, the more he brought. And the happier he was. And guess what? I became his knight, too.—Kimberly, on her insights into her husband of fifteen years

The Habit of Acting from Enlightened Selfishness goes hand-in-hand with Dedication. This habit comes from understanding that in helping your partner give to you, you are giving to him. You are furthering his sense of competence as a loving, dedicated man. Whenever your needs and wants are fulfilled, you can, in turn, give more back to him. Because you are content, soothed, recharged, and in a state of appreciation and gratitude, you can give in a whole, real way, with your full time and attention.

Often, the Habit of Acting from Enlightened Selfishness is hard for women, since they are used to being the givers. Nonetheless, this habit must be followed. If the giving flows only one way, the relationship becomes boring, stagnant, and rigid. Healthy relatedness is based on a rhythmic give-and-take where the partners fluidly play out different roles. Partners may function as best friends, teammates, lovers, mentors, parents, or children with each other. Fulfilling each other's needs in the many roles helps them to develop all the different sides of themselves.

In a loving, happy couple, each partner acknowledges their own TTLC needs *and even their more superficial wants* and shapes the other partner to succeed in fulfilling them either directly or indirectly. This includes pursuing one's real interests and dreams at play and at work that may be separate and apart from the other partner. He plays golf on Saturday mornings and she supports it. She studies tai chi Monday and Tuesday nights and he supports that. As the poet Rilke wrote:

> *Once the realization is accepted that even between the closest human beings infinite distances continue, a wonderful living side by side can grow, if they succeed in loving the distance between them which makes it possible for each to see the other whole against the sky.*

The partners are free to be their authentic selves. Acting from Enlightened Selfishness, they explore themselves, learning how to self-soothe when they are upset and self-validate when they need it. In this way, they are more whole as individuals and not so dependent on the relationship to fill all of their needs. Each partner becomes more mature and capable of delaying self-gratification. Having given themselves needed attention, support, or space and time alone, they are less anxious, irritable, or needy in the relationship.

The partners not only know but also appreciate their differences. He loves sports while she hates watching games. He is a Republican while she is a Democrat. And it is okay. As one study points out, over 69 percent of long-term couples have a few irreconcilable differences and yet still stay together. What is more important is the couple's self-and-other love and self-and-other caretaking. In a healthy relationship the inner world of the self is more fulfilled and mirrors the outer world of the couple's interactions.

Skill-Building

- Build on the positive shaping work you have already done with yourself, family, and friends. Pay close attention to what you need or want and get it for yourself or ask someone to get it for you. Attention, a warm bath, that crazy turquoise ring, a trip to St. Lucia? It's all okay. People who really love you love to make you happy.

- Practice Enlightened Selfishness with dates. Experiment by asking for more than "what you deserve." Do you want him to take you to the Four Seasons for dinner? For a stroll on a faraway beach? To come hear you play guitar at a student concert? Go for it.

- Consider taking a personal growth course that will help you get more in touch with your authentic self and what you really want. My clients and students have successfully used Dahn Yoga, the Star's Edge Avatar course, the Landmark Forum, Transcendental Meditation, the Art of Living, Byron Katie's courses, and many other classes.

THE HABIT OF CONSIDERING THE COST OF LOSS

He can be oblivious, self-centered and come back way late from surfing
sometimes. Then I think about moving out. But I don't. I don't want to
be crying, up nights, restless in a cold bed. Plus the rent would be so high.
Then I think: but we love each other. And he warms my feet at night.—Zoe,
35, *on thoughts of leaving her live-in love*

Healthy spouses are realistic in thinking about and considering the
costs of losing their relationship. First and foremost is the major cost of
a broken heart: the emotional, psychological, and physical pain of loss.
In Chapter 11 we looked at the high stress, the depressive spiral, the
aches and pains, sleeplessness, appetite problems, loss of motivation,
and other negative changes in brain chemistry that separation or rejection create. Even the immune system goes downhill. Second, there are
the economic and other real costs, including a lower standard of living,
division of assets, extra labor, and potential loss of custody or time with
the children. Many researchers believe that these exit costs serve as barriers to separation and therefore are major underpinnings of stability.
Healthy partners can look ahead and assess the harsh realities a breakup
would bring. This possible future helps keep them together through the
hard times. It also helps them appreciate what they have in each other.

But healthy partners do not stay together simply out of need. They
do have the emotional capacity to leave each other, which engenders a
healthy respect and creates the reality that loss could really occur. This
frightening possibility tends to keep the members on their toes and min-
imizes verbal and nonverbal abuse. Each person knows that he or she
cannot get away with repeated disrespectful, thoughtless, mean, or cold
treatment of the other.

Oftentimes in healthy couples a partner will use a fear-of-loss maneuver when the other partner steps too far out of line, say, after an affair.
At that point the offended person may be on the verge of moving out

or starting divorce proceedings. Fear of loss hangs over the emotionally devastated couple like a deadly saber. Nonetheless, the potential for growth at this time in a healthy couple is very high because they are willing to consider the emotional turmoil, depressive disentangling, economic hardships, child-rearing difficulties, and other costs that they will have to pay.

The odds of this being a coming together for the partners are good if they start couples therapy with a therapist who is a knowledgeable sea captain and can guide the couple through the straits and help them avoid the dangerous reefs. As they heal, the unfaithful partner becomes contrite, cuts off the other relationship, and makes it up to the Beloved. The Beloved expresses anger but over time accepts reparations that have symbolic meaning. This often leads to a rekindled relationship, which has grown out of the Habit of Considering the Cost of Loss.

Skill-Building

- When a friend, family member, or a guy you are seriously dating does something that offends you, where you might normally distance or cut off from the relationship, consider the cost of losing this person. How would you feel? What would your life be like without him or her in it? What would you miss? How valuable are these things to you?
- If you have had the experience of losing a relationship that had a lot of good aspects, what do you wish you had said to yourself about the cost of loss before it ended?

THE HABIT OF SHOWING APPRECIATION AND GRATITUDE

He who is in love is wise and becoming wiser, sees newly every time he looks at the object beloved, drawing from it with his eyes and his mind those virtues which it possesses.—Ralph Waldo Emerson

Because they know that loss can occur, loving couples appreciate and are grateful for each other. Each partner appreciates who the Beloved is, who he or she can be—that is, the Beloved's Diamond Self—and what is received from the Beloved. Both live in a state of gratitude. This habit leads to great personal and shared happiness in the couple.

Healthy partners tend to see each other's positive qualities rather than their negative ones. Everyone has flaws; there is no perfect person. In the practice of this habit of loving, the partner's flaws are not the focus. Instead of grimacing about her husband's flabby paunch and being grumpy about his snoring, a happy wife sees a sandy-haired hunk getting into her bed. Instead of zoning in on his wife's cellulite and complaining about her failed MLM business, a happy husband sees a warm, funny vixen who lights up his life.

This is why I taught you about Positive Paranoia. Healthy, happy couples live most of the time in a state of Positive Paranoia. They give their partners the benefit of the doubt when they do something that is disappointing or hurtful. They often see good or simply uninformed intentions underlying what their partners do or say instead of mean-spirited criticism, rejection, or attack. In contrast, in unhappy couples, the partners can never win. Even when one spouse tries to be nice, he or she is greeted with negative paranoia; the other spouse is suspicious about underlying intentions and thinks that the loving act is simply a setup to be disappointed and hurt once again. This makes it hard and, at the very end, almost impossible to simply take in a love gesture. There are few such barriers for healthy couples.

Because happy couples are naturally focused on blessings and feel grateful in their relationship, they are happier. As you now know, research clearly shows that appreciation and gratitude lead to happiness. Daily counting of one's blessings leads to less depression and a more elevated mood. A "gratitude visit," where you write a letter of thanks to a person who has helped you and then go to them and read it, has been associated with turbo-charging your joy. Members of a healthy couple are continuously making gratitude mini-visits to each other in verbal or written form. They express thanks, give each other appreciative, gratitude-based gifts, and exchange loving e-mails, notes, and cards.

The Habit of Showing Appreciation and Gratitude is critically important. When you are in a state of appreciation and happier in general, it is a lot easier to make your partner happy. Conversely, when you are depressed, worried, or busy counting your misfortunes, it is next to impossible to create happiness in your relationship.

This Living Love Habit also lays the foundation for Care-Full Communication.

Skill-Building

- You already have a head start on this if you have been doing your exercises and homework. I hope you have been. Make it a point to notice and appreciate all the wonderful qualities, large and small, that your family members and friends have. Practice telling them about it. Notice how they respond.
- Be truly appreciative of the guys you are dating. Be sure to thank them for outings, gifts, or helpfulness.
- With problematic people, polish up your Positive Paranoia skills. When someone seems unsupportive, negative, or ignores you, think thoughts like, *I bet Mom is proud of my music gig even though she hasn't called.* Or *My boss wants to help me succeed, even though he's critical.* See how that changes your relationship with these difficult people. You can tip the scales to the plus side and reap more positives from them by changing the focus of your own outlook.

THE HABIT OF PRACTICING CARE-FULL COMMUNICATION

Mend your speech a little,
Lest you may mar your fortunes.
—Shakespeare

This is the habit of caring and positive verbal and nonverbal communication. Psychologist John Gottman, PhD, a leading love researcher, found that healthy couples, no matter what their communication style is, show a five-to-one ratio of positive to negative interactions. That is, they are very kind to each other and their words and actions are full of care. Some loving couples have an even higher ratio of positive to negative strokes, like ten to one! Politeness, affection, humor, benevolence, praise, and niceness count—big time. When there are disagreements, the partners agree to talk about them, appreciate each other's point of view, and may agree to disagree.

Listening and paying attention are linchpins here. Couples who are making it listen and know each other's fears, problems, wishes, and dreams. When I did couples therapy, a simple prescription for daily ten-minute listening sessions, where one spouse played therapist by just listening with full attention and reflecting back what the other was saying, could remake a failing marriage.

Positive Shaping Talk, the process you learned earlier in the Program, is the other side of the Habit of Practicing Care-Full Communication. The spouses warmly and clearly explain what they want and need so that they help each other win, and come through for each other. Gottman calls this having a "soft start-up," where, instead of accusing or complaining, you simply tell your partner what you need and give him or her a way to succeed with you. "Honey, I need attention," and "Sweetheart, I would really love it if you rubbed my back," are the kind of requests that can work miracles.

Healthy couples do fight, and fighting is an important way to air anger and be authentic. However, they return to and maintain a more kind and loving way of relating most of the time. Their pattern is a mirror image of the heart-rending dance that is characteristic of a couple that is dying. Partners on the verge of breaking up live in a cascade of criticism, defensiveness, stonewalling, and contempt that color almost all of their interactions. They feel caught in a whirlpool of anger, insults, disinterest, dismissal, eye-rolling, and undermining. This downward-spiraling pattern leads to the hopelessness, loneliness, and lack of intimacy that in the end kill off love.

In contrast, happy partners work to avoid nitpicking, harsh judgments, belittling, abusing, or freezing each other out. When such incidents occur, they repair them as soon as they can. In great measure, loving couples speak and act out of honor, respect, and appreciation; they speak as the best of best friends.

Skill-Building

- Notice how you communicate with friends, family members, and the guys you are dating. How many positive interactions do you have for each negative one?
- Notice whether you tend to be negative, pessimistic, critical, defensive, or withholding of positive prizing statements or gestures.
- Examine how you act with your parents or stepparents. Oftentimes we can be quite unconsciously (or consciously) negative with parents or stepparents.
- Go into Care-Full Communication mode: practice listening to people with your full, undivided attention.
- Try giving people five positives for every negative comment and see what happens.

THE HABIT OF FOLLOWING FIGHT CLUB RULES

Beware of entrance to a quarrel.

—Shakespeare

All couples belong to what I call the Fight Club because they all fight. Couples who don't fight are the ones therapists worry most about. In fact, couples who do not fight have double the mortality rate of those who do. Loving couples air their differences, but they follow certain rules to make sure that their disagreement does not turn into World War III with mutual assured destruction.

- **Fight Club Rule #1: Anger and Criticism Do Not Take Over**
  Anger and criticism lead to "flooding," a stress explosion in which the heart beats more rapidly, blood pressure soars, and adrenaline surges. The whole body tenses up as fear, confusion, and then more anger take over. Reason goes out the window. In experimental studies of conflict, even when couples are asked to calm down, men simply aren't able to, while women can. Biologically speaking, men are wired to react more quickly and for a longer time period, probably for vigilance and safety reasons. So that's why it's best to start an interaction that could become a fight in a *soft, sweet, or affectionate way* with Positive Shaping Talk. While a man can often be triggered by mere criticism, it usually takes contempt or strong denigration to flood a woman.

  Loving couples tend to avoid flooding and practice Positive Shaping Talk with each other. They keep anger and upset levels down. And if anger swirls out of control, they may use breathing, time out, humor, or other Fight Club Rules to defuse the situation.

- **Fight Club Rule #2: Agree to Disagree**
  A healthy couple agrees to disagree, discussing differences with respect and self-control. They often show each other that they understand the other's point of view. The partners realize that ultimately they both want the same thing: closeness and a sense of shared love. If they feel heard and understood, like their opinion matters, they can often let go of the issue, back down, and reenter an intimate connection. In loving couples, who is right and who is wrong matters much less. In fact, these couples operate out of a fundamental paradox: "I accept you as you are," on the one hand, and, on the other, "Now will you please change." This paradox is so well known that it became the title of a long-running off-Broadway show, written by a long-term couple, called *I Love You, You're Perfect, Now Change.*

- **Fight Club Rule #3: End Conflict in a Win-Win Way**
  There are several ways you can help end conflict on a positive note. I have often used the Take Two technique with couples, where either of

them was able to call out "Take Two" when a fight erupted and they would start their "scene" all over again, *but from a loving place.* Couples do this naturally when one of them says something like, "Can we talk about this in a different way?" Or perhaps one partner affectionately teases or soothes the other who is in the midst of flooding and the fight is over then and there. Or they might compromise. The couple may follow a rule, like, Don't let the sun rise on your wrath. Of course, one key to ending a fight is that a partner realizes he or she is wrong, apologizes, and/or makes it up to the Beloved.

In general, healthy couples fight, but their fighting is less out of control and ends on a sweet note that carries them back to laughter, closeness, and intimacy. Here is how Gina, a therapist who is a graduate, describes following Fight Club Rules with her husband:

> *He gets so wounded and growls a lot if he thinks I am criticizing him. So I usually bring stuff up when we are lying in bed, feeling close, with our feet touching. It's funny, but doing it this way means we fight a whole lot less.*

Skill-Building

- Notice whom you fight with. Maybe it is siblings. Maybe other family members or certain friends.
- Practice doing whatever it takes to come out of your anger and create a dialogue. In the midst of a disagreement, take a break, breathe, soothe or calm yourself, and try on the other person's point of view. Ask yourself honestly whether you need to back down or make an apology to this person. When you are fighting, which is more important—being right, or being close?
- If the other person entangled in your disagreements gets flooded with anger, practice using humor, giving him or her space, or soothing him in some way so that he can calm down.

THE HABIT OF COLLABORATING AS TEAMMATES

There is no "I" in team.

—*Anonymous*

Partners in a loving relationship recognize that they are co-managers of their life together. They cooperate and team together with mutual support, respect, affection, and emotional connection. And this habit of effectively teaming and coordinating activities is a key factor in their happiness. Each partner takes into account the other's thoughts, feelings, and opinions before making a major decision. In other words, there is shared power where both members of the couple influence each other. There is also a fair distribution of household chores, child care, and management of the couple's intimacy. Studies show that men who do housework are more likely to be healthier and have more sex. This is because they have better relationships with their partners: women love this type of gender-stereotype-bending support and teaming.

In happy couples, teamwork is often shaped and informed by master Love Mentoring and filling each other's deeper TTLC needs. For example, when one of the students in our coaching program and her fiancé hit a roadblock with her controlling mom in wedding planning, the couple discussed it with their Love Mentor. Her Beloved sweetly offered to stand up to her mother in an assertive but positive way. This resulted in two things: a heartfelt and real ceremony with a cooperative mom—which was exactly what the couple wanted—and a healing experience for the bride, who needed to feel protected and encouraged to be real. Feeling radiantly happy and grateful, she then spent extra time teaming and brainstorming with her Beloved about his next career move.

If there are biological children or stepchildren, commitment to their well-being and teaming as parents contributes to the partners' respect and love for each other. This is true even with adult children. When I ask Sam to help my daughter dig through an onerous tax bill and he does it, I identify with her and feel like he is doing it for me.

I feel more appreciative and loving toward him. As I touched on in the last chapter, in healthy, happy stepfamilies, a specific role division where the biological parent is more of the disciplinarian and limit-setter while the stepparent is the nurturer promotes family bonding and harmony.

It is important to note that more men than women tend to balk at allowing themselves to be influenced. They can become critical, defensive, distant, or even show contempt. According to Gottman, when this occurs there is an 81 percent chance the marriage will be damaged. This kind of rigid unwillingness to accept constructive suggestions is something to watch out for when you are selecting the One.

In happy couples, teamwork is not thwarted; it actually gets better and better over time. The partners work out any issues of control or needing to be right. Instead they come to realize that their goals are met at a higher level when they partner. They come to know, respect, honor, and utilize each other's strengths and gifts more and more as they work together, making their dreams come true on the home front, with the children, and in their careers. When we studied healthy couples at the institute, it was inspiring to see how a couple would pull together seamlessly and get down to business when one was in a crisis or facing a major opportunity. Sam and I learned a tremendous amount from watching them.

Guess who is helping me fill in all the tedious details in the endnotes for this book.

Skill-Building

- When you plan outings, dates, or vacations with family members, friends, or guys you are dating, share your thoughts and opinions about the experience and ask for theirs.
- If you tend to be the one running the show, practice stepping back so that you can become more flexible. If you tend to be more passive, practice taking a leadership role.

- After you graduate from the Program of Three and are dating the One, make sure you implement these teaming skills.

- When you are farther along in your love relationship, plan a trip or activity that requires a lot of coordination and see if the two of you can work well together to create a positive experience. Research shows that even if the sex is good and you love each other and feel like friends, an inability to team could prevent you from being fully happy together.

These are the Eight Habits of Living Love. Remember, happy couples are not practicing the Habits all the time, just most of the time. And healthy partners hone their skills and get more and more competent at loving as the years go by. That is the very best news! I just met an affectionate couple from Belgium who have been married for fifty years. When I asked what their secret was, the wife smiled and charmingly answered, "Laugh, say, and do love every day." The interesting thing is that this couple has seven happily married children—with no divorces!

Now back to you and your journey. In the first few months of a relationship, when the dopamine infatuation levels are high, you should see many of these Habits in action already, at least in some rudimentary form. *Think about this whenever you are considering whether to stop the Program of Three and choose the One.* Ask yourself, Are the Habits of Living Love happening with this guy?

✎ The Eight Habits of Living Love: Exercises _____

Choose from among the following suggestions, according to your own intuition.

Total Time for Completing All of Them: 30 Minutes

EXERCISE 1: *SELF-PRACTICE*

Look through the Habits once more, but this time think about practicing them toward yourself via your own self-talk and actions. Almost all of them can be adapted this way. Partners in a loving couple automatically do this through the Habit of Acting from Enlightened Selfishness. Imagine new levels of: cultivating intimacy, that is, knowing yourself; being self-dedicated; considering what you might lose if you give in to an addiction; appreciating and talking sweetly to yourself; soothing and calming yourself when your temper flares. Remember, the outer world of relationships comes to mirror the inner world of the self.

EXERCISE 2: *WHICH HABITS ARE MOST CHALLENGING?*

Reread each of the Eight Habits and notice any negative thoughts or pessimistic feelings about being able to implement them in your life. Write these thoughts/feelings down in your journal.

EXERCISE 3: *YOUR SKILL-BUILDING AFFIRMATIONS*

Make a list of affirmations that counter your negative self-talk and any other problematic beliefs that came up in doing Exercises 1 and 2. For example, if intimacy sounds scary, you could create an affirmation like, *I open to the experience of intimacy.* If your temper tends to explode and take over, create an affirmation like, *Anger means I need to breathe.*

EXERCISE 4: *LETTER OF GRATITUDE TO YOURSELF*

In your journal write a letter of appreciation and gratitude to yourself for all the growth you have accomplished and for giving yourself the Love in 90 Days Program.

EXERCISE 5: *LETTER OF GRATITUDE TO YOUR BELOVED*

Now write a letter of appreciation and thanks to a perfectly loving partner, as if he were partnered with you right now. Here is an excerpt from Dawn's letter, which reflected the guy she met and married *after* she wrote it:

> *To my Beloved,*
> *You are a gift from God, the man I have been waiting for all my life.*
> *Thank you for loving me and accepting me as I am, for always finding*
> *the humorous side in me, for listening and caring about how I feel. And*
> *thank you for reassuring me that you are there for me, that you appre-*
> *ciate and adore me and that I am beautiful and amazing. Thanks*
> *for supporting me in my work, being real with me and encouraging*
> *me to grow…thank you for making our relationship the first and top*
> *priority. I am so grateful for your gentleness and kindness. I love you!*
>   *Your loving partner and wife,*
>   *Dawn*

 Homework

Choose from among the following suggestions, according to your own intuition:

1. Practice the Habit(s) that seem most problematic from Exercise 2 with appropriate friends and family.
2. Continue practicing Positive Paranoia and Positive Shaping Talk with family, friends, and guys you are dating so that they give you more of what you need.
3. Fill out your Field Reports on DUDs and STUDs with an attitude of total appreciation and gratitude.
4. Discuss your Field Reports on DUDs and STUDs with your master Love Mentor and Team Love.
5. Get more Beauty, Advice, or Matchmaker Mentors as needed.

6. Keep up the networking. Have the new people you meet set you up with guys.

7. Work two online dating sites/apps using all the search-engine optimization secrets *for at least one-half hour every day (including weekends).*

8. Fill out your Love in 90 Days Online Dating Report. Make any changes as needed.

9. Have at least three dates this week. Work your Program of Three!

10. If you are thinking about choosing the One and graduating from the Program of Three, review "Choose the One Only after Months on the Program" and "Follow the Guidelines for Graduating from the Program of Three," which are sections 10 and 11 in Chapter 4. If you feel that your current number one guy is your own true love, ignore the last three assignments, follow the guidelines, and complete your graduation. Big congratulations!

11. Once you have graduated from the Dating Program of Three, continue to focus on developing yourself—do all the personal growth and goal-setting exercises in the final chapter. Also, consciously practice the Eight Habits of Living Love in your relationship. Mark up this chapter so that you can refer to it as needed. Use Positive Paranoia and Positive Shaping Talk to help your Beloved fulfill your needs. Then come through for your Beloved and fill his deepest desires so that love takes root and grows. Most important: Don't forget to have lots of fun together!

In one way, we are near the end of our journey together. Yet, on a deeper level we are not, because love shared is a timeless thing. You are seeking, growing; you are amazing. I want to leave with you the words of the Buddha, who summarizes this chapter's teachings for us:

The thought manifests as the word. The word manifests as the deed. The deed develops into habit. And the habit hardens into character. So watch the thought and its ways with care. And let it spring from love, born out of concern for all beings.

15

Launch to More Love

What did I learn in 90 days
To get myself out of this haze?
To find a partner for my life
What will I do to claim that right?
I promise to date 3 times per week
And give up my deadly dating streaks
To use my Dud and Stud report,
Online Service and Deserve Log support
I promise to date without the drama
And let love in from a Love Mentor
To look for a partner with intention and
Make hot my style by reinvention
Don't you date just one on one
While he's out there having all the fun
Don't jump right straight into bed
Or else you'll turn gold into lead
Don't drift away from your goal
Or dreams will die and futures fold
Walk the walk with Princes and Frogs
Make the dates, Keep the logs
Think of all those marriage kisses
When the Miss becomes the Mrs.
—*Shelly, who is happily hunting with her generous*
Beloved for their dream home

Here we are in our final chapter, and I am delighted that we have taken this journey together. It's time to take a look at what you have accomplished in terms of your assignments, how much you have grown, and where you are on the Goals list. We will appreciate and celebrate all those accomplishments, no matter how small or big. I'll also ask you to sign an Acknowledgment and Commitment Contract that you should share with your Love Mentor(s). The contract lists the gains you have made and contains the steps you need to take in order to reach the next milestone on the road to living love.

Your gift for graduating from the Love in 90 Days Program is a copy of the Eight Steps to Love. These are like your CliffsNotes for the course—a summary sheet that allows you to take me along as you wish on your further love adventures.

Your Assignment Checklist

This is a time to take stock of what you did and did not complete in the Love in 90 Days Program. Depending on where you started, check off in your mind which of the assignments applied to you and whether or not you need to do more work on them. Did you:

- Reprioritize love?
- Work on your Deadly Dating Patterns?
- Follow a Dating Program of Three?
- Use two online sites?
- Get Love Mentors?
- Do Diamond Self work?
- Network where the men are?
- Handle Frenemies?
- Start practicing the Eight Habits of Living Love?

Even if you have just read and begun to think about doing these things, you have taken an important step! I salute you and want you to appreciate yourself for that. Appreciation and gratitude constitute one of the most fundamental Habits of Living Love, and I want you to be first and foremost an appreciative soulmate for yourself. So give yourself a big hug from me, even if just for exploring some new ideas.

If you have gone much farther than that, I am standing and applauding you. These are challenging assignments that fly in the face of all your fears. You are trekking up the Mount Everest of the heart. But I know you can do it. Just keep on going and you can take yourself as high as you wish.

If you are on the Love in 90 Days Program, you can think of this as a makeup week. You can go back to anything you skipped or intuitively feel you need more work on. Even in one week's time you can jump ahead dramatically. You could meet the One tonight.

Your Transformation

Now let's take a look at how far you have come. Think about your answers to the questions below. Notice, own, and enjoy your own dating progress:

- Are you putting out feminine "go" signals? Do you dress or act in a more attractive way?
- Has the number of text and phone interactions with potential dates increased since the beginning of the Program?
- Has the number of actual dates each week increased?
- Are you dating better-quality men?
- How have your dating habits changed?
- Which Deadly Dating Patterns have you broken through?
- Are you looking for something different in a relationship now?

Even the smallest gains on these items indicate significant improvement.

Now let's look at the big-picture gains you've made, your transformation in terms of creating affirming attitudes and positive beliefs. Read over the following list and put a plus sign by any areas in which you have made progress. Be generous and appreciative:

Self-esteem and Self-love
Ability to Connect with People
Clarity of Love Intention
Understanding and Fulfilling Your Needs
Femininity
Attractiveness to Men
Confidence with Men
Hopefulness About Creating a Love Relationship
Being Your Diamond Self with Men

Paula, a hospital administrator and graduate, describes her changes as follows:

> I'm deepening my love and appreciation for myself and others. My mind and heart are more open. I'm better understanding my patterns, forgiving myself for mistakes and placing my attention on what's desired. In learning to trust the Program, I'm making different decisions than I did in the past. I know it didn't work the old way. I'm attracting new attention and a better kind of guy. This makes me believe I will have a healthy, loving relationship.

Look over the pluses you have put on the list. These indicate that you are emerging from the chrysalis.

Plato once said:

> In that communion only, beholding beauty with the eye of the mind, [s]he will be enabled to bring forth, not images of beauty, but realities.

Let's look at more of the realities you have brought forth. Is your heart more open and connected to others? Have people been reacting differently to you? Are they more complimentary? Do you have more loving and helpful people around you, people who truly see and help you manifest your shining qualities, your true passion and beauty?

Announce and describe each gain you've made to your master Love Mentor and/or Team Love and celebrate with them. Enjoy and take pleasure in your changes, as you birth and rebirth yourself.

Goals Revisited

Check the goals you have reached on the Love in 90 Days Goals list on page 341:

Did you meet your course goal? You can't fail. There is no failure. Thomas Edison put it this way: "I never failed once—inventing the light bulb was a 2000-step process." You may miss your markers, but you are learning. Everything is unfolding perfectly. Where you are is just right for you: you are evolving inside your own unique chrysalis and when the time is ripe, you will become a one-of-a-kind butterfly. Just be grateful for whatever has happened and stay firmly and utterly committed to your vision for yourself. Persistence wins.

If you did make the goal you had chosen for yourself, how wonderful. Bravo! Did you exceed it? Even more wonderful! We have much to celebrate. Take yourself out, do a little victory dance, kiss your Beloved. Have a "New You" party with your master Love Mentor, Team Love, and other close friends. Have them make toasts and salute you and your inspiring transformation.

Love is a lifelong ascension into the realms of light. If you would like to choose a new, higher goal for yourself, look over the list and pick one that excites you right now. What do you want to create in the next 90 days? Six months? In the next year? Write it all down in your journal. It is so important to look ahead and decide where you want to go. Perhaps

you would like to make a brand-new love intention or work on Diamond
Self skills. Maybe you would like to find your STUD and graduate from
the Program of Three. Or maybe you have your STUD and want to
move in together or get engaged or married.

The Ten Love in 90 Days Goals

1. Create an exciting love intention or affirmation.

2. Create greater self-esteem, deservedness, and self-love.

3. Break out of Deadly Dating Patterns and create a successful
   Dating Program of Three.

4. Move up the ladder to better men.

5. Meet someone who has tremendous potential for a love relationship with you and graduate from the Program of Three.

6. Declare love for each other.

7. Talk seriously with your Beloved about what each of you
   needs and wants in a fulfilling love relationship.

8. Create a loving win-win contract that gives each of you roots
   (stability and dedication) and wings (fulfilling your dreams).

9. Commit to moving in together or getting engaged to your
   Beloved.

10. Marry or make a lifetime commitment to live out your
    dreams together.

Acknowledgment and Commitment Contract

There is a contract you can sign to acknowledge your gains and commit to continue using the Love in 90 Days work to meet new goals in the coming months on page 343. Copy it and fill in what you have accomplished, your next milestones, and the steps you need to take to achieve them. Some steps can be targeted immediately and others slated for later. For example, let's say your accomplishment is finding a STUD (we will call him Jose in the example) and graduating from the Program of Three. Write that in. If your next milestone is getting engaged to him, you might add the following steps:

1. Use Care-Full Communication. Be authentic and real with Jose about the vision of couplehood I have committed to creating for my own future.
2. Use Positive Paranoia to focus on how much he does love me, wants to marry me, and wants to spend the rest of his life with me.
3. When the time is right, use Positive Shaping Talk to tell Jose that I need and want a commitment.

   Note: Usually it is best to wait to do this step until you have dated for at least nine months. Also, if you have followed the Program of Three rules, chances are your boyfriend is crazy about you and will propose.
4. Be ready to reenter the Program of Three if Jose does not come through for me.

   Note: This last step will help a guy consider the cost of loss and uncover his deeper attachment and longing to commit! You have to be ruthless in your own commitment to creating love for yourself and willing to risk loss for that vision. If a STUD turns DUD on you, you need to get right back on the Dating Program of Three and let him know about it so that he can consider the high cost of losing you. So if you are at this point in a relationship, be sure to add this step to your Contract. Now that you know how to work the Program of Three, there is no reason to waste time with a Peter Pan who can't commit.

LOVE IN 90 DAYS ACKNOWLEDGMENT AND COMMITMENT CONTRACT

I, _____, hereby note and congratulate myself on my recent transformative gains, which include:

_____

_____

I deeply appreciate what I have created using the Love in 90 Days Program. And I am now making a new commitment to myself and creating the love that I want. My new goal is to: _____ _____ by (date) _____.

In order to meet this goal, I am prepared to do the following steps:

_____

_____

_____   _____
Signature   Date

After you fill in your Contract, discuss it with your master Love Mentor and/or Team Love. Then amend it as needed.

The Eight Steps to Love

It is time for you to receive your gift for going through the Program. On the next page is a summary of the Eight Steps. Post a copy where you will see it every day. The Steps will help you take me and the Love in 90 Days Program with you to create ever-increasing love.

Now you have the summary in hand, and we are almost ready to say good-bye. But at this point we have spent a good deal of time together and, chances are, I will be in your head, even if you are disagreeing with me. Know that you are very special to me, that I wrote this for you. Richard Bach expresses how I feel about our parting:

> *Fly free and happy… across forever, and we'll meet now and then when we wish, in the midst of the one celebration that never can end.*

If you have only read through the book, it is time to go back and do the exercises. Take each chapter as a week's assignment and you will work your way through and change your life in the next three months. Or just pick and choose what you want to work on. As I said in the beginning, there is no wrong way to work the Program, as long as you use the principles and practices.

If you have worked the Love in 90 Days Program all the way, know that while this might seem like the end of a process, it is really just the beginning. You can always come visit me at www.Lovein90Days.com or https://www.Facebook.com/DrDianaKirschner/ to ask questions and get daily affirmations and the support of a community dedicated to helping you create the love you want.

This is your launch to a life filled with soaring heights and sweet depths as you go on the greatest adventure, the adventure of the heart. Go on, risk, play full out, savor, and enjoy!

May You Have Love Beyond Measure,
Your Love Mentor, Diana

Love in 90 Days
The Eight Steps

1. Being your incredible Diamond Self

2. Telling yourself the truth—especially about reenacting your Deadly Dating Patterns

3. Setting a love intention and asking for what you want

4. Giving yourself helpful, devoted, and loving mentors

5. Being in the great feminine-masculine dance: showing your beauty, being receptive, and flirting

6. Dating three men and peeling back the wrappings to find true love, which almost always comes in a surprise package

7. Appreciating a good guy who is crazy about you and willing to grow

8. Practicing the Eight Habits of Living Love:

   - Cultivating Intimacy

   - Acting Out of Dedication and Service

   - Acting from Enlightened Selfishness

   - Considering the Cost of Loss

   - Showing Appreciation and Gratitude

   - Practicing Care-Full Communication

   - Following Fight Club Rules

   - Collaborating as Teammates

APPENDIX A

Creating Your Own Team Love Informally or with a Coach

Running the Love in 90 Days processes with other women is one of the greatest gifts you can give yourself. It can jump-start your program, increase your accountability in completing the course, and assist you in continuing your journey after the formal Program is over. Ask around and see who might be interested in having Love in 90 Days meetings weekly or bimonthly. You can either create a Team Love Group with your friends or join one led by one of my professional Love Mentor® coaches at www.Lovein90Days.com.

You can also consider having one of my professional coaches work with you one-on-one. Just go to http://lovein90days.com/dating-coach/ and enjoy a gift session by phone or Skype. We've helped thousands of women find love that is often beyond their wildest dreams through our unique process of one-on-one support, guidance, structure and uplifting inspiration.

Whether you work with your own Team Love or a dedicated Love Mentor® you can choose to follow the 90-day program and work on one chapter each week or you can have an open format working on different Love in 90 Days principles and strategies completely at your own pace.

Below you will find the Team Love Mission Statement, Philosophy, Team Love in Action guidelines, and suggested Meeting Structure.

TEAM LOVE MISSION STATEMENT

The Love in 90 Days Team Love groups are dedicated to helping women develop self-love and love with a partner. They promote the discovery and evolution of each member's Diamond Self, and her unique choice and expression of love with a partner.

THE TEAM LOVE PHILOSOPHY

Love is real. Love is a decision. Love is a co-creation by, with, and for oneself and one's Beloved. Radiant self-love and love with a devoted partner are available for any woman—at any age, weight, ethnicity, level of success, and in the face of any personal challenge.

TEAM LOVE IN ACTION

The group members hold each other's deep trust. They have a sacred responsibility to function as Love Mentors who hold the space of unconditional appreciation for each member, for each meeting, and for the group as a whole. Team Love members encourage, empower, and uplift each other. They hold everything each member says and does strictly confidential. They do not disclose the fact that a woman is a member to outsiders.

Acting out of Dedication, Team Love members celebrate each other's small and large steps as they work the Love in 90 Days Program. They help each other develop and use Diamond Self names within the group. The members help each other with beauty and dating tips, role modeling and inspiration, and introductions to possible STUDs.

Acting from Enlightened Selfishness, each member uses Positive Shaping Talk to ask for her needs to be met by group members in a win-win way.

Acting with Care-Full Communication, members listen to each other with unconditional positive regard and focus on the underlying love that members have for one another (practice Positive Paranoia). They make validating and uplifting comments and avoid being judgmental of each other. They do not gossip.

Acting as Collaborative Teammates, members operate in the spirit of all-for-one and one-for-all. Each group is self-governing. All decisions about meeting structure, times, and places are reached by discussion and a majority vote and if possible through unanimous agreement.

If conflict arises, the members do not allow anger to take over, but instead follow Fight Club Rules: calming down angry feelings, visiting each other's point of view or apologizing, making reparations, and actively healing any rift.

MEETING STRUCTURE

These guidelines will create the most stable and powerful Team Love group. However, each group is self-governing and can modify them as needed.

Create an initial meeting. At that meeting:

- Set up an e-mail distribution list and a schedule of meeting places and times for the next 90 days. Meeting weekly is ideal, though every other week can also work. Figure on about twenty minutes per member in calculating total meeting time. It is best to have real face-to-face meetings, but if need be, you can also have a virtual Team Love group. If you are creating a virtual team, you can have your meetings via conference call: www.freeconference.com will set the call up for free and the only cost is the long-distance charge individual members may incur.

- Select three team leaders (one for each month) to remind all members via e-mail about the meeting places and times. (You can continue the group after the Program as well.)
- The leader ensures that the agreed-upon Team Love meeting structure is followed:

1. *Opening:* The leader reads the Mission Statement. Then she asks other members to read the Philosophy and Team Love in Action items, with each person reading one paragraph. She asks for or designates a timekeeper.
2. *Positive Shares:* Each member takes one to three minutes to describe one success she experienced since the last meeting, no matter how small.
3. *Exercise and Homework Shares:* The remainder of the time is divided up among the members for the exercise and homework shares, including weekly DUD (Definitely Unworkable Dude) and STUD (Seriously Terrific, Utterly Devoted Dude) Reports.

   Note: Bring your journals. Read some exercises aloud—especially the loveless eulogies. Be creative with the work. For example, break into dyads and have a member read each person's perfect parent letter to her.
4. *Closing:* The leader asks each member to read aloud one of the Love in 90 Days Eight Steps on page 346.
5. *Group Hugs or Closing Ritual Created by the Group.*

Recommendation: Introduce other helpful books, ideas, or other resources only *after* the formal meeting is over. Otherwise the group could easily be derailed from the Love in 90 Days Program.

APPENDIX B

Love in 90 Days
THE EIGHT STEPS

1. Being your incredible Diamond Self
2. Telling yourself the truth—especially about reenacting your Deadly Dating Patterns
3. Setting a love intention and asking for what you want
4. Giving yourself helpful, devoted, and loving mentors
5. Being in the great feminine-masculine dance: showing your beauty, being receptive, and flirting
6. Dating three men and peeling back the wrappings to find true love, which almost always comes in a surprise package
7. Appreciating a good guy who is crazy about you and willing to grow
8. Practicing the Eight Habits of Living Love:
   - Cultivating Intimacy
   - Acting Out of Dedication and Service
   - Acting from Enlightened Selfishness
   - Considering the Cost of Loss
   - Showing Appreciation and Gratitude
   - Practicing Care-Full Communication
   - Following Fight Club Rules
   - Collaborating as Teammates

Love in 90 Days Online

WWW.LOVEIN90DAYS.COM

You are invited to join me and an entire community of supportive, like-minded women at lovein90days.com. The site is designed with one goal in mind: helping you create exactly the love you want. There, you can read my blog and learn what to do when there are setbacks or breakups, or if you get "stuck" in taking a relationship to the next level. You can also get my *Dating and Relationship Advice Newsletter* and daily inspirational affirmations.

So go to www.lovein90days.com now and sign up for all the free love support—it's all there for you.

See you soon!

Love in 90 Days Online University

WWW.LOVEIN90DAYSUNIVERSITY.COM

There is another powerful option for you that can make all the difference in the world in your love journey: I have developed a Love in 90 Days Certification course, which consists of eight weeks of experiential video trainings. And I hold your hand every step of the way. It is a two-mints-in-one course that boosts your own self-love and dating success and teaches you how to become a dating and relationship coach, should you choose to do this kind of work. In addition, www.Lovein90DaysUniversity .com provides a variety of courses designed to amplify self-confidence, increase dating success, and show you how to have lasting soulmate love. I'm very excited about being able to offer this new online university! Just go to http://www.Lovein90DaysUniversity.com/ and you will be able to watch complimentary videos on:

- The #1 Mistake That's Keeping You from the Love, Life and Career You Want.
- The Ultimate Secrets for Turning Setbacks and Heartbreaks into Triumphs.
- My Secret Method for Creating Soulmate Love that Lasts.

Facebook

Join me and more than 150,000 followers for daily inspiration and Facebook Live coaching sessions on my Facebook page, "Dating to True Love Mentor"! During the Live events, you'll have an opportunity to ask questions and share how your Love in 90 Days Program is going. I can't wait to hear about it! It's your opportunity to be part of a global community devoted to living a loving life each and every day. https://www.facebook.com/DrDianaKirschner.

NOTES

Introduction

xvii "When love beckons to you" Kahlil Gibran, *The Prophet* (New York: Alfred A. Knopf, 1983), 11.

xviii "a single forty-year-old woman" June 2, 1986, "The Marriage Crunch," *Newsweek*.

xviii "*Newsweek* recanted its own story" May 23, 2006, "The Marriage Crunch: Twenty Years Later," *Newsweek*.

xix "There is no mistaking love" Elisabeth Kubler-Ross, *The Wheel of Life: A Memoir of Living and Dying* (New York: Touchstone/Simon and Schuster, 1998), 192.

PART I. THE FIRST MONTH

Chapter 1: Your Love in 90 Days Program

3 "Love is everything it's cracked up to be" Erica Jong, *How to Save Your Own Life* (New York: Tarcher/Penguin, 2006), 263.

4 "Study after study has shown" For a thorough review of the literature, see R. Wood, B. Goesling, and S. Avellar, "The Effects of Marriage on Health: A Synthesis of Recent Research Evidence," Department of Health & Human Services, June 19, 2007, 1–68.

4 "a higher sense of self-worth" W. Gove, C. Style, and M. Hughes, 1990, "The Effect of Marriage on the Well-Being of Adults," *Journal of Family Issues*, 23, 4–35.

4 "provide intimacy and emotional support" J. House, D. Umberson, and K. Landis, 1988, "Structures and Processes of Social Support," *Annual Review of Sociology*, 14, 293–318.

4 "lead to greater wealth" R. Lerman, July 2002, "Marriage and the Economic Well-Being of Families with Children: A Review of the Literature," The Urban Institute and American University.

4 "married people may be happier" See M. Seligman's 1992 classic *Learned Optimism* (New York: Pocket Books). Among the many studies, Seligman cites a 35,000-person poll on happiness conducted by the National Opinion Research Center. The survey found that 40 percent of married folks reported they were "very happy" as compared with only 24 percent of the unmarried Americans.

4 "including depression" Wood et al., op. cit.

4 "better physical health" See, for example, J. Glaser, and T. Newton for a review of the literature, 2001, "Marriage and Health: His and Hers," *Psychological Bulletin*, 127, 472–503.

4 "greater health-seeking behavior" R. Kaplan and R. Kronick, 2006, "Marital Status and Longevity in the U.S. Population," *Journal of Epidemiology and Community Health*, 60, 760–765.

4 "lower rates of alcoholism" P. J. Curran, B. O. Muthen, and T. C. Harford, 1998, "The Influence of Changes in Marital Status on Developmental Trajectories of Alcohol Use in Young Adults," *Journal of Studies on Alcohol*, 59, 647–658.

4 "studies around the world" For an analysis of forty studies from both U.S. and global researchers on the relationship between marriage and longevity, see L. Manzoli, P. Villari, G. Pirone, and A. Boccia, 2007, "Marital Status and Mortality in the Elderly: A Systematic Review and Meta-Analysis," *Social Science and Medicine*, 64, 77–94.

5 "Love is a fruit in season at all times" Mother Teresa. Unsourced Wikiquote.

7 "Since love is the most delicate" José Ortega y Gasset, *On Love: Aspects of a Single Theme*, translator, Toby Talbot (New York: Meridian Books, Inc., 1958), 192.

17 "The irony of commitment" Anne Morriss, quoted on Web site http://www .getthenack.org/member.htm and on Starbucks coffee mugs.

19 "Top U.S. Online Dating Sites" ComScore Media Metrix, January 2006. Sites ranked by unique visitors.

20 "Top U.K. Online Dating Sites" ComScore Media Metrix, December 2006. Sites ranked by unique visitors.

21 "To reach the port of heaven" Oliver W. Holmes, Sr., *The Autocrat of the Breakfast Table* (New York: The Akadine Press, 2002), 78.

Chapter 2: The Deadly Dating Patterns

22 "It's not true that life" A. R. MacDougall, ed., *Letters of Edna St. Vincent Millay* (New York: Grosset & Dunlap, 1952). Letter, October 24, 1930.

22 "psychologists have studied" For a complete review of cognitive and cognitive-behavioral approaches and their effectiveness, see S. Holon and A. Beck, 1994. Cognitive and Cognitive-Behavioral Therapies in *Handbook of Psychotherapy and Behavior Change*, A. Bergin and S. Garfield, eds. (New York: John Wiley & Sons), 428–466.

23 "They play lead roles" First described by Albert Ellis, in *Reason and Emotion in Psychotherapy* (New York: Lyle Stuart, 1962).

23 "They underlie anxiety" S. Holon and A. Beck, op. cit., 428–430.

23 "the clinically proven tools" Many of the skills and exercises taught here rely on cognitive-behavioral techniques. Holon and Beck review the efficacy of these methods.

29 "alcoholic or drug-addicted parent" S. Kirschner, D. A. Kirschner, and R. L. Rappaport, *Working with Adult Incest Survivors: The Healing Journey* (New York: Brunner/Mazel, 1993).

32 "Your fellow is your mirror" Attributed to Rabbi Israel Baal Shem Tov at his official site, www.chabad.org.

43 "If you want to get somewhere" Norman Vincent Peale, *The Power of Positive Thinking* (New York: Prentice Hall, 1987), 96.

Chapter 3: Dating Games Men Play

44 "You come to love" Sam Keen. Quoted in *Perfecting: Webster's Quotations, Facts and Phrases* (San Diego: Icon Group International, 2008), 8.

70 "for the sole purpose of seducing as many women as possible" Read Neil Strauss's description of the seduction community and its techniques, in *The Game* (New York: William Morrow, 2005).

75 "It doesn't matter" *Good Will Hunting* script. Quoted in *Perfecting: Webster's Quotations, Facts and Phrases* (San Diego: Icon Group International, 2008), 2.

Chapter 4: Dating Three to Find the One

76 "Love moderately" W. Shakespeare, *Complete Works of William Shakespeare: Romeo and Juliet*, 2.6.14 (New York: Wordsworth Edition, 1997).

76 "By following this program" The Program of Three was first published in *Comprehensive Family Therapy* (New York: Brunner/Mazel, 1986), a book I co-authored with my husband, Sam Kirschner. Dr. Arthur Stein, my mentor, taught me an early form of the program. See Chapter 9.

77 "romantic love is a real addiction" Helen Fisher, *Why We Love: the Nature and Chemistry of Romantic Love* (New York: Henry Holt & Co., 2004).

77 "serotonin levels fall" D. Marazziti, H. Akiskal, A. Rossi, and G. B. Cassano, 1999, "Alteration of the Platelet Serotonin Transporter in Romantic Love," *Psychological Medicine*, 29, 741–745.

78 "the heat of Love" Homer, *The Iliad*, translator, R. Fagles (New York: Penguin Books, 1990), 376.

78 "Oxytocin...creates a strong biological attachment" See a review of the literature in M. Kosfeld, M. Heinrichs, P. J. Zak, E. Fehr, 2005, "Oxytocin Increases Trust in Humans," *Nature*, 435, 673–676.

79 "Those who want to trigger romance" H. Fisher, op. cit., 202.

79 "The world is full of abundance" M. David Dealy, Andrew R. Thomas, *Defining the Really Great Boss* (Westport, CT: Praeger Publishers/Greenwood Publishing Group, 2004), 50.

80 "more than 51 *million* single men" The 2017 Current Population Survey available at www.census.gov/.

85 "people who are emotionally aroused" D. G. Dutton and P. Aron, 1974, "Some Evidence of Heightened Sexual Attraction Under Conditions of High Anxiety," *Journal of Personality and Social Psychology*, 30, 510–517; A. Aron, D. G. Dutton, E. N. Aron, and A. Iverson, 1989, "Experiences of Falling in Love," *Journal of Social and Personal Relationships*, 6, 243–257; E. Hatfield and S. Sprecher, 1986, "Measuring Passionate Love in Intimate Relationships," *Journal of Adolescence*, 9, 383–410; E. Hatfield and R. Rapson, 1987, "Passionate Love/Sexual Desire: Can the Same Paradigm Explain Both? *Archives of Sexual Behavior*, 16, 259–278.

85 "Adrenaline makes the heart grow fonder" E. Walster and E. Berscheid, June 1971, "Adrenaline Makes the Heart Grow Fonder," *Psychology Today*, 47–62.

89 "86 percent of guys stress after a date" Cosmo Web poll, *Cosmopolitan*, December 2007, 56.

90 "guys were more likely to say" C. Meston and D. Buss, 2007, "Why Humans Have Sex," *Archives of Sexual Behavior*, 36, 477–507.

91 "An anonymous poll" www.match.com/magazine.

91 "the upsurge falls back down" M. R. Murphy, J. R. Seckl, S. Burton, S. A. Checkley, and S. L. Lightman, 1987, "Changes in Oxytocin and Vasopressin Secretion

During Sexual Activity in Men," *Journal of Clinical Endocrinology and Metabolism*, 65, 738–741.

95 "Mantra-based meditative processes" See the excellent review of the literature by R. K. Wallace, *The Neurophysiology of Enlightenment* (Fairfield, IA: MIU Press, 1991).

97 "The biggest human temptation" Thomas Merton, *Forbes* (New York: Forbes Publishing, April 4, 1980), 104.

Chapter 5: Secrets of Rapid Online and App Dating Success

98 "200 million singles" https://www.reuters.com/article/us-facebook-f8confer ence/facebook-to-play-cupid-in-online-dating-debut-idUSKBN1I23YV.

98 "one in three marriages" http://www.nydailynews.com/life-style/one-third-u -s-marriages-start-online-dating-study-article-1.1362743.

98 "59 percent of Americans" what-makes-us-click-how-online-dating-shapes-our -relationships.

99 "50 million people around the world" https://medium.com/the-mission/how -tinder-obtained-more-than-50-million-users-through-word-of-mouth-5d6105d24280.

99 "49 percent who message a match" https://www.theatlantic.com/health/archive /2016/10/the-unbearable-exhaustion-of-dating-apps/505184/.

101 "Singles in America Survey" singles-in-america-match-releases-largest-study -on-us-single-population-for-eighth-year-300591561.

101 "people aged 18 to 24" http://www.pewinternet.org/2016/02/11/15-percent-of -american-adults-have-used-online-dating-sites-or-mobile-dating-apps/.

102 "many of the online sites' personality tests" Industry white paper co-authored by M. Thompson, P. Zimbardo, and G. Hutchinson, 2005, *Consumers Are Having Second Thoughts About Online Dating*. Available at http://www.weattract.com/images /weAttract_whitepaper_v1_4.pdf, 1–51.

102 "You are never given a dream" Richard Bach, *Illusions: The Adventures of a Reluctant Messiah* (New York: Dell, 1989), 120.

103 "men are fourteen times more likely" www.match.com.

104 "dopamine...increases in activity" I. Aharon, N. Etcoff, D. Ariely, C. F. Chab-ris, E. O'Connor, and H. C. Breiter, 2001, "Beautiful Faces Have Variable Reward Value: fMRI and Behavioral Evidence," *Neuron*, 32, 537–551.

104 "Men consciously and unconsciously choose" V. S. Johnston, *Why We Feel: The Science of Human Emotions* (Cambridge, MA: Perseus Books, 1999).

112 "Top Online U.S. Dating Sites" ComScore Media Metrix, January 2006. Sites ranked by unique visitors.

113 "Top Online U.K. Dating Sites" Ibid.

121 "lost more than $230 million" https://www.consumerreports.org/dating-rela
tionships/online-dating-romance-scams/.

127 "Don't wait until everything is just right" J. Canfield and M. V. Hansen, *The Aladdin Factor* (New York: Berkley Books, 1995), 262.

PART II. *THE SECOND MONTH*

Chapter 6: Finding Love Mentors

132 "are more successful in their careers" S. Seibert and M. L. Kraimer, 2001, "A Social Capital Theory of Career Success," *The Academy of Management Journal*, 44, 219–237.

132 "and in school" M. Jacobi, 1991, "Mentoring and Undergraduate Academic Success: A Literature Review," *Review of Educational Research*, 61, 505–532.

132 "Women, in particular, have greatly benefited" R. A. Noe, 1988, "Women and Mentoring: A Review and Research Agenda," *The Academy of Management Review*, 13, 65–78.

132 "a heightened ability" M. Davidson and R. J. Burke, *Women in Management: Current Research Issues* (New York: P. Chapman Publishing, 1994).

132 "They do even better" Seibert, op. cit.

134 "You must be fearless enough" Oprah Winfrey, July 2001, "What I Know for Sure," *O, the Oprah Magazine*.

135 "Their failures" The original work in this section is found in Chapter 1 in Kirschner and Kirschner, *Comprehensive Family Therapy*, op. cit.

141 "Love's gift cannot be given" Rabindranath Tagore, *Fireflies*. Available in its entirety and translated from the Bengali at www.terebess.hu/english/tagore5, 21. With photo of original manuscript.

142 "Beauty is truth's smile" Tagore, *Fireflies*, Ibid., 12.

144 "Love adorns itself" From an essay by R. Tagore, "Modern Poetry," 1–8. Available at www.cscs.umich.edu/~crshalizi/Poetry/Tagore/modern-poetry.html.

Chapter 7: Discovering and Using Your Diamond Self

152 "Most of the shadows" Ralph Waldo Emerson, in Larry Chang, ed., *Wisdom for the Soul* (Washington, DC: Gnosophia Publishers, 2006), 644.

152 "The overwhelming majority" Madden, Pew Internet and American Life Project, op. cit., 11.

153 "Love is what we are born with" M. Williamson, *A Return to Love* (New York: HarperCollins, 1992), from Chapter 7.

155 "Every person is interesting" Jack teaches in New York and Los Angeles and can be reached at www.jackplotnick.com.

155 "He was Real...." Margery Williams, *The Velveteen Rabbit* (Philadelphia: Running Press, 1981), 24.

156 "creating happiness" R. A. Emmons and M. McCullough, 2003, "Counting Blessings vs. Burdens: An Experimental Investigation of Gratitude and Subjective Well-being in Daily Life," *Journal of Personality and Social Psychology*, 84, 377–389.

156 "contentment" L. J. Walker and R. C. Pitts, 1998, "Naturalistic Conceptions of Moral Maturity," *Developmental Psychology*, 34, 403–419.

156 "pride, and hope" F. Overwalle, I. Mervielde, and J. De Schuyter, 1995, "Structural Modeling of the Relationships Between Attributional Dimensions, Emotions, and Performance of College Freshmen," *Cognition and Emotion*, 9, 59–85.

156 "extremely happy" or "happy" G. H. Gallup, Jr., May 1998, *Thankfulness: America's Saving Grace*. Paper presented at the National Day of Prayer breakfast, Thanksgiving Square, Dallas.

157 "gratitude research suggests" Emmons and McCullough, op. cit.

157 "In three different studies" Ibid.

162 "confrontation is the single best approach" For a complete review of the effectiveness of exposure therapy, see S. Holon and A. Beck, op. cit.

164 "Each friend represents a world in us" Anais Nin, *The Diary of Anais Nin, Volume 2 (1934–1939)* (New York: Harvest/HBJ Book, 1970), 193.

164 "they are taught to share problems" Deborah Tannen, *You Just Don't Understand: Women and Men in Conversation* (New York: Ballantine Books, 1991).

164 "positive phenomenon of empowerment" A. Bandura, op. cit.

165 "Mighty I am" J. Karl, *Original Tribe Handbook of Angels* (Happy Camp, CA: Naturegraph, 1997).

166 "almost all of us come from one group" See Chapter 13 for the latest studies.

166 "you have from six to thirty seconds" N. Ambady and R. Rosenthal, 1993, "Half a Minute: Predicting Teacher Evaluations from Thin Slices of Non-Verbal Behavior and Physical Attractiveness," *Journal of Personality and Social Psychology*, 64, 431–441.

174 "Shine on you crazy diamond" Pink Floyd, 1975, "Shine on You Crazy Diamond" from *Wish You Were Here*, Capitol Records.

Chapter 8: One Simple Secret to Irresistible Self-Confidence

179 "positive self-talk which is very powerful" D. H. Meichenbaum, *Cognitive Behavior Modification: An Integrative Approach* (New York: Plenum Press, 1977). See a more recent and thorough review of the literature in D. Sherman and G. L. Cohen, 2006, "The Psychology of Self-Defense: Self-Affirmation Theory," in M. P. Zanna, ed., *Advances in Experimental Social Psychology*, 38, 183–242.

179 "change behavior in underachieving students" J. Schimmel, J. Arndt, K. Banko, and A. Cook, 2004, "Not All Self-Affirmations Were Created Equal: The Cognitive and Social Benefits of Affirming the Intrinsic Self," *The Art and Science of Self-Defense*, 22, 75–99.

179 "increase nurses' and doctors' well-being" G. Yamey and M. Wilkes, 2001, "Promoting Well-Being Among Doctors," *British Medical Journal*, 322, 252–253.

179 "reduce breast cancer patients' cortisol levels" Ibid.

179 "heighten athletic performance" K. Mills, K. Munroe, and C. Hall, 2001, "The Relationship Between Imagery and Self-Efficacy in Competitive Athletes," *Imagination, Cognition and Personality*, 20, 33–39.

179 "Participants in one study" S. Spencer, S. Fein, and C. Lomore, 2001, "Maintaining One's Self-Image vis a vis Others: The Role of Self-Affirmation in the Social Evaluation of the Self," *Motivation and Emotion*, 25, 41–65.

182 "You can be the prime and sole architect" Meichenbaum, op. cit.; A. Bandura, 1997, op. cit.

192 "Be to yourself" W. Shakespeare, "Henry VIII," *Complete Works of William Shakespeare* (New York: Wordsworth Edition, 1997), 1.1.135.

192 "May you not forget" https://www.coraevans.com/blog/article/14-Of-The-Most -Powerful-Peace-Quotes-From-St-Teresa-Of-Avila.

Chapter 9: Field Report on DUDs and STUDs

209 "married men were more likely" D. Popence and B. Whitehead, 2004, *The State of Our Unions*. The National Marriage Project, Rutgers University, 6–14.

209 "Those who came from traditional backgrounds" Ibid., 11.

209 "these men are seeking a 'soulmate'" Ibid., 2002 Gallup poll commissioned by the National Marriage Project and cited on p. 14.

209 "significant differences" Popence and Whitehead, op. cit., 13.

209 "'if you marry'" Ibid., 12.

210 "Does there within thy dimmest dreams" Adelaide Procter, "A Woman's Question," *Library of World Poetry*. W. C. Bryant, ed. (New York: Avenel Books, 1976), 63.

213 "Without words, without even understanding" Lao Tzu, *The Tao Te Ching of Lao Tzu* (New York: St. Martin's Griffin, 1996).

Chapter 10: Ditching Deadly Dating Patterns Forever

215 "Autobiography in Five Short Chapters," Portia Nelson, from the book *There's a Hole in My Sidewalk* (Hillsboro, OR: Beyond Words Publishing, 1993), 2.

222 "You have to realize" *Al-Anon's Twelve Steps and Twelve Traditions* (Virginia Beach, VA: Al-Anon Family Group Headquarters, Inc., 2005).

230 "you will maximize your odds" F. Mosteller, *Fifty Challenging Problems in Probability with Solutions* (Boston: Addison-Wesley, 1987).

230 "you will have entered the sweet spot" Ibid.

235 "When two people are at one" Richard Wilhelm, Cary F. Baynes, *I Ching or Book of Changes* (New York: Pantheon Books, 1955), 329.

PART III. *THE THIRD MONTH*

Chapter 11: First Aid for Heartache

239 "For even as love crowns you" Gibran, op. cit., 11.

240 "the process of growth always includes setbacks" S. Kirschner and D.A. Kirschner, 1991, "The Two Faces of Change: Progression and Regression," in R.C. Curtis and G. Stricker, eds., *How People Change: Inside and Outside Therapy* (New York: Plenum Press), 117–127.

240 "Love anything" C. S. Lewis, in *Simply C. S. Lewis* by Thomas C. Peters (Wheaton, IL: Good News Publishers, 1997), 179.

241 "Your brain is in a state" Fisher, op. cit., 183.

242 "being divorced is the number two" T. H. Holmes and R. H. Rahe, 1967, "The Social Readjustment Rating Scale," *Journal of Psychosomatic Research*, 11, 213–218.

242 "number one, being widowed" Ibid.

242 "Researchers at UCLA" N. Eisenberger, J. Jarcho, M. Lieberman, and B. D. Naliboff, 2006, "An Experimental Study of Shared Sensitivity to Physical Pain and Social Rejection," *Pain*, 126, 132–138.

242 "They call it broken heart syndrome" I. S. Wittstein et al., 2005, "Neurohumoral Features of Myocardial Stunning Due to Sudden Emotional Stress," *New England Journal of Medicine*, 352, 539–548. Posted online on February 10, 2005, at www.nejm.org.

243 "being with close friends" Eisenberger, op. cit.

243 "Johns Hopkins researchers" Wittstein et al., op. cit.

243 "a regular relaxation or meditation program" Wallace, 1991, op. cit.

244 "People who have imaginary conversations" K. Shear, 2005, "Treatment of Complicated Grief: A Randomized Controlled Trial," *Journal of the American Medical Association,* 293, 2601–2608.

245 "we are wired genetically" See Koestler's work reviewed in D. Kirschner and S. Kirschner, 1984, op. cit., Chapter 1.

245 "Your old identities" D. W. Winnicott, *Maturational Processes and the Facilitating Environment* (London: Karnac Books, 1996).

246 "turning to your Love Mentors" Kirschner and Kirschner, 1984, op. cit.

248 "A vengeful lack of forgiveness" The Stanford Forgiveness Project. See D. Tibbits, G. Ellis, C. Piramelli, F. Luskin, and R. Lukman, 2006, "Hypertension Reduction Through Forgiveness Training," *Journal of Pastoral Care and Counseling,* 60, 27–34.

251 "there is a positive and healing physical effect" Dozens of studies cited in L. Dossey, *Healing Words: The Power of Prayer and the Practice of Medicine* (San Francisco: Harper, 1993).

256 "Look lovingly on some object" Paul Reps, Nyogen Senzaki, *Zen Flesh, Zen Bones* (Boston: Tuttle Books, 1998), 199.

256 "Realize that we are not alone" Sri Daya Mata, *Enter the Quiet Heart* (Los Angeles: Self-Realization Publishers, 1998), 10.

256 "a wild delight" Ralph Waldo Emerson, *Emerson: Essays and Lectures* (New York: Library of America, 1983), 10.

257 "New research shows" N. Wolfinger, 2006, *Does the Rebound Effect Exist?* Available at http://paa2006.princeton.edu/download.aspx?submissionId=61125.

258 "Both psychotherapy and antidepressant drugs" A. L. Brody, 2001, "Regional Brain Metabolic Changes in Patients with Major Depression Treated with Either Paroxetine or Interpersonal Therapy," *Archives of General Psychiatry,* 58, 631–640.

262 "It is by going down" Joseph Campbell, Joseph Campbell with Bill Moyers, *The Power of Myth* (New York: Doubleday, 1988), 37.

Chapter 12: Beware of Frenemies

263 "It is difficult to say" Attributed to the novelist Edward Bulwer-Lytton in Wikiquote.com.

263 "Frenemies" was first coined by the group the New Radicals, in their hit song

"You Get What You Give" (1999) and then later was used as the title of an episode on *Sex and the City* (HBO, 2000).

264 "I have no trouble with my enemies" Attributed to President Harding in N. Miller, *New World Coming: The Making of Modern America* (New York: Scribner's, 2003), 116.

265 "your friend or family member airs a complaint" Tannen, op. cit.

265 "you will tend to re-create" Meichenbaum, 1977, op. cit.

266 Term "cynics" coined by J. Pressler, December 2007, "Wedding Belle Blues," *Philadelphia*, 82–88.

266 "wish for you to remain as the old you" In systems theory this dynamic is called homeostasis—the tendency in close relationships to maintain the status quo. See Kirschner and Kirschner, *Comprehensive Family Therapy*, op. cit., 2–3.

267 "the crucial role of our childhood experiences" John Bowlby, *Attachment and Loss* (New York: Rand, 1997).

267 "attachment behavior" Ibid.

268 "annihilation fear" Ibid.

268 "In cases of sexual and physical abuse" See S. Kirschner, D. A. Kirschner, and R. Rappaport, *Working with Adult Incest Survivors: The Healing Journey* (New York: Brunner/Mazel, 1993).

268 "therapy for survivors" Ibid.

281 "Let us be grateful" Marcel Proust, in *The Columbia Dictionary of Quotations* by Robert Andrews (New York: Columbia University Press, 1993), 393.

Chapter 13: Love Secrets Just for You

282 "Every situation, properly perceived" Helen Schucman and W. Thedford, eds., *Jesus' Course in Miracles* (Omaha: Course in Miracles Society, 2000), 188.

282 "Our strength often increases" Multiple sources including, C. N. Catrevas, 1960, *The New Dictionary of Thoughts: A Cyclopedia of Quotations from the Best*, 173.

283 "there are fewer *available* African-American men" There are about 85 males for every 100 females. See www.census.gov/population for 1998 survey.

283 "the rate of incarceration" See Bureau of Justice statistics on race and crime at www.ojp.usdoj.gov/bjs/crimoff.htm.

283 "an underground practice called the 'down low'" B. Denizet-Lewis, August 3, 2003, "Double Lives on the Down Low," *The New York Times*. Nytimes.com. M. Miller, M. Semer and M. Wagner, 2006, "Sexual Diversity Among Black Men Who Have Sex with Men in an Inner City Community," *Journal of Urban Health* 82, 26–34.

283 "increasing the number of HIV/AIDS cases" Fact Sheet: HIV/AIDS Among African-Americans. Revised June 2007, www.cdc.gov/hiv/topics/aa/resources /factsheets.

283 "Research has also shown" National Center for Health Statistics, U.S., 1999. Hyattsville, MD: U.S. Dept. of HHS, CDC.

283 "college-educated black women" Bob Herbert, December 4, 1994, "Who Will Help the Black Man?" *The New York Times*.

283 "the 'marriage squeeze'" Kyle D. Crowder and Stewart E. Tolnay, August 14, 2006 "A New Marriage Squeeze for Black Women: The Role of Racial Intermarriage by Black Men" *Newsweek*.

284 "You may encounter many defeats" Quoted in C. Cosby and R. Poussaint, eds., *A Wealth of Wisdom: Legendary African-American Elders Speak* (New York: Simon & Schuster, 2004).

284 "The support of extended kin" Cynthia Fuchs Epstein, 1973, "Positive Effects of the Multiple Negative: Explaining the Success of Black Professional Women," *The American Journal of Sociology*, 78, 912–935.

284 "modern man first evolved" C. Stringer and P. Andrews, 1988, "Genetic and Fossil Evidence for the Origin of Modern Humans," *Science*, 239, 1263–1268.

285 "DNA research" See Rebecca Cann, M. Stoneking, and A. C. Wilson, 1987, "Mitochondrial DNA and Human Evolution," *Nature*, 325, 3 1–36; Leonard Lieberman and F. Jackson, 1995, "Race and Three Models of Human Origin," *American Anthropologist*, 97, 235–239; Hua Liu et al., 2006, "A Geographically Explicit Genetic Model of Worldwide Human-Settlement History," *The American Journal of Human Genetics*, 79, 230–237.

285 "Mitochondrial Eve," Cann et al. Ibid.

285 "detailed interviews of very accomplished black men" Lois Merriweather Moore, *Voices of Successful African-American Men* (Lewiston, NY: Edward Mellen Press, 2004).

285 "recently married black men" http://www.pewresearch.org/fact-tank/2015 /06/12/interracial-marriage-who-is-marrying-out/.

285 "college educated black men" https://www.thoughtco.com/the-top-myths -about-black-marriage-2834526.

285 "the more educated you are" Elaina Rose, 2004, *Education and Hypergamy in Marriage Markets*. Also see Rose, 2005, *Education and Hypergamy and the "Success Gap."* Both papers available at www.csss.washington.edu/Papers.

286 "marital satisfaction and dissatisfaction" J. Taylor 1990, "Relationship Between Internalized Racism and Marital Satisfaction," *Journal of Black Psychology*, 16, 45–53.

287 "We must recognize" Interview dated October 15, 2007.

289 "Ask for what you want" Unreferenced quote from en.wikiquote.org/wiki /Maya_Angelou.

289 "there are 12 million single parent households" https://singlemotherguide.com /single-mother-statistics/.

289 "more prone to psychological distress" See, for example, Lorraine Davies, William R. Avison, Donna D. McAlpine, 1997, "Significant Life Experiences and Depression Among Single and Married Mothers," *Journal of Marriage and the Family*, 59, 294–308.

291 "reasons why single men might prefer" Available at www.boston.per sonals.yahoo.com/us/static/single-mom_guys.

291 "engage in sexual activity sooner" Les B. Whitbeck, Kevin A. Yoder, Dan R. Hoyt, and Rand D. Conger, 1999, "Early Adolescent Sexual Activity: A Developmental Study," *Journal of Marriage and the Family*, 61, 934–946.

292 "sets your man up" See Chapter 10 in Kirschner and Kirschner, *Comprehensive Family Therapy*, op. cit.

294 "men would rather marry" John Schwartz, December 14, 2004, "Glass Ceiling at Altar as Well as Bedroom," *New York Times*.

294 "another *Times* column" Maureen Dowd, October 30, 2005, "What's a Modern Girl to Do?" *New York Times*.

294 "both online and offline media" Amanda May, *Successful Women: Undateable?* posted on match.com, December 2007.

295 "Researchers tested 120 male undergraduates" S. Brown and B. Lewis, 2004, "Relational Dominance and Mate Selection Criteria: Evidence That Males Attend to Female Dominance," *Evolution and Human Behavior*, 25, 406–415.

295 "responsibility for disciplining absence" Ibid., 412.

295 "men with MBAs" T. W. Harrell, 1993, "Women with MBAs Marry Up While Men with MBAs Marry Down," *Psychological Reports*, 72, 1178.

296 "spouses tend to show similar educational achievements" See, for example, Blossfeld and Tim, 1997.

296 "partners who are similar in attitudes" L. Shanhong and E. C. Klohnen, 2005, "Assortative Mating and Marital Quality in Newlyweds: A Couple-Centered Approach," *Journal of Personality and Social Psychology*, 88, 305–326.

296 "educational homogamy rates have *increased*" Blossfeld and Tim, op. cit.

296 "For women in their forties" Blossfeld and Tim, eds., *Who Marries Whom?: Educational Systems as Marriage Markets in Modern Societies* (New York: Springer, 2003).

Notes

296 "a study of educational homogamy in marriage" H. Domanski and D. Przybysz, 2007, "Educational Homogamy in 22 European Countries," *European Societies,* 9, 495–526.

296 "a college graduate brought her man" S. M. Worner, 2007, *Marriage and Education in Australia,* discussion Paper #550, Australian National University, 1–69. Available at http://econrsss.anu.edu.au/pdf/DP550.pdf.

297 "men in the 1990s" https://www.smh.com.au/opinion/marrying-down-why-men -are-the-ones-now-looking-for-wealthy-wives-20170831-gy7ykl.html. See also https://www .academia.edu/32056972/Womens_Progress_for_Mens_Gain_Gender-Specific _Changes_in_the_Return_to_Education_as_Measured_by_Family_Standard-of-Living _1990_to_2009-11.

297 "71 percent of high-earning or graduate-educated men" C. Whelan, 2007, *SWANS Song: Why Gentlemen Prefer Brains?* Posted August 7, 2007, on huffingtonpost.com.

297 "smarter women actually tend to take better care of their bodies" C. Whelan, *Why Smart Men Marry Smart Women* (New York: Simon & Schuster, 2006).

297 "Being visually appealing" S. W. Gangestad and R. Thornhill, 1997, "The Evolutionary Psychology of Extra-Pair Sex: The Role of Fluctuating Asymmetry," *Evolution and Human Behavior,* 18, 69–88.

297 "Gentlemen prefer brains" C. Whelan, 2007, op. cit.

298 "a delay in the age at which women marry" The 2005 CPS, op. cit.

298 "education is becoming less of an impediment" In addition see also Elaina Rose, 2004, op. cit., 14.

299 "there are demographers" J. W. Rowe, 1997 editorial: "A New Gerontology," *Science,* 278, 367.

299 "the giddy swirl of romantic passion" H. Fisher, 2004, op. cit., 4–6. She conducted her own study on romantic love at Rutgers University with more than eight hundred subjects.

299 "Seventy percent of single baby boomers" *AARP Survey: Study Reveals Baby Boomers' Dating Habits,* posted on www.NBC4.com, April 3, 2006.

299 "Boomers have also taken to online dating" Vanessa Juarez, 2006, *Boomers and Sex,* posted on Newsweek.com, February 20, 2006.

299 "positive changes in the emotional brain" L. M. Williams et al., 2006, "The Mellow Years?: Neural Basis of Improving Emotional Stability Over Age," *The Journal of Neuroscience,* 26, 6422–6430.

300 "it releases endorphins" See the literature review in N. E. Rosenthal, *The Emotional Revolution: How the New Science of Feelings Can Transform Your Life* (New York: Citadel Press Books, 2002).

302 "Exercise creates happiness" N. E. Rosenthal, 2002, Ibid.

303 "Meditation and other mind/body practices" See the complete review of more than six hundred studies in R. K. Wallace, 1991, op. cit. More recent work on meditation published on February 6, 2003, by research team at University of Wisconsin, posted at www.news.wisc.edu/packages/emotion.

303 "A comprehensive study" S. T. Lindau, L. Waite, P. Schumm, C. A. O'Muircheartaigh, and W. Levinson, 2007, "A National Study of Sexuality and Health Among Older Adults in the U.S.," *New England Journal of Medicine*, 357, 762–774.

304 "66 percent of relationships" Pew Internet and American Life Project, 2006, op. cit.

304 "Sixteen million singles" Ibid.

305 "only 39 percent of those who were having regular sex" AARP Survey, op. cit.

305 "number of AIDS cases in women age fifty and older" Vanessa Juarez, 2006, op. cit.

308 "Life shrinks or expands" Anais Nin, *The Diary of Anais Nin, Volume Three (1939–1944)* (New York: HBJ Inc., 1969), 125.

Chapter 14: How Happy Couples Work

309 "Married people are healthier" Gove, Style, and Hughes, op. cit.

309 "Marital happiness contributes far more" Ibid.

310 "From every human being there rises a light" Attributed to Rabbi Israel Baal Shem Tov and used in the Jewish wedding document, the Ketuba.

311 "After about two to three years" I. Kerner, *Sex Detox* (New York: Collins Living, 2008).

313 "spouses in long marriages shape each other" John M. Gottman, *The Marriage Clinic: A Scientifically Based Marital Therapy* (New York: W. W. Norton, 1999).

313 "a flow of brain chemicals that generates attachment" Fisher, op. cit., 89.

313 "All happy families resemble one another" L. Tolstoy, *Anna Karenina* (New York: Signet Books, 2002), 1.

314 "Researchers have identified almost all" J. M. Gottman, 1999, op. cit.

315 "In long-term healthy couples" R. W. Levenson, L. Carstensen, and J. M. Gottman, 1993, "Long-Term Marriage: Age, Gender and Satisfaction," *Psychology and Aging*, 8, 301–313.

315 "Loving couples share rituals" W. J. Dougherty, *The Intentional Family: How to Build Family Ties in Our Modern World* (Reading, MA: Addison-Wesley, 1997).

315 "Celebrations of each partner's triumphs" S. L. Gable, G. Gonzaga, and

A. Strachman, 2006, "Will You Be There for Me When Things Go Right? Social Support for Positive Events," *Journal of Personality and Social Psychology*, 91, 904–917.

315 "spending time alone as a couple" Jerry. I. Kleiman, 1981, "Optimal and Normal Family Functioning," *The American Journal of Family Therapy*, 9, 37–44.

315 "about 80 percent of people who divorce" L. Gigy and J. Kelly, 1992, "Reasons for Divorce: Perspectives of Divorcing Men and Women," *Journal of Divorce and Remarriage*, 18, 169–187.

316 "three primary ways" D. Mosher, 1980, "Three Psychological Dimensions of Depth of Involvement in Human Sexual Responses," *Journal of Sex Research*, 16, 1–42.

316 "At the highest level of partner engagement" Vatsyayana and R. Burton, *The Kama Sutra of Vatsyayana* (New York: Dover Publications, 2006).

317 "sensate focus" W. H. Masters and V. E. Johnson, *The Pleasure Bond* (New York: Bantam Books, 1974).

317 "Stephen did all the research" B. Katie and S. Mitchell, *A Thousand Names for Joy: Living in Harmony with the Way Things Are* (New York: Harmony Books, 2007).

317 "It is dedication and commitment" S. Nock, 1995, "Commitment and Dependency in Marriage," *Journal of Marriage & the Family*, 57, 503–514.

317 "Commitment is related to better relationship quality" S. M. Stanley and H. J. Markman, 1992, "Assessing Commitment in Personal Relationships," *Journal of Marriage & the Family*, 54, 595–608.

317 "Faithfulness is a key to a happy marriage" Gigy and Kelly, op. cit.

317 "it is not infidelity that usually kills marriages" Ibid.

317 "many couples have weathered an affair" Diana A. Kirschner and S. Kirschner, 1990, "Reparation and Forgiveness in Marital Life," *The Family Psychologist*, 6, 30–31.

318 "the needs of the couple or the other partner" Stanley and Markman, op. cit.

318 "Dedication also involves a willingness" D. A. Kirschner and S. Kirschner, 1984, op. cit., Chapter 2.

318 "he encourages his Beloved" Ibid.

319 "as study after study has shown" R. W. Levenson et al., op. cit.

320 "Once the realization is accepted" R. M. Rilke, *Rilke on Love and Other Difficulties* (New York: W. W. Norton, 2004).

321 "over 69 percent of long-term couples" Gottman, 1999, op. cit.

321 "the inner world of the self is more fulfilled" D. Schnarch, *Passionate Marriage* (New York: Henry Holt & Co., 1997).

322 "Healthy spouses are realistic" Stanley and Markman, op. cit.

322 "pain of loss" Bowlby, op. cit.

322 "economic and other real costs" Gary Becker, *A Treatise on the Family* (Cambridge, MA: Harvard University Press, 1981), 224.

322 "a partner will use a fear-of-loss maneuver" D. Kirschner and S. Kirschner, 1990, "Reparation and Forgiveness in Marital Life," *The Family Psychologist*, 6, 30–31.

323 "He who is in love" Ralph Waldo Emerson, "The Method of Nature" in *The Works of Ralph Waldo Emerson* (London: Macmillan & Co, 1884), 176.

324 "appreciation and gratitude lead to happiness" M. Seligman, op. cit.

325 "Mend your speech a little" W. Shakespeare, *King Lear*, 1.1.96.

326 "healthy couples…show a five-to-one ratio" J. Gottman, 1999, op. cit., 38.

326 "soft start-up" Ibid., 224.

326 "fighting is an important way" J. M. Gottman, *Why Marriages Succeed or Fail* (New York: Simon & Schuster, 1994).

326 "Partners on the verge of breaking up" Ibid.

327 "Beware of entrance to a quarrel" W. Shakespeare, *Hamlet*, 1.1.65.

327 "double the mortality rate" E. Harburg, M. Julius, N. Kaciroti, L. Gleiberman, and M. Schork, 2008, "Expressive/Suppressive Anger-Coping Responses, Gender and Types of Mortality," *Journal of Family Communication*, January.

328 "when couples are asked to calm down" D. Zillmann, *Hostility and Aggression* (Hillsdale, NJ: Lawrence Erlbaum, 1979).

328 "these couples operate out of a fundamental paradox" N. S. Jacobson and A. Christensen, *Integrative Couple Therapy: Promoting Acceptance and Change* (New York: Norton, 1996).

330 "Partners in a loving relationship recognize" Ibid.

330 "this habit of effectively teaming and coordinating activities" M. Kumashiro, E. J. Finkel, C. E. Rusbult, 2002, "Self-Respect and Pro-Relationship Behavior in Marital Relationships," *Journal of Personality*, 70, 1006–1050.

330 "there is shared power" John Gottman and Nan Silver, *The Seven Principles for Making Marriage Work* (New York: Three Rivers Press, 1999).

330 "a fair distribution of household chores" Jay Belsky and John Kelly, *The Transition to Parenthood* (New York: Dell, 1994).

330 "men who do housework" J. M. Gottman, 1994, op. cit.

330 "If there are biological children or stepchildren" D. A. Kirschner and S. Kirschner, 1984, op. cit., Chapter 10.

331 "in healthy, happy stepfamilies" Ibid.

331 "an 81 percent chance the marriage will be damaged" J. M. Gottman, 1999, op. cit., 101.

332 "an inability to team" Kumashiro et al., op. cit.

335 "The thought manifests as the word" Buddha, in *Meditation for Life* by Martine Batchelor (Somerville, MA: Wisdom Publications, 2001), 156.

Chapter 15: Launch to More Love

339 "In that communion only" Plato, *Symposium* (Sioux Falls, SD: NuVision Publications, 2007), 48.

340 "I never failed once" Attributed to Thomas Alva Edison in Jack Canfield and Mark Victor Hansen, *A 2nd Helping of Chicken Soup for the Soul* (Deerfield Beach, FL: HCI, 1995), 253.

344 "Fly free and happy" Richard Bach, *There's No Such Place as Far Away* (New York: Dell, 1998), 44.

INDEX

Abuse Recycle Deadly Dating
  Pattern, 29–30, 134, 268
Abuse Recycle Deadly Dating Pattern
  Fix, 223–224
activity level and breakups, 243
affirmations. *See* self-affirmations
African-American men, 283, 284,
  285, 289
African-American women
  availability of African-American
    men, 283, 284, 285
  dating exercises, 306–307
  dating sites and apps for, 289
  digital dating and, 283, 285
  homework, 308–309
  interracial dating and, 286–288
  tips for, 288–289
age. *See also* over forty-fives
  apps and, 19, 101
  Dating Program of Three potential
    candidates and, 194–195
  meditation and, 303
  "mellowing" of brain with, 299
  online profiles and, 110–111
  transformation of physical
    appearance and, 143

AIDS
  African-American women and, 283
  over forty-fives and, 305
Alcoholic Men's Deadly Dating
  Pattern, 70
alcoholics, 69–70
American Psychological Association,
  258
Angelou, Maya, 284, 289
anxiety
  handling, 162
  as helpful, 161
  self-sabotage and, 23
appreciation
  expressing, and happiness of
    married couples, 323–325,
    333–334
  in healthy relationships, 312–313
  letter to Beloved, 334
  letter to self, 33
  lists, 170
  practicing, 156–158
  as result of teamwork, 330–331
  self-, exercise, 170
  showing, 324–325
apps. *See* dating sites and apps

authentic self
    exercise for rediscovering, 170
    of happily married partners,
        320–321
    rediscovering, 154–155
    reframing painful memories and,
        156–157

Baal Shem Tov, 310
baby boomers
    dating exercises, 306–307
    Dating Program of Three and, 305
    dating sites and apps, 299, 304
    flirting by, 305
    happiness of, 299
    homework, 308–309
    makeover of physical appearance,
        303
    meditation and, 303
    need to youthify, 302–303
    negative self-talk by, 298–299,
        303
    physical exercise and, 302–303
    sexual activity of, 303, 305
    tips for, 305–306
Bach, Richard, 102
Batson, Susan, 286–287, 288
beauty
    Diamond Self name and, 160
    making over, 303
    Outer Work Mentors to nurture,
        142
    own perception of body, 188
    physical health and, 117
    prayer for, 165
    relationship between love and, 144
    self-confidence and, 186–189
    self-love and, 143–144
    of smarter women, 297
    to-do list, 149
being-in-the-moment meditation,
    255–256
blended families, 292–293
body blues, 187, 189
bot profiles, 99

Bowlby, John, 267–269
brain
    breakups and, 206, 242
    deliberate stimulation, 183
    Higher Power and, 252
    malleability of structure, 158
    meditation and, 252
    "mellowing" of, with age, 299
breakups
    brain and, 206, 242
    depression and, 258
    dopamine and, 241
    emotions brought out by, 245
    heartache as inevitable, 240–241
    learning from, 248–250
    letters and, 247
    master Love Mentors and, 243,
        250
    physical exercise for, 244
    physical health and, 206–207
    revenge and, 248–250
    self-talk after, 244–245, 249
broken heart syndrome (BHS),
    206–207, 242–243
Buddha, 335
Bulwer-Lytton, Edward, 263
Burns, Khephra, 288
Burnt Toast Men's Deadly Dating
    Pattern, 55–56

Campbell, Joseph, 161
Canfield, Jack, 127
Care-Full Communication, 325–327,
    342, 349
Chase Me Deadly Dating Pattern,
    33–34, 268
Chase Me Deadly Dating Pattern Fix,
    226–227
chemistry of love
    dating without, 84–85
    stimulating, 85, 86
    visual images and, 104
Chicken Soup for the Soul series
    (Canfield and Hansen), 127
Chopra, Priyanka, 300

coaching program
about, xv, xxi
website, 82, 132, 248
college educated African-American
men, 285
college educated women
with advanced degrees, 295, 296
African-American, 285
dating exercises, 306–307
homework, 308–309
as at marriage disadvantage,
294–295
as at marriage disadvantage as
myth, 296–298
tips for, 298
commitment
exercise for self-, 42
of happy couples, 317–319
men's fears and, 45
signs of lack of, 92
Commitment Phobe Men's Deadly
Dating Pattern, 61–63
committed partner, as master Love
Mentor, 138–139
competitiveness and Dating Program
of Three, 78–79
confidence. See self-confidence
constructive criticism, 331
Contract of Acknowledgment and
Commitment Contract of Love in
90 Days, 15–17, 342–344
control freaks, 72–73
Cosmo, 89
Coward Men's Deadly Dating
Pattern, 53–54
Cross, Marcia, 18
Crumbs Deadly Dating Pattern,
26–27, 267
Crumbs Deadly Dating Pattern Fix,
220–221
cynics, 266

dating
interracial, 285, 286–288
journaling reasons for not, 212

maximizing odds of finding best
candidate, 230
self-affirmations for, 190
DatingDirect.com, 112
Dating Program of Three
African-American women and, 286
basics of, 76
exercises, 94–96
finding men to date, 79–81
getting rid of stinking thinking,
81–82
guidelines, 93–94
healing heartbreak with, 257
homework, 96–97
Jealousy Trap Fix and, 228
over forty-fives and, 305
putting on hold, 203
questions to ask about candidates,
194–196
reasons for success of, 77–79
replacement hunt, 91
rule 1. DUD/STUD test, 82–84
rule 2. dating against type, 84–85
rule 3. use OPEN Technique,
85–86
rule 4. working, for special guy,
86–87
rule 5. honesty about dating others,
87–88
rule 6. allocating time for each guy,
88–89
rule 7. making Proactive Moves,
89–90
rule 8. no sex, 90–91
rule 9. ranking in order guys dating,
91–92
rule 10. choosing the One, 92
teamwork and, 332
TTLC list and, 202
dating sites and apps. See also Secrets
of Rapid Online and App Dating
Success
African Americans and, 283, 289
challenges to using, xiv–xv
choosing, 111

dating sites and apps (*cont.*)
DatingDirect.com, 112
Facebook, xiii–xiv, 354
finding, 19
homework, 150
interracial marriage and, 286
JDate.com, 113–114
leading to marriages, 102
listing productivity of, 100, 114
Match.com, 91
myths about, 101–102
negative aspects, 99, 123
number of monthly users, xiii, 98
online profiles, xiv, 106–108,
    109–111
over forty-fives and, 299, 304
personality tests, 102
popularity of, 101
safety tip for initial in-person
    conversation, 119
switching, 115
Tinder, xiv, 99, 286
top European, 112, 113
top U.K., 20, 113
top U.S., 19–20, 112
wading through many DUDs,
    122–123
Deadly Dating Patterns
Abuse Recycle, 29–30, 134, 268
Chase Me, 33–34, 268
Crumbs, 26–27, 267
exercises for facing, 38–42
Fade Away, 34–35
Fantasy Relationship, 24–26
Flame-Out, 23–24, 77, 86–87
Grass Is Greener, 37–38, 268
Hermit, 27–28, 267
homework for overcoming, 42–43
I'll Make You Love Me, 28–29, 268
Jealousy Trap, 35–36
Just Buddies, 36–37
Not Perfect—I'll Pass, 31–33
parental attachments as cause,
    267–268
resurfacing of, 215

Safety Net, 30–31
self-sabotage, 22–23
Deadly Dating Patterns Fix-It Kit
about, 216–217
Abuse Recycle Fix, 223–224
Chase Me Fix, 226–227
Crumbs Fix, 220–221
exercises, 232–234
Fade Away Fix, 227–228
Fantasy Relationship Fix, 219–220
Flame-Out Fix, 217–219
Grass Is Greener Fix, 230–231
Hermit Fix, 221–222
homework, 235
I'll Make You Love Me Fix,
    222–223
Jealousy Trap Fix, 228–229
Just Buddies Fix, 229
Not Perfect—I'll Pass Fix, 225–226
Safety Net Fix, 225
depression
breakups and, 258
divorce and, 242
dopamine and, 241
Desert Island exercise, 212
Diamond Self
dedication to development of
    partner's, 318–319
described, 132, 152, 153
destroying Disappointing Self with,
    160
exercises for discovering and using,
    169–172
Fade Away Deadly Dating Pattern
    Fix and, 227
Five-Minute Manifestation Miracle
    Exercise and, 183, 184–185
homework, 173–174
life-changing exercise, 158–161
mini-exercises, 157, 166
name and Crumbs Deadly Fix,
    220
name and physical appearance,
    160
name and self-confidence, 179

name in affirmation, 181
networking and, 152, 164–165
step 1 to creating: rediscovering
    authentic self, 154–155
step 2 to creating: practicing
    gratitude, 156–158
step 3 to creating: life-changing self
    exercise, 158–161
step 4 to creating: facing fear,
    161–163
digital dating. See dating sites and
    apps
disagreements, 327–329
Disappointing Self
    bringing forth with self-
        affirmations, 177
    described, 160
    destroying, 160, 182
    Five-Minute Manifestation Miracle
        Exercise and, 183–184, 190
Dispenza, Joe, 158, 177, 186
Divine Consciousness/Presence. See
    Higher Power
"Divine Has Your Back" Exercise,
    254–255
divorce, 242
dopamine
    depression and, 241
    endurance of, 311
    intimacy and, 316
    sexual activity and, 78
    visual images and, 104
Dowd, Maureen, 294
DUDs (Definitely Unworkable
    Dudes)and STUDs (Seriously
    Terrific, Utterly Devoted Dudes).
    See also Field Reports on DUDs
        and STUDS
    apps and, 99
    chemistry and, 196–198
    exercise for pulling away from
        DUDs, 232
    need to wade through, 122–123,
        194
    ranking, 198

red flag warning signs, 120
test, 82–84
turning Safety Net DUDs into
    STUDs, 225

Edison, Thomas, 340
education, 296–297. See also college
    educated women
Eight Habits of Living Love, 314
    1. cultivating intimacy, 315–317
    2. acting out dedication and service,
        317–319
    3. acting from Enlightened
        Selfishness, 319–321, 349
    4. considering cost of loss, 322–323
    5. showing appreciation and
        gratitude, 323–325
    6. practicing Care-Full
        Communication, 325–327, 342,
        349
    7. following Fight Club rules,
        327–329
    8. working as team, 330–332
    exercises, 332–334
    homework, 334–335
    practicing, as lifelong endeavor, 310
Eight Steps to Love, 337, 344–346,
    351
Emerson, Ralph Waldo, 152, 256, 323
emotional health. See also happiness;
    happiness of married couples
    breakups and, 258
    divorce and, 242
    dopamine and, 241
    handling anxiety, 162
    self-sabotage and, 23
encouragement letter to self, 259
Enlightened Selfishness, 319–321, 349
Enter the Quiet Heart (Mata), 256
exercises
    accounting for time spent, 12–13
    African-American Women,
        306–307
    being-in-the-moment meditation,
        255–256

exercises (*cont.*)
  breakups, physical for exercises, 244
  building habit of positive self-
    affirmations, 170
  college educated women, 306–307
  commitment to self, 42
  creating Diamond Self, 157, 159–160
  Dating Program of Three, 94–96
  Deadly Dating Patterns Fix-It Kit,
    232–234
  Desert Island, 211
  Diamond Self discovery and using,
    169–172
  Diamond Self life-changing, 158–161
  Diamond Self minis, 157, 166
  Ditching Deadly Dating Patterns
    Forever, 232–234
  "Divine Has Your Back," 254–255
  Eight Habits of Living Love,
    332–334
  facing Deadly Dating Patterns, 38–42
  facing fears, 171–172, 184
  Field Report on DUDs and STUDs,
    210–212
  figuring out TTLC needs, 147
  financially successful women,
    306–307
  finding Love Mentors, 147–149
  Five-Minute Manifestation Miracle
    Exercise, 183–186, 190
  forgiveness, 259–260
  Frenemies, 277–279
  goals envisioning, 13–14, 233–234
  gratitude, 170
  healing heartbreak, 254–255,
    258–261
  heart affirmation, 260–261
  identifying secret negative beliefs,
    39–40, 259
  listing needs from Frenemies,
    278–279
  loveless eulogy, 40–41
  love letter to self, 232
  Miracle Day, 233
  networking mini, 166

  opening, 11–17
  over forty-fives, 306–307
  personal love intention, 41–42
  physical appearance to-do list, 149
  physical for, breakups, 244
  positive thinking, 159
  pulling away from DUD, 232
  rediscovering authentic self, 170
  remembering positive experiences,
    157
  Secrets of Rapid Online and App
    Dating Success, 123–125
  self-appreciation, 170
  sound-bite introduction, 172
  spirituality practice commitment,
    260
  Team Love group letters, 148–149
  during Team Love group meetings,
    350
  turning TTLC needs into
    affirmations, 147
  uncovering Frenemies, 277–278
  writing own prescription for love, 41
expectations, lowering of, 103

Facebook, xiii–xiv, 354
Fade Away Deadly Dating Pattern,
  34–35
Fade Away Deadly Dating Pattern
  Fix, 227–228
family/families
  African American, 284
  commonality among healthy, 313–314
  as Frenemies, 267–269
  healing of childhood wounds, 313
  letters to difficult members of,
    269–271, 278
  parents as prototypes for mates, 311
  websites for blended, 293
Fantasy Relationship Deadly Dating
  Pattern, 24–26
Fantasy Relationship Deadly Dating
  Pattern Fix, 219–220
fear/fears
  affirmation making and, 176–177

conquering, 162–163
facing, 161–163, 171–172
Five-Minute Manifestation Miracle
    Exercise and, 184
forward-backward transformational
    process and, 245
as learned, 153
meditation and, 252
practicing Habits of Living Love
    and, 310
of rejection, 32, 45
signals to follow, 161
fidelity, 317–318
Field Reports on DUDs and STUDS
    about, 193–195, 198, 202
    exercises, 210–212
    Grass Is Greener Fix and, 230
    gratitude and appreciation in, 334
    homework, 212–213
    importance of, 205
    journaling and, 211, 213, 235
    questions, 195–196, 199–201
    samples, 197–198, 202–208
Fight Club rules, 327–329
financially successful women
    dating exercises, 306–307
    homework, 308–309
    at marriage disadvantage, 294–295
    at marriage disadvantage as myth,
        296–298
    tips for, 298
Finding Your Own True Love (PBS
    special), xv–xvi, xx
Fisher, Helen, 77
Five-Minute Manifestation Miracle
    Exercise, 183–186, 190
Flame-Out Deadly Dating Pattern,
    23–24, 77, 86–87
Flame-Out Deadly Dating Pattern
    Fix, 217–219
Flame-Out Men's Deadly Dating
    Pattern, 65–66
Flight Club, 328
flirting
    insecurity of men and, 152–153

Just Buddies Fix and, 229
key techniques, 168–169
by over forty-fives, 305
forgiveness, 248, 249, 259–260
forward-backward transformational
    process
    described, 177
    emotions brought out by, 245–246
    examples of, 246–247
    master Love Mentors and, 245, 246
Frenemies
    building boundary around,
        275–277
    characteristics, 264, 266–267
    effect of, 263
    exercises, 277–279, 278
    family members as, 267–269
    homework, 279–281
    journaling about, 269–271
    letters to family, 269–271, 278
    needs from, 278–279
    negative patterns of, 272
    turning into friends, 271–275
    types of, 264–266
    uncovering, 277–278
    understanding, 266–267
Frost, Robert, 175

Gamble, Corey, 300
Gandhi, 271
Geek Men's Deadly Dating Pattern,
    50–51
generosity, 167, 191
ghosting, 99, 122–123
Gibran, Kahlil, xvii, 239
goals
    celebrating achievement, 340
    choosing new, 340–341
    envisioning exercise, 233–234
    establishing, 13–14
    self-assessment of progress toward,
        338–340
    of Ten Love in 90 Days, 14, 126,
        234, 341
    updating, 125

God
    "Divine Has Your Back" Exercise,
        254–255
    turning to, 250–251, 252, 253
Good Morning America (television
    program), xviii
Gottman, John, 326, 331
Grass Is Greener Deadly Dating
    Pattern, 37–38, 268
Grass Is Greener Deadly Dating
    Pattern Fix, 230–231
Grass Is Greener Men's Deadly
    Dating Pattern, 63–64
gratification, delaying, 320–321
gratitude
    exercise, 170
    expressing, and happiness of
        married couples, 323–325,
        333–334
    in healthy relationships, 312–313
    letter to Beloved, 334
    letter to self, 33
    lists, 170
    practicing, 156–158
    as result of teamwork, 330–331
    showing, 324–325
Green, Tamara, 132–133

Habits of Living Love. See Eight
    Habits of Living Love
Hansen, Mark Victor, 127
happiness of married couples, 309.
    See also Eight Habits of Living
    Love
    Care-Full Communication and,
        325–327, 342, 349
    commitment to each out, 317–319
    envisioning, 309
    expressing gratitude, 323–325,
        333–334
    fear-of-loss maneuvers, 322–323
    fighting and, 327–329
    growth potential, 323
    helping partner give, to you,
        319–321

intimacy builders, 316–317
as master Love Mentors, 138–139,
    312, 318
need for each other, 322
overlooking partner's flaws, 324
physical and sexual activity,
    315–316
shared rituals, 315
time alone as couple, 315
TTLC and, 312–313
working as team, 330–332
Harding, Warren, C., 264
Hayek, Selmak, 187
heartache/heartbreak
    brain area activated, 242
    broken heart syndrome and,
        242–243
    dopamine and, 241
    exercises for healing, 254–255,
        258–261
    getting over, 243–245
    healing, 250–256, 261–262
    as inevitable with breakups,
        240–241
    Inner Work, 250–256
    revenge and, 248–250
    spirituality, 250–253
heart attacks, 242–243
Hermit Deadly Dating Pattern,
    27–28, 221, 267
Hermit Deadly Dating Pattern Fix,
    221–222
Higher Power
    "Divine Has Your Back" Exercise,
        254–255
    turning to, 250–251, 252, 253
HIV/AIDS
    African-American women and,
        283
    over forty-fives and, 305
Homer, 78
homogamy, 296
honesty about dating multiple men,
    87–88
hookups and apps, 99, 123

identity
  brain structure's malleability, 158
  exercise for rediscovering, 170
  of happily married partners,
    320–321
  letting go of, and reframing painful
    memories, 156–157
  old, brought out by forward-
    backward transformational
    process, 245–246
  rediscovering, 154–155
I'll Make You Love Me Deadly Dating
  Pattern, 28–29, 268
I'll Make You Love Me Deadly Dating
  Patterns Fix, 222–223
imaginary conversations. See self-
  affirmations; self-talk
infidelity, 317–318
initial contact tips, 118–119
Inner Work. See also self-affirmations;
  self-love
  being-in-the-moment meditation,
    256
  described, 7
  healing heartbreak, 250–256
  Love Mentors and, 132–133
  positive self-talk, 179–180, 228,
    287, 288
in-person conversations
  initial contact tips, 118–119
  safety tips, 119
Institute for Comprehensive Family
  Therapy, xix
interracial dating, 285, 286–288
intimacy, 315–317
"it" factor. See self-confidence

JDate.com, 113–114
Jealousy Trap Deadly Dating Pattern,
  35–36
Jealousy Trap Deadly Dating Pattern
  Fix, 228–229
Jenner, Kris, 300
Jonas, Nick, 300
Jong, Erica, 3

journaling/journals
  commitment to, 16
  Dating Three to Find One, 94
  Deadly Dating Patterns, 39, 42
  DUD/STUD Field Reports and,
    211, 213, 235
  finding secret negative beliefs by,
    259
  goals, 340–341
  Grass Is Greener Fix, 230
  gratitude to self, 33
  as location for letters, 211
  negative thoughts, 33, 259
  online dating and, 119
  reactions to friends and Frenemies,
    269–271
  reasons why not dating, 212
  for relaxation, 243
Just Buddies Deadly Dating Pattern,
  36–37
Just Buddies Deadly Dating Pattern
  Fix, 229

Karl, JoAnne, 165
Katie, Byron, 304
Keen, Sam, 44

Lao Tzu, 213
letters
  appreciation to Beloved, 334
  breakups and, 247
  to difficult friends, 275–276
  to family Frenemies, 269–271, 278
  forward-backward transformational
    process, 247
  of gratitude, 324
  location for, 211
  to self, 33, 232, 259
  as Team Love group exercises,
    148–149
Lewis, C. S., 240–241
lovability/love. See also self-love
  affirmations for believing in, 11
  as cycle of benevolence, 312–313
  dopamine and, 241, 311

lovability/love (*cont.*)
  heartache as inevitable, 240–241
  of original self, 153, 154–155
  personal love intention exercise,
    41–42
  physical health and, 24, 25
  positive entitlement, 191–192
  prioritizing, 4
  writing own prescription for, 41
Love in 90 Days
  Acknowledgment and Commitment
    Contract, 15–17, 342–344
  assignment checklist, 337–338
  Certification course, 10, 353
  complimentary videos, 353
  Eight Steps to Love, 337, 344–346,
    351
  on Facebook, 354
  goals, 14, 126, 234, 341
  homework, 17–20
  opening exercises, 11–17
  program basics, 6–10
  tailoring program, 8
  website, 352
Love in 90 Days Online Dating
    Report
  form, 116
  keeping regularly, 125, 335
  love intention rating, 115
  productivity at sites and apps, 100,
    114
  updating, 335
loveless eulogy exercise, 40–41
Love Mentors. *See also* master Love
    Mentors
  about, xv, xxi
  being own, 260–261
  exercises for finding, 147–149
  as gift to self, 133
  importance of, 132
  for Inner Work, 132–133
  for Outer Work, 133
  as providers of TTLC needs,
    135–136, 139–140
  website, 9, 132, 248

Mantra Affirmation Activation,
    181–182
Marcia Cross Technique, 18
marriage. *See also* happiness of
    married couples
  African Americans and, 283, 284,
    285
  benefits of, 4
  characteristics of men likely
    interested in, 208–210
  characteristics of men likely to
    avoid, 209
  envisioning happy, 309
  infidelity and, 317–318
  interracial, 285, 286–288
  online dating and, 102
  parents as prototypes for mates, 311
  professional, college-educated, or
    financially successful women and,
    294–295, 296–298
  single mothers, 292–293
  social networks as source of
    partners, 152
  uniqueness of bonds of mates, 312
master Love Mentors
  Abuse Recycle Fix and, 224
  becoming own, 140–141
  breakups and, 243, 250
  Chase Me Fix and, 226–227
  committed partners as, 138–139,
    312, 318
  Crumbs Deadly Fix and, 220–221
  cultivating relationship with, 139
  discussing FIELD reports with, 334
  Fantasy Relationship Fix and, 219
  finding, 137–138, 147–149
  Flame-Out Fix and, 218
  forward-backward transformational
    process and, 245, 246
  homework, 150
  I'll Make You Love Me Fix, 223
  Just Buddies Fix and, 229
  Not Perfect—I'll Pass Fix and, 226
  as providing reparenting, 134–135
  qualities of, 137

Safety Net Fix and, 225
  training, 141, 352
  website, 132, 248
Mata, Sri Daya, 256
Match.com, 91
Matchmaker Mentors, 144, 229
meditation
  Abuse Cycle Fix, 223
  aging process and, 303
  being-in-the-moment, 255–256
  brain and, 252
  breakups and, 243
  Chase Me Fix, 226
  to connect with Higher Power, 251
  Dating Program of Three, 87
  Flame-Out Fix, 217
  mantras and, 95, 182
  stress and, 252
  Your Love Intention, 94–95
men
  accepting constructive criticism,
    331
  African-American, 283, 284, 285
  broken heart syndrome and, 227,
    242
  closure with, from past, 211–212
  as competitors, 78–79
  education levels, 296–297
  fear of commitment by, 45
  flirting and insecurity of, 152–153
  honesty about dating multiple,
    87–88
  importance of photos to, 103–104
  as likely interested in long-term
    relationship or marriage, 208–210
  as likely to avoid marriage, 209
  as marrying down, 294, 295–296
  number of single, in U.S., 80
  as problem solvers, 229
  stressing after dates, 89
Men's Deadly Dating Patterns
    (MDDPs)
  Alcoholic, 69–70
  Burnt Toast, 55–56
  Commitment Phobe, 61–63

Coward, 53–54
Flame-Out, 65–66
Geek, 50–51
Grass Is Greener, 63–64
growth willingness of men with,
    74–75
Mama's Peter Pan, 57–58
New Ager, 58–60
Not Perfect—I'll Pass, 68
Peter Pan, 56–58
Player, 70–72
Pr*ck, 72–74
Savior, 51–53
Shy Guy, 48–50
Slacker, 66–68
Trophy Seeker, 60–61
understanding, 45–47
mentors, importance of, 132
Millay, Edna St. Vincent, 22
Miracle Day exercise, 233
Mitochondrial Eve, 285
Moore, Lois Merriweather, 285
Mosteller, Frederick, 230

narcissistic people, 265, 268
negative thoughts
  exercise for identifying, 39–40, 259
  getting rid of, 81–82, 225–226
  journaling, 33, 259
  of over forty-fives, 298–299, 303
  sharing with Frenemies, 265
Nelson, Portia, 215–216
networking
  with Diamond Self, 164–165
  Fade Away Deadly Dating Pattern
    Fix and, 227
  importance of, 152
  keys to successful, 165–167
  leads, 335
  mini exercises, 166
  speed dating as, 173
New Ager Men's Deadly Dating
    Pattern, 58–60
Newsweek, xviii
New York Times, xvi, xx

Nin, Anais, 164
Not Perfect—I'll Pass Deadly Dating
　Pattern, 31–33
Not Perfect—I'll Pass Deadly Dating
　Pattern Fix, 225–226
Not Perfect—I'll Pass Men's Deadly
　Dating Pattern, 68

100 Black Men of America, Inc., 285
online dating sites. *See* dating sites
　and apps
OPEN (Opening Possibility Exercises
　Now) Technique, 85–86, 196
Original Tribe Handbook of Angels
　(Karl), 165
Ortega y Gasset, José, 7
Outer Work. *See also* physical
　appearance
　described, 7
　Diamond Self name and, 160
　healing heartbreak, 257–258
　homework, 150
　Love Mentors and, 133
　making over, 303
　own perception of body, 188
　physical health and, 117
　prayer for, 165
　relationship between love and, 144
　self-confidence and, 186–189
　of smarter women, 297
　to-do list, 149
Outer Work Mentors, 142, 144–146
Out of Africa Model, 284–285
over forty-fives
　dating exercises, 306–307
　Dating Program of Three and, 305
　dating sites and apps, 299, 304
　flirting by, 305
　happiness of, 299
　homework, 308–309
　makeover of physical appearance,
　　303
　meditation and, 303
　negative self-talk by, 298–299, 303
　physical exercise and, 302–303, 305
　sexual activity by, 303, 305
　tips for, 305–306
overinvolvement
　as addiction, 77–78
　Dating Program of Three avoids, 77
　Flame-Out Deadly Dating Pattern
　　and, 23–24, 77, 86–87
　Flame-Out Deadly Dating Pattern
　　Fix, 217–219
　Flame-Out MDDP, 65–66
oxytocin, 78, 91, 316

paranoia, 273, 274–275, 324, 335, 342
parental attachments, 267–269
partner engagement, described, 316
Peale, Norman Vincent, 43
perfection
　men's Not Perfect—I'll Pass Deadly
　　Dating Pattern, 68
　women's Not Perfect—I'll Pass
　　Deadly Dating Pattern, 31–33
　women's Not Perfect—I'll Pass
　　Deadly Dating Pattern Fix,
　　225–226
personal growth courses, 321
Peter Pan Men's Deadly Dating
　Pattern, 56–58
phone, initial contact tips, 118–119
photos
　creating your look, 104–105
　importance of, 103–104
　taking, 105–106
physical appearance
　Diamond Self name and, 160
　making over, 303
　Outer Work Mentors to nurture,
　　142
　own perception of body, 188
　physical health and, 117
　prayer for, 165
　relationship between love and, 144
　self-confidence and, 186–189
　self-love and, 143–144
　of smarter women, 297
　to-do list, 149

physical distress and rejection, 242
physical exercise
  breakups and, 244
  over forty-fives and, 302–303, 305
physical health
  beauty and, 117
  breakups and, 206–207
  heartache and, 242–243
  loss of partner and, 322
  love and, 24, 25
  meditation and, 252
  revenge and, 212
  spirituality and, 250–253
Player Men's Deadly Dating Pattern,
  70–72
Playing God, 253
Plotnick, Jack, 154
positive entitlement, 191–192
Positive Paranoia, 273, 274–275, 324,
  335, 342
positive self-talk, 179–180, 228, 287,
  288. See also self-affirmations
Positive Shaping Talk
  Acknowledgment and Commitment
    Contract, 342
  Frenemies and, 273–275, 276–277
  happiness of married couples and,
    326, 328, 335
  Team Love groups and, 349
positive thinking
  developing self-affirmations, 180
  exercise, 159
  reframing past and, 157
  subconscious negative feelings and,
    177
The Power of Myth (Campbell), 161
Pr*ck Men's Deadly Dating Pattern,
  72–74
prescription for love exercise, 41
Pressler, Jessica, 266
Proactive Moves, in beginning, 89–90
Procter, Adelaide Anne, 210
professional women
  dating exercises, 306–307
  homework, 308–309

as at marriage disadvantage,
  294–295
as at marriage disadvantage as
  myth, 296–298
tips for, 298
psychotherapy, 258

Rapin, Paul de, 282
rejection
  brain area activated, 206, 242
  control freaks and, 72
  cowards and, 53
  dopamine levels and, 241
  fear of, 32, 45
  geeks and, 50
  ghosting and, 122–123
  learning to handle, 124–125
  shyness and, 48
relaxation, 162, 171–172, 243
revenge, 212, 248–250
reverse-image search engines, 122
right time to believe in love exercise,
  11
Rilke, Rainer Maria, 320
role model, Diamond Self as, 164–165
role playing sexually, 316
romance scams
  money lost to con artists, xiv
  warning signs, 121–122
Rose, Elaina, 285

safety
  fear signals and, 161
  in-person conversation tips, 119
  sexual activity and, 93
Safety Net Deadly Dating Pattern,
  30–31
Safety Net Deadly Dating Pattern
  Fix, 225
Savior Men's Deadly Dating Pattern,
  51–53
Scamalytics, 122
Schucman, Helen, 282
Schwartz, John, 293, 294
Scott, Jess, 160

screen names, 106–108
secret negative beliefs
    exercises for identifying, 39–40, 259
    getting rid of, 81–82, 225–226
    journaling, 33, 259
    of over forty-fives, 298–299, 303
    sharing with Frenemies, 265
Secrets of Rapid Online and App
    Dating Success
    about, 100
    choosing sites and apps, 111
    describing ideal mate, 108
    exercises, 123–125
    homework, 125, 127
    initial phone and in-person
        conversation tips, 118–119
    lowering expectations, 103
    mastering search-engines, 113–114
    messaging tips, 117–118
    photos, 103–106
    responding to those not your type,
        114
    screen name and profile, 106–108,
        109–111
    suggesting connecting, 108–109
    using Love in 90 Days Online
        Dating Report, 100, 114–116
selectivity, 82
self-affirmations
    believing in love, 11
    building body self-confidence, 188
    building habit of positive, 170
    countering negative self-talk, 33,
        305
    for dating, 190
    Disappointing Self brought forth
        by, 177
    exercise for turning TTLC needs
        into, 147
    finding, for self-confidence,
        180–182
    Five-Minute Manifestation Miracle
        Exercise and, 184
    heart, 260–261
    Jealousy Trap Fix and, 228

loss of confidence and, 176–177
    positive entitlement and, 191–192
    power of, 179–180
    self-love and, 191
    using Diamond Self name in, 181
    website, 10
self-appreciation to-do list, 170
self-assurance. See self-confidence
self-commitment exercise, 42
self-confidence
    definition of confidence, 178
    Diamond Self name and, 179
    in physical appearance, 186–189
    self-affirmations and, 176–177,
        180–182
    as transformational, 178–179
self-discipline, 149
self-doubts
    acknowledging, 182
    forward-backward transformational
        process and, 245
self-love
    importance of, 13, 14, 126, 234, 341
    letter to self, 232
    physical appearance and, 143–144
    self-affirmations and, 191
    self-declaration of, 181–182
    Team Love groups and, 348
    yoga and, 149
self-marketing, dealing with issues
    about, 124
self-sabotage habit, 22–23. See also
    Men's Deadly Dating Patterns
    (MDDPs)
    exercises for identifying, 39–40, 259
    exercises for overcoming, 39–41
    forward-backward transformational
        process and, 245
    getting rid of, 81–82, 225–226
    journaling, 33, 259
    sharing with Frenemies, 265
self-talk. See also self-affirmations
    after breakups, 244–245, 249
    countering negative, 33
    healing heartache with, 258–259

of over forty-fives, 298–299, 303
practicing Eight Habits of Living
Love with, 333
stopping negative, 162
serotonin levels, 77
service, as act of love, 317–319
sexual activity
benefits of, 300
of children of single mothers,
291–292
Dating Program of Three and, 78,
90–91
exercise program and, 303
Flame-Out Fix and, 218
I'll Make You Love Me Fix, 222
intimacy and, 315–316
of over forty-fives, 303, 305
primary ways of interacting during,
316
rule changes, 299
safely, 93, 305
sexual trance, described, 316
Shakespeare, William, 76, 192, 325,
327
Shinn, Florence Scovel, 183
Shy Guy Men's Deadly Dating
Pattern, 48–50
Shy Guys and Proactive Moves, 90
shyness
as inverted need for attention, 221
overcoming, 96, 221–222
rejection and, 48
single mothers
challenges of, 289–290
dating behavior, and children of,
291–292
remarriage of, 292–293
Special Time, 290–291, 293
tips for, 293–294
Slacker Men's Deadly Dating Pattern,
66–68
sleep and breakups, 243
social networks, 152. See also
networking
soulmates, 310

sound-bite introductions, 166, 172
spam, 99
Sparks, Nicholas, xiii
Special Time, 290–291, 293
speed dating
as networking, 173
for overcoming shyness, 96, 222
website for, 173
spirituality
commitment to practicing, 260
exercise, 254–255
as ultimate first aid for heartache,
250–253
stepfamilies, 292–293
stinking thinking
exercise for identifying, 39, 259
getting rid of, 81–82, 225–226
journaling, 33, 259
sharing with Frenemies, 265
stress
divorce as major, 242
meditation and, 252
revenge and, 248
turning to Higher Power and, 251
style, developing own, 142

Tagore, 141, 142, 144
Take Two technique, 328–329
Taylor, Susan, 285, 288
Team Love groups
about, 9, 347
in action, 348–349
breakups and, 243
discussing FIELD reports with,
334
forward-backward transformational
process and, 246
importance of, 231
letters as exercises, 148–149
meeting structure, 349–350
mission statement, 348
as Outer Work Mentors, 144–146
philosophy, 348
self-love and, 348
teamwork, 330–332, 349

388   Index

Tender and Tough Loving Care
(TTLC) needs
acknowledging own, 320
asking for ones you need, 139–140
fulfilling partner's, 318
in healthy relationships, 312–313
identifying, 135–137, 147
list and Dating Program of Three,
202
Love Mentors as providers of,
135–136, 139–140
teamwork and, 330
turning, into affirmations exercise,
147
Ten Love in 90 Days goals, 14, 126,
234, 341
Teresa of Avila (Saint), 192
testosterone, 316
texting, 99
thankfulness, 76
"three-date rule," 76
time, squandering exercise, 12–13
Tinder
average number of monthly users,
99
beginning of, xiv
interracial marriage and, 286
Today Show (television program), xx
Tolstoy, Leo, 313
Trophy Seeker Men's Deadly Dating
Pattern, 60–61
twelve-step programs, 253–254, 257

vasopressin, 316
vicariousness, 164–165
Voices of Successful African-American
Men (Moore), 285

warning signs
Abuse Recycle Deadly Dating
Pattern, 30
Alcoholic MDDP, 70
Burnt Toast MDDP, 56
Chase Me Deadly Dating Pattern,
34

Commitment Phobe MDDP, 63
Coward MDDP, 54
Crumbs Deadly Dating Pattern, 27
DUD, 120
Fade Away Deadly Dating Pattern,
35
Fantasy Relationship Deadly
Dating Pattern, 26
Flame-Out Deadly Dating Pattern,
24
Flame-Out MDDP, 66
Geek MDDP, 51
Grass Is Greener Deadly Dating
Pattern, 38
Grass Is Greener MDDP, 64
Hermit Deadly Dating Pattern, 28
I'll Make You Love Me Deadly
Dating Pattern, 29
Jealousy Trap Deadly Dating
Pattern, 36
Just Buddies Deadly Dating
Pattern, 37
New Ager MDDP, 60
Not Perfect—I'll Pass Deadly
Dating Pattern, 33
Not Perfect—I'll Pass MDDP, 68
Peter Pan MDDP, 58
Player MDDP, 71
Pr*ck MDDP, 73
romance scams, 121–122
Safety Net Deadly Dating Pattern,
31
Savior MDDP, 53
Shy Guy MDDP, 48–49
Slacker MDDP, 68
Trophy Seeker MDDP, 61
websites. See also dating sites and apps
American Psychological
Association, 258
blended families, 293
coaching program, 82, 132, 248
complimentary videos, 353
increase in use by over forty-fives,
299, 304
Love in 90 Days, 352

Love in 90 Days Certification
    course, 10, 353
Love in 90 Days on Facebook, 354
Love Mentors, 9, 132, 248
    religion-oriented, 304
    Scamalytics, 122
    self-affirmations, 10
    speed dating, 173
Whelan, Christine, 297
Why Smart Men Marry Smart Women
    (Whelan), 297
Why We Love (Fisher), 77
Williams, Margery, 155
Williamson, Marianne, 153

Winfrey, Oprah, 134
Wolf, Naomi, 187
Woolsey, Midge, xvi

yoga
    Abuse Cycle Fix, 224
    Chase Me Fix, 226
    Dating Program of Three, 87
    to help end suffering, 253
    New Agers and, 58–59
    self-love and, 149
Your Love Intention meditation,
    94–95
youthifying, 302–304, 305